The Devils is a celebrated 1971 picture based on the
Loudun demonology trials in the 17th century, scripted by Ken
Russell from Aldous Huxley's *The Devils of Loudun* (1952) and
the 1961 play by John Whiting (1918-63). *The Devils* was
undoubtedly Russell's most notorious hour as a film director. It
was the site of conflicts between the filmmakers, the studio
(Warners), the censors and the critics. And it wasn't seen in the
form the filmmakers desired for decades.

MEDIA, FEMINISM, CULTURAL STUDIES

The Sacred Cinema of Andrei Tarkovsky
by Jeremy Mark Robinson

Jean-Luc Godard: The Passion of Cinema/ Le Passion de Cinéma
by Jeremy Mark Robinson

Mel Brooks: Genius and Loving It!
by Thomas A. Christie

Liv Tyler: Star In Ascendance
by Thomas A. Christie

John Hughes and Eighties Cinema
by Thomas A. Christie

Stepping Forward: Essays, Lectures and Interviews
by Wolfgang Iser

Wild Zones: Pornography, Art and Feminism
by Kelly Ives

'Cosmo Woman': The World of Women's Magazines
by Oliver Whitehorne

Andrea Dworkin
by Jeremy Mark Robinson

Cixous, Irigaray, Kristeva: The Jouissance of French Feminism
by Kelly Ives

Sex in Art: Pornography and Pleasure in the History of Art
by Cassidy Hughes

The Cinema of Richard Linklater
by Thomas A. Christie

The Christmas Movie Book
by Thomas A. Christie

The Erotic Object: Sexuality in Sculpture From Prehistory to the Present Day
by Susan Quinnell

Women in Pop Music
by Helen Challis

Detonation Britain: Nuclear War in the UK
by Jeremy Mark Robinson

Luce Irigaray: Lips, Kissing, and the Politics of Sexual Difference
by Kelly Ives

Helene Cixous I Love You: The Jouissance of Writing
by Kelly Ives

Julia Kristeva: Art, Love, Melancholy, Philosophy, Semiotics
by Kelly Ives

Feminism and Shakespeare
by B.D. Barnacle

FORTHCOMING CINEMA BOOKS

Akira: The Movie and the Manga
Ghost In the Shell
Legend of the Overfiend
Fullmetal Alchemist
Tim Burton
George Lucas
Francis Coppola
Orson Welles
Pier Paolo Pasolini
Ingmar Bergman
Contempt
Pierrot le Fou
The Pirates of the Caribbean Movies
The Twilight Saga
The Harry Potter Movies

THE DEVILS
KEN RUSSELL

POCKET MOVIE GUIDE

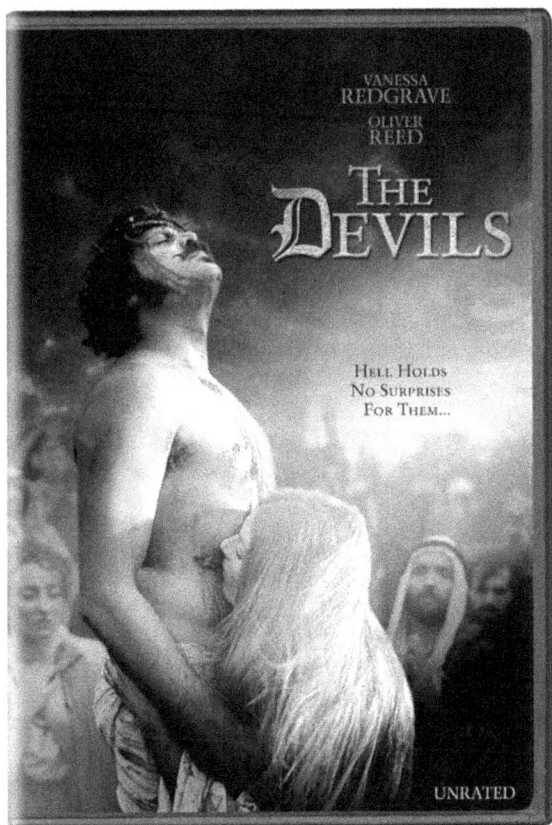

Jeremy Mark Robinson

Crescent Moon

First published 2015. © Jeremy Mark Robinson 2015.

Printed and bound in the U.S.A.
Set in Bodoni Book, 9 on 12pt.
Designed by Radiance Graphics.

British Library Cataloguing in Publication data available for this title.

ISBN-13 9781861715067

Crescent Moon Publishing
P.O. Box 1312
Maidstone, Kent
ME14 5XU, Great Britain
www.crmoon.com

CONTENTS

ACKNOWLEDGEMENTS

Thanks to Ken Russell.
Thanks to John Baxter.

To the copyright holders of the illustrations.
To authors quoted and their publishers.

PICTURE CREDITS

Ken Russell. MGM. United Artists. Warner Bros. Vestron. Virgin Vision. Trimark Pictures. Major Motion Pictures. New World Pictures. Goodtimes Enterprises. BBC. Columbia. Associated British Picture Corporation. Channel 4 Films. London Films. RM Associates. HBO. RBT Stigwood Productions. Hemdale. British Film Institute.

British pounds have been converted to US dollars at a rate of 1:1.6.

ABBREVIATIONS

BP	*A British Picture* by Ken Russell
DL	*Directing Film* by Ken Russell
Bax	*An Appalling Talent* by John Baxter
G	*Ken Russell* by Joseph Gomez
PF	*Phallic Frenzy* by Joseph Lanza
RC	*Reel Conversations* edited by G. Hickenlooper

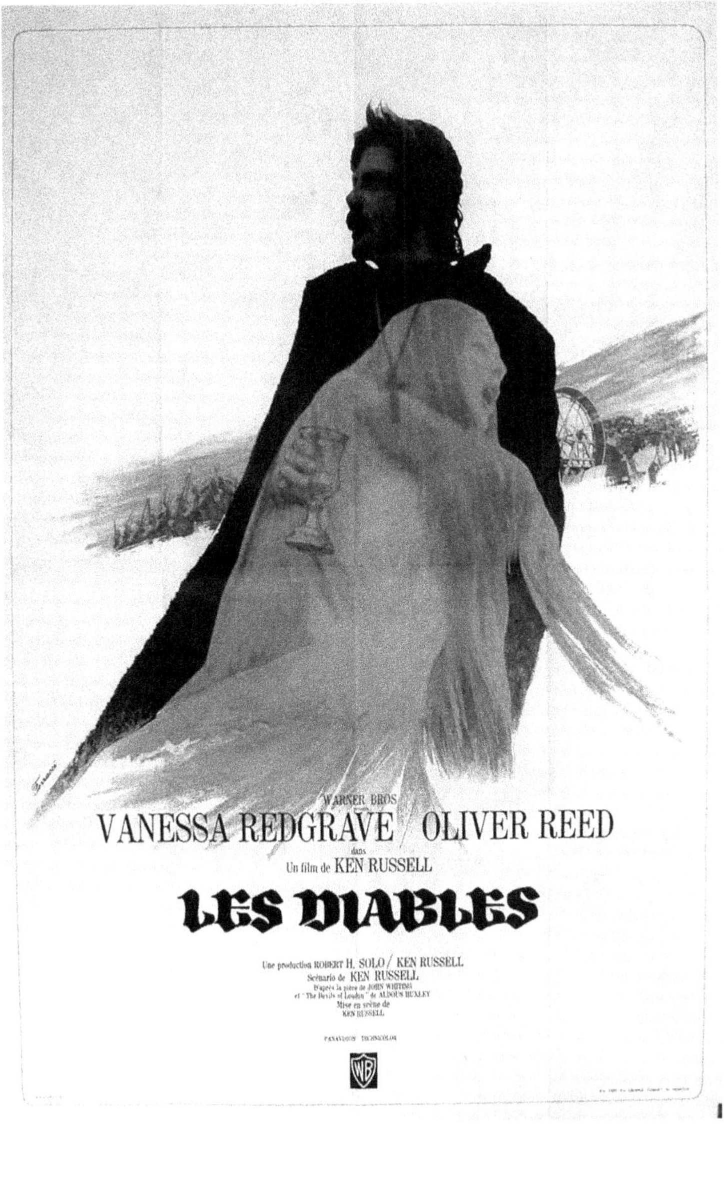

Video ★ WatchdoG ®

the Perfectionist's
Guide to
Fantastic Video

No. 35
$6.50

THE DEVILS

A Plea for Restoration

Ken Russell
On Film Censorship

Donald Cammell
Final Performance

ANIME   **SOUNDTRACKS**   DISCS   RETITLINGS

1
✝
THE DEVILS

The whole film was conceived as a black comedy, but the fact
that people don't laugh isn't very surprising... What the film is
saying is that this would be a terrible joke if it weren't all so
horrible and hadn't actually happened. I find it extraordinary
that Grandier was convicted and burnt on the strength of
ludicrous statements which even a young child would find
implausible these days in a fairy story.

Ken Russell (Bax, 202f)

Any film that sacrilegiously features frenzied nuns sexually
attacking a giant crucifix is pure enjoyment in my cinematic
book.

Raymond Murray, *Images In the Dark: An Encyclopedia of Gay
and Lesbian Film and Video*

Ken Russell's most notorious hour was undoubtedly *The Devils*
(1971),[1] based on the Loudun demonology trials in the 17th
century, scripted by Russell from Aldous Huxley's *The Devils
of Loudun* (1952) and the 1961 play by John Whiting (1918-
63).[2] The project did not originate with Russell, however: it
was set up by United Artists, who owned the property, and they
approached Russell to direct it.[3] Russell, though, wanted to do
the Peter Tchaikovsky movie first, and reluctantly UA agreed
(Bax, 183). However, the project passed to Warners.

A *tour-de-force* of direction (and organization and production), the most significant contribution to *The Devils* may

---

1 But Russell's had a few notorious moments, hasn't he? – more than many filmmakers!
2 A Polish version of the events in Aldous Huxley's book, *Mother Joan of the
Angels* (dir. Jerzy Kawalerowicz., b. 1926) had appeared in 1961, but Russell said
he saw it after making *The Devils*.
3 J. Gomez, 1976, 21.

well be the screenplay – and Ken Russell has the screen credit for the script. Which makes *The Devils* all the more remarkable. (As if writing the script and directing the movie wasn't enough, Russell also co-produced it.) Not enough credit is given to Russell as a screenwriter;[4] he also sometimes downplayed his contributions to scripts, and he also happily admitted that he re-used the ingredients of scripts in other movies (like large chunks of the unproduced *Angels* script in *Tommy*). Go watch *The Devils* and consider it in terms of screenwriting, and you'll appreciate even more what a masterpiece it is.

Aldous Huxley's 1952 book allowed the filmmakers,[5] Ken Russell explained, to go a little nuts (and *The Devils* certainly went just a little nuts!).[6] Huxley's treatment was a 'mind-blowing account of those fantastic events', and was

> just about the trippiest version of a historical event it has ever been my good fortune to happen upon. It was also largely responsible for the original look of the film. (DF, 41)

Although Ken Russell drew on both Aldous Huxley's book and John Whiting's play, the resulting screenplay – and movie – is very much his own interpretation. Russell reckoned he had employed Huxley's books for the atmosphere, but although he'd been knocked out by the play when he'd seen it in 1961,[7] he later found Whiting was too soft-centred in the end, and the play 'evaded the central issue'.

Aldous Huxley (1894-1963) was one of Britain's finest writers in the modern era, best known for novels such as *Brave*

4 Joseph Gomez commented: 'This film, more than any other, also best reveals Russell's genius as a creator-adaptor. He remains faithful to all of the major events in Huxley's book, captures the tone of the original, and, most importantly, delineates the major themes of the prose account in methods appropriate to the film medium. He also forcefully presents his own attitudes and responses, but in a way which never violates Huxley's vision' (1976, 161-2).

5 There have been fewer adaptions of Aldous Huxley's fiction than one might expect – fewer than contemporaries such as D.H. Lawrence or Graham Greene, for instance. Most adaptions have been on TV, rather than feature films. A BBC adaption of *Point Counterpoint*, and a couple of versions of *Brave New World*, have been made.

6 In his superb study of Ken Russell's cinema, Joseph Gomez described *The Devils of Loudun* as 'an apocalyptic statement which fuses biography, fiction, and essay to warn about present trends that can lead to world destruction, and to instruct people in the quest for the alternative "divine peace" which comes from upward self-transcendence.' (G, 125)

7 It had starred Dorothy Tutin, whom Russell would cast in *Savage Messiah*.

New World, Eyeless In Gaza, Chrome Yellow and *Point Counterpoint.* He also wrote books of essays and non-fiction, including the influential *The Doors of Perception* and *The Perennial Philosophy*, with their explorations of mysticism, religion and drugs, which were taken up by the counter-culture in the Sixties. *The Doors of Perception* has links with *Altered States*, and Huxley was part of the literary circle that included D.H. Lawrence (indeed, Huxley parodied Lawrence himself in his novel *Point Counterpoint*).

Aldous Huxley had considered a dramatic version of his book back in the early 1950s, and a movie adaption was being talked of in the early 1960s. Commissioned by the Royal Shakespeare Company, John Whiting's play opened in February, 1961, at the Aldwych Theatre in Londinium.

Aldous Huxley also went to Hollywood (in 1938), working on *Jane Eyre* and *Pride and Prejudice*, and a biography of Madame Curie (writing for the movies was a mixed blessing for Huxley, as it is for many writers). There's an excellent Huxley website at somaweb.org.

Urbain Grandier (1590-1634) was burnt at the stake in public in Loudun in 1634 after being charged with inciting the Mother Superior, Jeanne des Anges,[8] and other Ursuline nuns, to demonic possession. As well as combining characters (characters such as D'Armagnac were dropped completely), Ken Russell's script also grants Grandier the powers of governor (departing from the book), when the current governor, Saint-Marthe, dies (it's Saint-Marthe's funeral at the beginning).

Ken Russell commented in the *Toronto Star* on Dec 4, 1971:

> The church has always been appalling. I'm an ordinary run-of-the-mill sinner who only pays lip service to the church, but I was trying to tell the truth about how it uses totally illiterate people to seduce everyone through terror.

It's clear from the first few minutes of *The Devils* that Ken

---

8 Jeanne des Anges became Prioress of the Ursuline Convent of Loudun at 25.

Russell was on fire as a filmmaker[9] when he made this picture[10] (he was certainly on fire at the period in his film career – not only *The Devils* but also *The Music Lovers* and *The Boy Friend* were playing at the same time in central London theatres. Incredible – I can't think of another British movie-maker with three big (and very different) movies in release at the same time).

It was a highly productive period for the maestro: not long after *The Devils* and *The Boy Friend* in 1971, Russell and his team were making *Savage Messiah* for MGM-EMI. (Also in 1971, Russell received awards for best director from the National Board of Review). 'He was fantastically proud of *The Devils*, and was willing to defend it to the death,' remarked Mark Kermode (2013, 43).

You can only make a movie as good as *The Devils* if you're feeling very confident and have immense organizational skills. And you can only really do this kind of movie with the backing and resources of a major film studio. Yeah, and plenty of imagination and skill and 95% hard work.[11]

And Ken Russell was happy with what he'd achieved in *The Devils*. '*The Devils* is the most successful film I've done, insofar as what I expected is there. The effects I aimed at seemed to work' (G, 162).[12] In *The Devils*, Russell was operating with a giant canvas, and you can tell from the first few minutes that the director is in complete control of the form, and of this movie (which gives the audience confidence in the storytellers; this movie *really* knows what it's doing). With *The Devils* and *The Music Lovers*, Russell rises far above being merely an accomplished director, and joins the greats.

In fact, in this movie set in 17th century France, with French characters, filmed in England with a mainly British cast and crew (and drawing on two British writers), but paid for by a

9 Joe Gomez speaks of 'Russell's richly ornate images, his craving for the theatrical, his ambivalent attitudes towards his heroes, and his bizarre sense of humour' in *The Devils* (1976, 70).

10 As Jack Fisher noted, 'it seems impossible that anyone can watch *The Devils* and not be aware of Russell's brilliance as a visual artist. The film is so totally visual that one has the feeling of watching a series of single frame paintings being displayed' (55).

11 Elements of *The Devils* were arduous for cast and crew: as Ken Russell put it, '*The Devils* left many of us weak, miserable and shattered' (Bax, 211).

12 The Jesuit reverend Gene Phillips was a keen supporter of *The Devils*, and included it in the course he taught at Loyola University in Chicago.

North American studio, everyone is a star, producing their finest work.

The Devils was a big movie, and Ken Russell's production team should always be mentioned when discussing the movie: David Watkin, DP, camera operator Ronnie Taylor, editor Mike Bradsell, costume designer Shirley Kingdon, production designer Derek Jarman, art director Robert Cartwright, set dresser Ian Whittaker, production manager Neville C. Thompson, make-up Charles Parker, hairdresser Ramon Gow, A.D. Ted Morley, unit manager Graham Ford, choreographer Terry Gilbert, composer Peter Maxwell Davies, special effects by John Richardson, and sound by Gordon McCallum, Terry Rawlings and Brian Simmons. Let's not forget that Russell also produced the film, along with Robert H. Solo, and his regular producer, Roy Baird.

The Devils was filmed on 35mm in Panavision widescreen (ratio: 1:2.35). Technicolor produced the prints. Running time was 111 minutes, and 117 minutes (restored). Released: July, 1971 (G.B.), and July 16, 1971 (U.S.A.).

Ken Russell's extravagant, over-the-top take on the Loudun martyrs starred Oliver Reed, Vanessa Redgrave, Gemma Jones, and British character actors (such as Dudley Sutton, Murray Melvin, Michael Gothard, Georgina Hale, Kenneth Colley, Andrew Faulds, Judith Paris, and Max Adrian). Many of the actors were Russell regulars – the whole repertory of Russellians is here. Sutton and Gothard played the State emissaries sent in to break Loudun; Redgrave was the chief sister, Jeanne, deformed, and tormented by 'sinful thoughts';[13] Hale and Jones were Grandier's lovers (Hale would later star in *Mahler*).

The Devils may be Ken Russell's masterpiece (tho' for him his favourite movie was *The Music Lovers*– not least because it's a pæan to that most miraculous event in human history: music).[14] You can tell when filmmakers are really engaged with their material and when they are really reaching for something and extending themselves. And Russell and his

---

13 Giving Vanessa Redgrave the OTT movie hump of Igor in *Frankenstein* fits perfectly in this savage satire.
14 '*The Devils* stands as Ken Russell's major achievement, in part, because the flamboyance of his style is so perfectly suited to the film's subject matter,' remarked Joseph Gomez (G, 161).

team were certainly going for it big time in *The Devils*. Look at the staging and the way the camera is used, for instance: *The Devils* contains muscular, confident blocking and filming of scenes – from the big, crowd scenes to the small, intimate scenes. The subject matter and the themes are fully in tune with Russell's own sensibilities, and his form of cinema. With *The Devils*, as with *The Music Lovers* Russell really found a way of exploiting his talents on a very grand scale.

The control of *mise-en-scène* in *The Devils*, as Joseph Gomez has demonstrated in his excellent close analysis of the movie (in his 1976 study of Ken Russell), is superb. Russell and DP David Watkin compose shots, for instance, which subtly underscore the drama, as well as images which express the key themes of the piece in an OTT manner. The blocking of actors within shots, for instance, illustrates many of the tensions inside the drama, such as having the people opposed to Urbain Grandier on the issue of the walls being demolished on one side of the frame (Mignon and Trincant), and two that support him (Rangier and Legrand) on the other side of the frame.

✟

In terms of production, *The Devils* displayed a slightly larger budget[15] than the usual Ken Russell film: there was an impressive French, 17th century town square set, all in white, contrasting with the predominantly black costumes (the sets[16] were designed by Derek Jarman, with set dressing and art direction by Robert Cartwright and Ian Whittaker; Jarman would later make films such as *The Tempest, Caravaggio* and *The Last of England*, clearly influenced by Russell).[17] It's a stylization of Loudun, of a 17th century, French town (Russell wasn't interested in the real place, for the purposes of this

---

15 Look at what Ken Russell and his film crews put on screen for budgets of $1-2 million, compared to other movies of this period like *Paint Your Wagon* (1969, 26 million bucks), *Catch 22* (1970, $24m), *Fiddler On the Roof* (1970, $40.5m), *Dr Doolittle* (1967, $20m), and *Star!* (1968, $14m).
16 But the film studio – Warners – asked the filmmakers to cut back on some of the sets: the royal palace, for instance, and a court and garden for King Louis (PF, 107).
17 Derek Jarman had met Ken Russell through Janet Deuters (PF, 103). Russell found Jarman full of ideas and enthusiasm for the movie. 'We talked for days and days on end'.

movie). The first scenes in Loudun show off the big sets[18] (which took up a large portion of the backlot at Pinewood Studios), the many extras, and the costumes.

Derek Jarman is often praised and singled out by critics in relation to the look of *The Devils*,[19] but it's the way the design fuses with the other elements that really makes it work (on their own sets are just... sets). In *The Devils*, everyone is working at their best.[20]

As accomplished and visionary as the sets are, for example, one could cite the dazzlingly brilliant, widescreen cinematography as being more important, or the editing, or the music – no one can forget Peter Davies' score for *The Devils*, by turns parping, florid, irreverent, stark, mawkish and nihilistic (there isn't a score quite like this one anywhere!).

When we're talking about such a stunningly visual movie like *The Devils*, the DP is incredibly important. David Watkin turns in a performance as lighting cameraman the equal of the superstar DPs of the period, like Vittorio Storaro, Geoffrey Unsworth, Gordon Willis, Vilmos Zsigmond or Sven Nykvist. In terms of the cinematography, *The Devils* is sensational. Illuminating the black Cathedral, for example, required an inventive approach to lighting (Ken Russell recalled that Watkin employed a giant searchlight from WW2 and blasted it thru the stained glass, to throw colours onto the performers. It was very effective). The cinematography in *The Devils* is crisp, stylized yet also naturalistic.

The hair and make-up is particularly fine in *The Devils*, with Ramon Gow, Charles Parker and their teams delivering fabulous results, as well as gruesome visualizations of the

18 Urbain Grandier's apartments comprise a circular room at the top of an Italian-style tower, containing a circular staircase. The luxury of such rooms emphasizing the vanity of Grandier, of course, and how he appears to be above everyone else.
19 Ken Russell and Derek Jarman drew on a Russell favourite movie, *Metropolis* (Bax, 207), a hugely influential picture of course; Jarman looked at Giovanni Piranesi (his *Imaginary Prisons*, 1760s), Étienne-Louis Boulée, and Claude-Nicolas Ledoux (PF, 107).
20 Including the camera department, headed by David Watkin, with Ronnie Taylor as camera operator; the costume department, headed up by Shirley Kingdon; the editing team led by Mike Bradsell (with Stuart Baird as assistant editor); the music by Peter Maxwell Davies and David Munrow; the hair by Ramon Gow; the make-up by Charles Parker; the set dressing and art direction by Robert Cartwright and Ian Whittaker; the choreography by Terry Gilbert; and the special effects by John Richardson.

plague, hunch-backs and torture.[21] Hairdresser Gow gives Vanessa Redgrave a deliberately over-the-top, long wig for Sister Jeanne's fantasies.

Masks (and masquerades) are favourite props in a Ken Russell movie, and *The Devils* has masks aplenty, as if everyone is wearing a disguise and no one is quite what they seem. It was a stroke of genius, for instance, to have Georgina Hale's Philippe Trincant sporting a face done in pale make-up.[22] And the king appears first in a high camp costume as the Goddess Venus.

There were crowd scenes, with many (maybe two hundred) extras in costume (for sequences such as the funeral procession; Urbain Grandier expelling the government from Loudun with the aid of soldiers bearing crossbows; and the climactic burning of Grandier). There were horses, animals, and numerous props (some were very large, like the wooden, wheeled engines).

And *The Devils* is a very grand, special effects movie – there are numerous special make-up jobs (for the plague victims, for instance, or Urbain Grandier as he's tortured), and a huge amount of practical effects (courtesy of special effects supervisor John Richardson and his team), ranging from fire and smoke to water and explosions (pretty much all of the exterior shots include smoke and many have fire). Richardson, a veteran of almost every movie made in Britain from the 1960s to today, commented in the *Times:* 'I was horrified sometimes at what we were doing. But seeing the picture I wasn't at all offended by it, it all had a rightful place in the film'.[23] Yes: *The Devils* is one of those movies that if people visited the set (such as studio executives or journalists, probably the people most resented on set by film directors), and observed some of the action, they might've come away with a negative impression (especially if they don't really know how movies are made – many journos don't): but put it all together, and it makes sense.

21 And of course the special effects make-up for Urbain Grandier's last moments on Earth.

22 The green lipstick and white face make-up was historically accurate, according to Ken Russell: it was a fashion of the period. 'I thought: yes, it makes her look corpse-like and it does go with her jealousy, her wish to kill Grandier' (Bax, 223).

23 *The Times*, December 7, 1971.

The fundamental design principle of *The Devils* was a scheme of black and white throughout the costumes, sets, props, and lighting. It's a film of opposites in everything: life and death, Protestantism and Catholicism, good and evil, God and the Devil, belief and non-belief, State and citizen, King and subject, Paris and Loudun.[24] Black and white, but with the red of blood, hate and fire superimposed over it, and running thru it (red's used in *The Devils* for Cardinal Richelieu's costume, the crosses on the costumes, and of course the blood – *The Devils* is Russell's bloodiest movie).

Ken Russell said he hated historical films, where everything is crumbling or in ruins.

> I really despise period films. Anything before the eighteenth century is automatically in crumbling ruins, all grey blocks of stone. It looks like a pageant with everyone in fancy dress. We wanted to do away with the cobwebs and grey stone and get a contemporary feeling. The people of Loudun who were so crazy about their city and trying to save it certainly didn't see it as an old museum relic. For them it was something new and modern. So we had to make if modern for people today. (Bax, 206).

So Ken Russell and his team went for a contemporary look. The simple, household brick was chosen as the basic building block for all of the architecture in the Loudun set (using Pinewood Studios' standard brick mould); everything was painted white (actually beige, so it photographed white), giving the set the look of a hospital, a clinic, an asylum, a prison, and a slaughterhouse. The chapel is extremely odd, with even the altar being built from white bricks. And the Catholic archive in Paris is constructed in the same way, looking like a prison that's been turned into an archive and library[25] – not only implying the continuity between the convent and a prison, but also between Paris and Loudun, and the whole of France (but France has seldom appeared like this on screen!).

Ken Russell and his team took a line in Aldous Huxley's

24 I wonder if the filmmakers were also linking the struggle between Catholics and Protestants in *The Devils* to the Irish Troubles: at the time of production, the acts of I.R.A. (including bomb attacks) were very much in the news.
25 The Catholic Church must've had enormous vaults holding information on everybody, Russell reckoned: hence the OTT archive set, complete with piles of books stored in prison cells and giant swing doors with a cross on them.

The Devils of Loudun as their starting-point: 'Barré had treated [Jeanne] to an experience that was the equivalent, more or less, of a rape in a public lavatory' (1970, 1924). The design æsthetic took that concept – 'a rape in a public lavatory' (a phrase guaranteed to get Russell's attention!) – and applied it on a grandiose scale. (Huxley is referring to gruesome tortures such as the 'miraculous enema'). The anachronistic sets of Loudun were analogous to Huxley's references to the present day – Huxley and Russell are sending out warnings about the present by using the past (like any decent production of a classic play, from say William Shakespeare or Sophocles, *The Devils* updates the material and makes it contemporary).

The score, by Peter Maxwell Davies, announces itself forcefully in the opening scenes of *The Devils*, too. It's a distinctive, modernist score which plays with dissonance. And in the later, hysterical scenes, the music comes close to cacophony, with instrumentation that emulates the mediæval street parade (horns, drums, flutes). Davies's music is vital to *The Devils*, partly because Mike Bradsell had edited some scenes to the music.

Peter Davies recalled that the musical language for *The Devils* was easy to find: it drew on the 1960s, and was meant to get louder and more disturbing as the narrative progressed: 'it becomes louder than it is because it's echoing back at you, and it begins to have a resonance which you want to get out of. There's a slight feeling that you don't want to stay there too long' (PF, 113).

It's not all rasps and hoots and drum-banging, however: many scenes are played alongside slow drones of strings; however, these are not the usual, soft strings of Hollywood movies, which gently enhance the mood. Rather, they are deliberately unsettling sounds, consciously melancholy and disturbing, underlining the fact that *The Devils* is *never* at rest: the entire film is in a state of flux and riot. Even the intimate scenes of Urbain Grandier with his two lovers, for instance, are not really respites from the hothouse atmosphere, because the audience is always aware that the whole town is on the edge of erupting into chaos or violence. (There are also versions of *Dies Irae* (*Day of Wrath*), deliberately cheesy, melodramatic music, and of course the 1920s popular song 'Bye Bye Blackbird' – included perhaps to further piss off purists! Warners likely hated the score as well as everything about *The Devils*).

✟

The Devils was Ken Russell's first of two productions for the Warner Brothers studio (the second being *Altered States*). At the time, in the early 1970s, Warners was presided over by Ted Ashley. Russell was not the only filmmaker to run afoul of Ashley's regime: for instance, George Lucas and Francis Coppola[26] fell out with Warners over *THX 1138*, and would not do business with them for years afterwards. Lucas loathed the way Warners treated his film. When four minutes were cut from *THX 1138* by Warners' editor Rudy Fehr, on Ted Ashley's orders, Lucas said it was 'like watching someone cutting the fingers off of his child'.[27]

Needless to say, it's unlikely that Warners would've developed and produced *Altered States* had Ken Russell been the initial director: Warners took up *Altered States* after Columbia Pictures had dropped it. In a familiar story, Russell insisted that Warners had approved the script of *The Devils* (but maybe they hadn't scrutinized it too closely), and he had shot what had been agreed in the screenplay (it's the famous scene in *Contempt*, Jean-Luc Godard's masterful 1963 satire on the film industry, when the producer (Jack Palance) berates the director (Fritz Lang) for not shooting the script as written and agreed; then, when he checks the script, he sees the rushes *are* as

---

26 Francis Coppola's relationship with Warners was rocky, to say the least: they backed his first three features (*You're a Big Boy Now*, *Finian's Rainbow* and *The Rain People*), all of which flopped; they invested in Zeotrope but backed out; they backed *Hammett* and *The Escape Artist* but these failed; later, there were lawsuits brought by Coppola against Warners over *Pinocchio* and *Contact*.
27 George Lucas hated the way Warners executive Fred Weintraub had spoken about it. Weintraub had liked the dwarfs, whom he called freaks, who appeared towards the end of *THX 1138*. Weintraub told Lucas that he ought to grab the audience's attention early on in the film: 'put the freaks up front', as Weintraub put it. Lucas later referred to the phrase to embody what he hated about the studio system, where the 'freaks' were the executives. 'Put the freaks up front' summed up for Lucas (and his contemporaries) the typical, dumb, Hollywood studio executive's mentality when it came to movies.

agreed. But he's still not satisfied).[28]

✤

The Devils, performance-wise, was monopolized by Ken Russell regular Ollie Reed (not easy in a film of many eccentric acting turns),[29] and Vanessa Redgrave's Sister Jeanne. Reed, with his substantial bulk, bulldog face, shaggy, black hair, moustache, and haunted look, was a formidable presence in *The Devils* (especially in the agonizing torture scenes, shaven-headed (and without eyebrows),[30] broken, surrounded by Sutton, Adrian, Gothard and Melvin hissing 'confess!' at him, and maintaining his dignity to the end). But all of the way through *The Devils*, Reed is at his best; it's a remarkable performance, undoubtedly the biggest challenge of Reed's acting career. But it also needs a great supporting cast, which *The Devils* has in spades.

Urbain Grandier was certainly a challenging role,[31] and one many an actor would jump at the chance to do[32] – these sorts of roles simply do not come along that often.[33] Oliver Reed's performance was certainly Oscar-worthy, and maybe the best performance of his career – although *The Devils* was probably just a tad too Out There for the Academy in L.A.

Altho' Oliver Reed recognized that Urban Grandier was his greatest role, he also thought that his performance had

---

28 That's also partly a joke about Jean-Luc Godard – he *never* shot what was in the script! And there wasn't a conventional script in the first place, anyway! The amusing incident may derive from something that happened to Fritz Lang when he was directing *Fury* (1936) for producer Joe Mankiewicz: according to Lang: 'When *Fury* was finished, the producer came out of a preview and called me to his office and accused me of changing the script. I said, "How could I change the script when I can't even speak English!" So they went and got a copy of the script and he read it and he said, "Damn you, you're right, but it *sounds* different on the screen." Perhaps it did – to him.' (In *Films & Filming*, 1962).
29 Oliver Reed found the dialogue difficult, and sometimes read from pieces of dialogue written on the set.
30 Russell said that Reed's eyebrows had been insured by Lloyd's of London (if they didn't grow back). Reed had been reluctant.
31 Oliver Reed sometimes wasn't confident about his dialogue and his voice (he had the Latin quotations in *The Devils* reduced, for instance, and the lines hidden off-camera). Critics have wondered if Reed might've done some William Shakespeare – an aged King Lear, perhaps, or Macbeth (in the 1971 adaption which starred Jon Finch).
32 Filming *The Devils* had been intense, Oliver Reed admitted – he likened working with Ken Russell on this challenging production to sitting on a firecracker.
33 John Whiting's play added a character called the Sewerman, so that Urbain Grandier could have someone to talk to, rather than playing scenes alone (or using monologues). Among his symbolic functions was to act as a court jester or commentator, and to embody the notion of the world as a sewer (G, 126).

been swamped somewhat by the extravagance of the film-making: 'there was so much going on that it was difficult to make a performance live. The performances got lost in the tirade of masturbation, flagellation and kissing God's feet', Reed complained when the movie was released. But when you consider Ollie's performance now, it seems magnificent.

Vanessa Redgrave (b. 1937) had not been Ken Russell's first choice to play Sister Jeanne: that was, as one might expect, Glenda Jackson. When she refused (not fancying the role),[34] Russell was furious – 'it produced the most bilious fury from him', as Jackson put it – it had seemed the perfect pairing, Reed and Jackson, and had proved so successful in *Women In Love*.

Glenda Jackson had liked the ending of *The Devils* in one (earlier) script version – when, after her death, Sister Jeanne's head was put on display in a casket and her followers approached it on their knees. In this version of the screenplay, the movie would've continued after Urbain Grandier's demise to show Sister Jeanne becoming something of a saintly celebrity, cosying up to Cardinal Richelieu and the King. But the movie would've been long. Jackson wanted that ending, and didn't like the revised ending: in the movie, the ending for Jeanne is rather downbeat and unresolved.

But if you can't sign up Glenda Jackson, Vanessa Redgrave will do! – Redgrave is absolutely spell-binding as the tormented soul in a hunchback's body – again it may be the performance of her career (at least in cinema – Redgrave has worked extensively on stage, and her cinema performances have been a little patchy). Redgrave thought very highly of *The Devils*, calling it the chief work of genius of the postwar period, along with *The Charge of the Light Brigade* (which had been directed by her husband Tony Richardson in 1968, in which she appeared). Russell was full of praise for Redgrave, how she would throw herself into the role, without worrying about how badly she looked.[35]

Prior to *The Devils*, Vanessa Redgrave had appeared in *Isadora, Morgan, The Charge of the Light Brigade, Blow-Up,*

34 'I was worried about playing another neurotic, sex-starved lady, albeit a nun,' Jackson remarked in the *New York Times* in 1971.
35 And it must have been difficult for Redgrave playing every scene with her head tilted to her left side.

A Man For All Seasons, Camelot, and *Oh, What a Lovely War!*
Redgrave became known for her outspoken left-wing political
opinions.[36] As well as *Isadora*, a 1968 movie version of the
dancer who'd been the subject of Russell's incredible, 1966 TV
biography, another connection with Russell was Redgrave's
daughters (by Tony Richardson) – Joely and Natasha – who
appeared in *Lady Chatterley* and *Gothic*.

The supporting players are also outstanding in *The Devils*.
Many were Ken Russell regulars, and actors such as Dudley
Sutton, Michael Gothard, Christopher Logue, Max Adrian,
Georgina Hale and Murray Melvin excelled themselves.
Although *The Devils* was by most reports at times a difficult
shoot, that never detracted from the performances. In every
respect, *The Devils* is filmmaking at its very, very finest. (The
roles played by Dudley Sutton, Michael Gothard and Christopher Logue – the chief heavies – perhaps called for more
well-known actors – Jack Palance, say, or Trevor Howard.
Logue, for instance, was a poet, not an actor, although he had
been impressive as Algernon Swinburne in *Dante's Inferno*.
Someone with more menace and weight on screen might've
been more suitable casting. But Sutton and Gothard were
terrific, and perhaps Logue playing the Cardinal as a scheming
tho' clearly weak person enhances the picture).

☙

The Devils is Ken Russell's *hommage* to the silent movie
classic *The Passion of Joan of Arc* (Carl-Theodor Dreyer,
1928). There are numerous affinities between the two: such as
stylistic motifs like big close-ups, or setting actors against
white and grey buildings (which comprise stylized, abstract
versions of mediæval architecture). And of course *Joan of Arc*
shares many themes with *The Devils* (including a French
setting), such as the satirical representations of the Church and
Catholicism, hypocrisy, religion, prayer, worship, religion vs.
politics, etc. And both movies conclude with a martyrdom at
the stake (the finale of *Joan of Arc* is evoked in many ways by
The Devils – such as the use of street performers (jugglers,
acrobats) mocking the event, the cuts back to big close-ups of
the victim, the shaved head, the skull in the dirt, and even the

---

36 She apparently sold copies of the *Communist Manifesto* outside the comm-
issary.

descent into violence, as the soldiers set upon the onlookers).

✟

In a classic Russellian fantasy sequence (not in the Aldous Huxley book or the John Whiting play, needless to say!), Oliver Reed's Urbain Grandier appeared as Christ, walking on water (in a lake), towards Vanessa Redgrave's Sister Jeanne, now clad in a white dress with long, ginger hair – a Mary Magdalene who prostrates herself before Reed's Jesus. She wipes his feet with her hair, like the Magdalene does in the Christian story. The fantasy, which occurred early in the 1971 picture (as Jeanne watches the funeral procession), served to illustrate Jeanne's suppressed erotic desires for Grandier, which she couches in religions terms (the fantasies 'are projected by a very sick lady in heat', as Jack Fisher put it [1976, 64]).

Typically for a Russellian fantasy sequence, it all goes horribly wrong, when a righteous hurricane rises, coming straight from God or the moral majority (or maybe the mob), and blows Sister Jeanne's dress up, revealing her ugly hump. By the end of the fantasy, Jeanne is rolling around on the stones in agony, as the nuns laugh at her. 'I'm beautiful!' she insists. Urbain Grandier looks down at her pityingly. Poor Sister Jeanne – even her sexual fantasies don't come out right. Even in a sexual fantasy, the one place you can get everything just right (you just close your eyes!), *jouissance* is disrupted.

The fantasy then cuts to Sister Jeanne in the little alcove[37] where she's been spying on the procession,[38] caught in a contorted posture, crouched on the floor. She's a twisted, deformed body in cramped, claustrophobic spaces.[39]

This's one instance of many in the 1971 film of highly physical acting: although he's never described as an 'actor's director', Ken Russell certainly knew how to extract extraordinary and visceral performances out of his ensemble in *The*

---

37 The alcove is put there just for this scene: it's an example of production design describing a personality: it demonstrates how Sister Jeanne has her own ways of circumventing convention, how she has her own little spying places, while the nuns have to fight over getting the top place at the window.
38 Narratively, the procession is there partly to offer an ensemble scene in which to introduce many of the main characters (G, 141). Such scenes also of course show off the production values of a movie. Ironically, Urbain Grandier will undertake the same journey in his own Calvary, at the end of the movie.
39 As Jack Fisher pointed out, those confined spaces and deformities embody the turmoil of Jeanne's sexual and religious repressions (58).

Devils (or he knew how to create an environment in which they could feel safe enough to experiment). It's something that critics tend to overlook – maybe because the visuals and behaviour in a Ken Russell movie are so compelling. But he is a master at drawing out from his actors really kinetic movements and gestures.[40]

And *The Devils* is full of them: actors lunge at other actors, gripping them tightly during the exorcism scenes; they fall to the floor; they loll about from the plague; and in the torture scenes and the frenzy in the church, all manner of contortions are on show (Vanessa Redgrave performs the 'hysteric's arc', for instance, and croaks in a demon's voice (at Grandier: 'devil!'), anticipating *The Exorcist* by a couple of years).[41] The actors throw themselves into these roles – they know that parts this juicy don't come along that often. How many times do you get asked to whip yourself up into (sexual/religious) hysteria in a major, historical movie?!

In a later erotic fantasy of Sister Jeanne's, the real Christ on the Cross transforms into Urbain Grandier crucified. The *mise-en-scène* comprises smoke, extras in Biblical costumes, and a rocky cliffscape (it looks like the Lake District again, or maybe a quarry near Pinewood).[42] It's a full-on, Golgotha sequence, in gnarly black-and-white,[43] with three people being crucified against a rock face (drawing on Renaissance art, of course – a *Crucifixion* out of Rogier van der Weyden or Hans Memling, perhaps).

---

40 Which's also partly why some of the later works are disappointing, because that feeling for physical acting and gesture, and the *sheer energy* that infuses the high-water mark works, from the late 1960s thru the 1970s, is lacking in some of the later pieces.

41 *The Devils* would make a great double-bill with *The Exorcist* – two Warners movies which explore very similar, hysterical, Catholic territory, by filmmakers at the height of their powers. The shoot of *The Exorcist* was by most accounts more difficult than *The Devils,* however.

42 *The Devils* was shot mainly at Pinewood Studios. Bamburgh Castle was also used for the approach road to Loudun (it was seen in *Macbeth* (directed by Roman Polanski) the same year). Locations near Pinewood Studios included Black Park for the forest scene, and a small lake, for the scene where Urbain Grandier walks on the water in Sister Jeanne's dream.

43 Joseph Gomez suggested that Ken Russell and the team employed b/w here because the scene is 'meant to parody such motion pictures as C.B. DeMille's *King of Kings* (1927)' (G, 162). In *An Appalling Talent,* Russell wished he'd filmed both dream visions in black-and-white, to maintain consistency (Bax, 209). The final image of *The Devils* is an optically printed shot which bleaches out to black-and-white.

Vanessa Redgrave's Sister Jeanne[44] overacts in a silent movie manner (as if she's Lillian Gish in a D.W. Griffith melodrama), again clad in white with long hair – a Mary Magdalene figure or bride of Christ (the nun here as a literal 'bride of Christ'). Jeanne approaches Urbain Grandier, who steps down from the Cross (Oliver Reed doing 'Moody 3', of course, complete with a crown of thorns and blood on his face). Grandier/ Jesus embraces the hysterical nun; they kiss while the crowd jeer, and she licks her dream lover's wounds. Finally, they roll on the ground in an erotic embrace, with the Grandier on top of Jeanne.[45]

And while Jesus/ Grandier is fucking Sister Jeanne, the movie cuts back again and again to Jeanne conducting a religious service on her knees, in close-up, surrounded by her nuns, all holding their rosaries. The music is working frantic-ally to enhance the atmosphere of intense eroticism and intense religious repression. At the climax, Jeanne digs a crucifix into her palm, creating a bloody hole that recalls stigmata. Wow! (The cross as phallus, the hole as vagina, plus menstrual blood). She hides, embarrassed (Jeanne is always being overtaken by her erotic desires).

The evocations of classical Hollywood cinema in Sister Jeanne's sexual fantasies (and in particular Cecil B. DeMille) is intentional, of course: DeMille famously sexed-up Biblical stories, happily conflating sex and religion (ancient world epics were a legitimate way of getting a lot of naked flesh on screen, for instance, in Production Code-era Hollywood: the Hays Office and the Legion of Decency might complain about lines of suggestive dialogue, or keeping one foot on the floor in a bedroom scene, but Salomé or Delilah or Cleopatra could just-ifiably be clad in skimpy costumes). And the *form* of a sword-and-sandal Biblical epic from the 1930s-60s also shows how corny and clichéd Jeanne's fantasies are, how she sees herself

44 Another echo of the *Gospels* has Sister Jeanne hanging herself on a tree in a rainstorm.
45 Igniting several taboos, principally those surrounding religion and religious imagery, *The Devils* was adding nothing new to well-known works on the margins of mainstream art. For instance, British artist Eric Gill (another passionate, Catholic Romantic, like Ken Russell, who exalted a particular brand of British/ English tradition), had portrayed a nude, long-haired Mary Magdalene embracing Christ on the Cross. (Gill had produced other images which combined sex and religion, such as his illustrations to the most erotic book in the *Bible*, the *Song of Songs*, in which couples fuck while blessed by the hand of God).

in camp, OTT settings. Because by 1971, when *The Devils* was produced, those sorts of toga sagas were very old hat.

Certainly the erotic fantasy aspects of *The Devils* have been noted by viewers. In one of American author Nancy Friday's books of women's sexual fantasies, for instance, we find this entry from 'Rose Ann', a 23 year-old college grad:

> When the movie *The Devils* came out, a whole new fantasy world opened to me. I don't know if you're familiar with it. The "nun-possessed-by-sexual-demons-that-must-be-exorcised-through-sexual-means" type of thing. Vanessa Redgrave, the nun in question, had to go through the most delicious tortures (having her breasts bound with barbed wire, etc). It turned me on so I had to leave in the middle to go home and masturbate.[46]

Filmmakers, like any artists, love it when people react powerfully to their work, so if they're leaving halfway thru a movie to get themselves off at home, wow! (Even the exhibitors're happy, 'cos they've already paid to see the movie!).

Yeah – take that crrritics Pauline Kael, Vincent Canby, Judith Crist and Alexander Walker: here's a happy customer!:

> It turned me on so I had to leave in the middle to go home and masturbate.[47]

Yes, the erotic fantasy scene in *The Devils* is the cliché of all nun movie genre clichés – taking the 'bride of Christ' fantasy to an erotic conclusion, and depicting Sister Jeanne and Jesus getting it on. Nuns and candles, nuns and lesbianism, nuns and Jesus – you can't expect Ken Russell *not* to include those clichés! So, yes, there're scenes of nuns jerking candles, nuns a-kissin' and a-frolickin' naked, and nuns getting intimate with Christ.[48]

Immediately after the gruesome death of the plague victim (played by one of the Russell regulars, Maggie Maxwell), which ironically brings together Urbain Grandier and Madelyn de

46 N. Friday, *Forbidden Flowers*, Arrow, London, 1994, 279.
47 That should be put on the ads and posters: 'this movie got me off five times!'
48 Even so, a movie such as *Behind Convent Walls* (1977, a.k.a. *Interieur d'un Convent, Sex Life in a Convent* or *Within a Cloister*), directed by Euro-art-'n'-erotica maestro Walerian Borowczyk, was more sexually explicit: the picture (set in a convent) depicted nuns carving dildos from wood and masturbating with them. But the filmmakers of *The Devils* probably knew that being so graphic wouldn't get past the studio or the censors in an American, studio-financed picture in 1971.

Brou (the victim's daughter), and the eternal themes of love and death (they pray over the dead body),[49] the 1971 Warners film shifts into a humorous moment.[50] The outraged father of Philippe, Magistrate Trincant (John Woodvine), accosts Grandier (and he's egged on by Adam and Ibert, the town fools and quacks, who love any social disruption). A little bit of *The Three Musketeers*style swordplay crops up here, when Trincant draws his sword on Grandier, and the priest employs a stuffed crocodile to defend himself (Adam and Ibert having been using crocodiles, among other crazy cures, to treat the plague victim).[51]

Ken Russell gleefully *refuses* to put a serious sword fight on screen in any of his movies – they are always sent up (in *Lisztomania* or *Dante's Inferno*, for instance). He just *won't* do it! He won't he won't he won't! Imagine Russell directing one of those Hollywood blockbuster, action movies, like *Lord of the Rings* or *King Arthur Decapitates the Pirates of the Caribbean In Troy*, which call for thirty-minute-long sword fights. After three seconds the swords would become stuffed crocodiles and ten foot bananas, everyone's costume would fall off to reveal silver bikinis, and on come the chorus girls dressed as nuns and Nazis!

Just writing these little skits on Hollywood movies, where a Hollywood Action Movie Sword Fight becomes an Over-The-Top Ken Russell Dance Number, reminds me just how ridiculous those Hollywood blockbuster movies are, with their incessant and insane insistence on (and glorification of) endless violence. They are far, far dumber, and far more perverse, twisted and sick, than anything Russell produced.[52] And just how much *fun* Russell's approach to movies can be. Oh, once again, I wish that a Hollywood studio had been ballsy enough to give Russell $150 million to see what he could deliver!

Detractors who dislike Ken Russell's movies could critic-

49 As they pray, Urbain Grandier has discovered a new potential lover.
50 Some of the in-jokes include the word 'RUSSEL' daubed on a building (but you'll miss it on panned-and-scanned versions).
51 Russell said he came up with the idea of wasps in glass jars as a cure (wasps?! How would that work?!).
52 The *Lord of the Rings* flicks, for instance, are *extremely violent*, at least in terms of what they are trying to portray – a world war in a fantasy land called Middle-earth. The body counts of *The Return of the King* (836) and *The Two Towers* (468) far excel those in *Saving Private Ryan*, *Hard-Boiled*, *Braveheart* or *We Were Soldiers* (according to www.moviebodycounts.com).

ize the sword-'n'-crocodile fight scene in *The Devils* for being
foolish and pointless, but it's not: first, it demonstrates that the
townspeople can't touch Urbain Grandier, and he knows it; it
shows that Grandier thinks he can get away with being a bad
boy (like horsing around with Important People's Daughters),
and not suffer any consequences; it shows that Philippe
Trincant is not going to take being thrown over by Grandier for
a younger model (Madelyn de Brou) lightly (she has already
appealed to her father, but he's ineffectual); and it lightens the
movie with some humour after the horrors of the death of the
ill woman. (Thus, the movie skilfully uses humour to get
across some key points. And that, folks, is clever screenwriting.
Not every bit of exposition or information in a movie needs to
be delivered in a solemn, sit-down-and-shut-up-and-listen
manner).

The instant rejection of poor Philippe Trincant when she
tells Urbain Grandier that she's pregnant (in their post-coital
scene), demonstrates his cold-hearted side ('so it ends', he
mutters). And once he's made his decision, none of her frustrated protestations have any effect on him: to emphasize his
indifference (and also his vanity), the movie has Grandier
looking in a mirror and combing his hair, in C.U., while the
nude Philippe frets and rages out of focus in the background.
(Her father, Trincant, presents her – naked – to the Baron in
attempt to obtain some justice. But that slur against Grandier
doesn't stick). However, Grandier's cavalier-Casanova attitude
to the town's women works against him in the end, persuading
Trincant to become involved in the conspiracy to oust
Grandier.

You could say that while all around him there is twisted
sexuality – repressed sexuality, too-intense desire, sexuality
that erupts via the suppressions of Christianity into something
tormented and self-loathing – Urbain Grandier's sexuality is
actually straightforward and simply heterosexual. The guy just
likes a good fuck. He's a Henry Miller character or Giacomo
Casanova who unfortunately finds himself in the middle of a
lunatic asylum putting on a play of Dante's *Inferno* at a time of
plague.

Yes, Urbain Grandier moves on from one mistress to the

next, and sometimes has to hear them confess in church, but his sex life is familiar, heterosexual, traditional. It's what men have always been like (yeah, men're shits, but what're you gonna do? Kill them all? 3 billion men?!). In fact, it is through Grandier that one sees much of the insanity of *The Devils*. Meanwhile, the other main viewpoint of the narrative, Sister Jeanne's, comes from someone who is literally twisted in her body as well as her mind (but the most twisted mind in *The Devils*, according to the filmmakers is the power behind the throne, Cardinal Richelieu. Twisted minds who have access to political power are the worst of all).

Thus the scene where Urbain Grandier and Philippe Trincant are seen making love is an important scene (rather than being merely titillating), because it offers a familiar and conventional, central, emotional/ psychological axis for the narrative: b4 the rest of the crazy story splatters across the screen, the audience has seen 'honest lovemaking between two loving people', as Jack Fisher put it (58). Similarly, there is a scene where Grandier and Madelyn de Brou share a meal and talk. Just that. A simple, non-dramatic and harmonious scene (but not a scene that critics who dislike Russellania, and this movie in particular, ever comment upon. What movie reviewer would discuss a modest scene like that? – but there are quite a few in *The Devils* (and loads in Russell's whole output), including a very lengthy two-shot of Madelyn and Grandier later on where they do naught but talk quietly).

✝

Who are the 'devils' in this movie? The nuns when they go nuts at the end? The State's bullies who persecute them and the townspeople of Loudun? Is it Urbain Grandier and Sister Jeanne? Is it Christianity, or Catholicism, or French society, or themes like sin and guilt and retribution?

No. Joseph Gomez is right when he states in his illuminating book on Ken Russell that the real devils in *The Devils* are Cardinal Richelieu and the King of France: because the movie opens not with Loudun, but with the pageant involving the King and Richelieu (presumably in Paris), and when the main title comes up, it is over close-ups of Richelieu and the King (that is, the movie *shows you* who the devils are, by placing the title right over their faces).

Church and State, religion and politics: when Cardinal Richelieu talks to the King in the prologue, he says, 'I pray that I may assist you in the birth of a new France in which Church and State are one' (Eh? Nobody wants that!). He also adds that he wishes to rid France of Protestants. At that point, dispensing with the usual opening credits (of who-did-what), the film cuts straight to a close-up of a maggot-filled skull, attached to the skeleton of a dead Protestant on a wheel on a post in the countryside.

The shock cut does a lot of narrative work: it's all about contrasts, for a start: life and death. It's about the hypocrisy and corruption of the ruling powers. It's about the relationship between mere talk at court and what that talk leads to in reality – death for people who follow the wrong religion. Words and acts.

And that close-up of the skeleton slowly rotating on a wheel functions as vivid *mise-en-scène* for the rest of the 1971 picture, evoking the setting of grim, political times, a world where death is a hair's-breadth away. It also defines the two primary settings: city and town, Paris and Loudun, and the ideological and social contrasts between them. The shock cut also defines where we're going in *The Devils* (and in our own lives): to d-e-a-t-h.

✝

The religious atmosphere in *The Devils* is at fever pitch. It's a hothouse – and the more the religious fervour emerges, the more the religious repression asserts itself – as well as the State oppression (the irony being, of course, that the more political pressure the State exerts on their hothouse, the crazier it gets, which in turn demands more policing and suppression).

Everyone's highly sensitive or already mad, like the Mother Superior. They're all praying, or confessing. (Once again, I insist on the elegance of the script written by Ken Russell, how it builds and builds, so that when the full force of the hysteria erupts, some of the key influences on it have been carefully established. The hysteria[53] doesn't explode out of nowhere: it has a number of dramatic motivations, and is given a historical-religious context. Of course, the structure was already in place in the play by John Whiting and the book by Aldous Huxley, but it was Russell who adapted that structure to make it work in a movie. Sounds easy? It's not: thousands of movies fail at exactly this. Scripts of this kind don't just write themselves: you can't just switch on a camera and point it at the actors in their costumes and tell 'em to recite the lines from Whiting's play or Huxley's novel).

✟

Perhaps the most infamous scene in *The Devils* was Oliver Reed's priest Urbain Grandier being tortured at length (having his tongue stretched and pierced, his limbs smashed with a hammer, his head shaved, pulled along the ground behind a donkey, crawling along the scaffold with his legs smashed), culminating in being burned at the stake. Some of the tortures that were historically enacted (i.e., people really did this stuff! those torture devices really did exist!) wouldn't pass any film censor,[54] but what's on screen is already tough enough to endure (it's how the victim is portrayed that really makes such scenes work, and Reed is marvellous in the torture sequence. Boy, he *really* sells it!).

Urbain Grandier is surrounded in these scenes by the venomous, scheming, manipulative Baron de Laubardemont, the vain, hysterical Father Barré, and the oily, sanctimonious Father Mignon (plus the two comic sidekicks, the chemist and the physician, Ibert and Adam,[55] who are always on hand with their collection of grotesque instruments and their crazy schemes and theories).

For Joseph Gomez, the anachronistic costume and look of

53 *Häxan* (Benjamin Christensen, 1922), also known as *Witchcraft Through the Ages*, is a truly remarkable, Scandinavian silent movie, which includes many scenes which prefigure *The Devils* (nuns in hysteria in a church, mediaeval torture devices, and trials where victims're accused of witchcraft). Produced by Svenska, photographed by Johan Ankerstjerne, *Häxan* starred Maren Pedersen, Clara Pontoppidan, Elith Pio, Oscar Stribolt and Tora Teje. The Danish director – Benjamin Christensen (1879-1959) – appears as the Devil (of course!).
54 Shots had to be curtailed, such as the close-ups of Grandier's mutilated legs (on screen for a brief flash only). The stake scenes took 3 weeks to film, according to Murray Melvin.
55 Adam and Ibert are inspired additions to the Huxley book, deriving from the Whiting play. Wherever there is the potential for mischief to be made, they slyly appear. In later eras, they would be journalists and film critics!

THE DEVILS ✟ 33

Father Barré was a misfire, even in Ken Russell's definition of using anachronisms to make a point. He sports hippy hair, wire-rim specs like John Lennon's in the late 1960s, and black and white garden gloves (G, 149f). I'm not convinced the present day trappings of Barré's costume work either (the hippy trappings form the wrong associations).

And sometimes it does seem as if Ken Russell allows Michael Gothard's portrayal of Father Barré to go too far, to be too silly and OTT. Yes it is a caricature performance, a send-up of the mediaeval exorcist and witch-finder (as played so solemnly and seriously by Vincent Price in *The Witchfinder General* (a.k.a. *The Conqueror Worm* 1968), and by Max von Sydow in *The Exorcist* (1973). But it does threaten to drag *The Devils* too far into farce.

It's a vital element of the overall impact of *The Devils* that Urbain Grandier is being tested and tortured by a gaggle of men who are either insane and sadomasochistic, or who *play* at being insane and vicious (but the result, for Grandier, is just the same!). Father Barré is as out-size in his hysteria as Sister Jeanne. It's wonderful the way that Barré doesn't hesitate for a second to launch himself at Jeanne or the nuns or Grandier; he only requires the slightest provocation, and he leaps into the fray. It's apt too that Ken Russell has Mike Gothard play Barré at fever pitch in many scenes, so that the persecutors turn out to be just as mad as the nuns or Jeanne. But during the scene where Barré enters the pit holding the quaking, weeping nuns, there's a look exchanged between Barré and the Baron: he's enjoying it.[56]

That scene is crucial to the narrative of *The Devils* too: the nuns don't get hysterical without a very good reason: Baron de Laubardemont has them corralled in a pit in the woods, and threatens them with death. If he sets them free, they are commanded to make merry hell. Which they do. (Just like a film director cajoling his actors to go nuts).

Spike Milligan had appeared in the scene where soldiers smash Urbain Grandier's home to bits. But although Milligan played it straight (without the comic flourishes he often

---

[56] In the book, Aldous Huxley described the nuns as 'cabaret performers and circus freaks', while Grandier 'behaves exactly like the proprietor of a sideshow at a fair'.

seemed unable to resist inserting into every performance, even if they were great), it was decided it didn't quite fit, so it was reshot with Dudley Sutton. It is a very effective scene, with obvious ideological symbolism (the thugs destroying Grandier's collection of classical nude statuary), which works (why be subtle when you're portraying the violence of the State?).

One of Hollywood cinema's curious traits is to combine contemporary and period fashion and appearance. Thus, although a film is supposed to be taking place in mediæval times, like *The Devils*, the film's stars will either retain a modern haircut or will have an approximation of a mediæval hairstyle but in modern terms. Costumes are rarely 'authentic' versions of period costume, down to the tiniest detail. Blatant and camp misrepresentations of costume occur in films such as *One Million Years BC* (1966), when Raquel Welch wore a 'prehistoric', Sixties-style bikini. In a film such as *In the Name of the Rose* (1986), Sean Connery went barefoot in mediæval garb, which seemed 'authentic' – but the film's dialogue was in a 20th century, 1980s idiom. Even if, as in BBC TV costume dramas, every detail is 'authentic' and of the period, the speech, language and interactions of the people will be distinctly 20th or 21st century. Movies can never be 'about' earlier times, it seems, but only about the era when the film was made. *The Devils* is no different: but it is also one of those movies which transcends its time.

Aldous Huxley wondered if the events he related in his book *The Devils of Loudun* would prove too much for some audiences. He wrote to playwright John Whiting about Whiting's early draft of the play:

> I wonder if some of the scenes in the last two acts may not prove almost too powerful. The possession, exorcism and torture episodes were hair-raising enough in the narrative (incidentally, I exaggerated nothing; everything in the book is drawn from original sources). Dramatized and well-directed and acted, they may be almost more than many people can take. In any case, it will be very interesting to see how an audience reacts to the horror and strangeness of the story.[57]

And in the end, Ken Russell and his team did tone down some of the wilder events described in Aldous Huxley's book

57 *Letters of Aldous Huxley* Chatto & Windus, London, 1969, 896.

(G, 137).[58]

The Baron de Laubardemont, Cardinal Richelieu's instrument in Loudun, is a wily and brutal politico, wonderfully performed by Dudley Sutton, an ever-dependable character actor (and it's a great role for an actor, too). The Baron is a wholly believable character, who is rightly kept this side of credibility by the filmmakers. It might have been tempting to let the Baron be played over-the-top. But there's no need to do that when you've got Father Barré doing all the crazy eye-rolling, Latin-spouting and larking about with the nuns. Instead, the Baron's cool, menacing quality and calm, cold efficiency as a military man renders the mania of the final scenes all the more unnerving. The Baron just wants to get the job done: he's a professional, a soldier, a tactician (yet he remains a commander all the way thru – you don't see the Baron getting his own hands dirty, such as physically attacking any of the townspeople himself, which makes the violence of what he and his underlings are doing in Loudun all the greater).

Again, if you consider the characterization of Baron de Laubardemont in the movie, and the way he's played by Dudley Sutton, you can once again appreciate just how good Ken Russell is as a film director, and as a film writer. If this were Sam Peckinpah or Howard Hawks, *cinéastes* would be marvelling at how brilliantly Russell creates a military leader, brutish and canny, worthy of standing alongside William Holden's Pike Bishop in *The Wild Bunch* or John Wayne's Ethan in *The Searchers.*

The Baron has a striking introduction in *The Devils,* too: the camera picks up a skull filled with maggots, then pulls back to reveal the skeleton chained to a wheel, and lastly to the Baron on horseback looking up at the victim (the first shot after the amazing prologue). The subsequent scene depicts the Baron ushering a convoy towards Loudun along a road lined with skeletons on wheels. There's a large wagon pulled by many people carrying something bulky but mysterious – it's foreshadowing: all will be revealed at the start of the second

---

58 Russell said that *The Devils* had to be harsh, because the topic was harsh. But the facts, from the book, were 'far more horrible than anything in the film' (PF, 105).

act, when the Baron's over-seeing the destruction of the walls of the town.

✟

The last third of *The Devils* has a marvellous, mesmeric and cruelly logical momentum. It begins when Cardinal Richelieu decides to do something about Loudun, in the archive scene set in Paris, where he confers with the Baron in a slow tracking shot. Once that decision has been made, the events accelerate in their unreality and horror.

For a start, it's not only Urbain Grandier who is tortured: Sister Jeanne is subjected to a horrific bout of punishment, culminating in stomach-churning enemas. It's staged with immense flair in the white-brick convent, with the spectators wearing black eye-masks, and Jeanne being man-handled by Father Barré, Ibert and Adam onto the altar. The camera is now handheld, and right next to Jeanne's legs as they're forced apart. The low angle shots of the large clyster used for the enema enhance the chaos and madness of the scene.

Yes, *The Devils* is a movie where someone's given an enema on an altar. It's not something you see everyday! (And if film censorship allowed it, Ken Russell and his team would surely have gone further, and been more explicit with the enema scene. Although they went way too far for many viewers and critics, and certainly too far for Warner Brothers).

So *The Devils* isn't one long bout of craziness from start to finish: there is a logic, cruel as it is, to the events, as the powers that be (headed up by Cardinal Richelieu and Baron de Laubardemont) try one thing after another. When the torture of Sister Jeanne doesn't turn up the required results, the State tries different tactics, such as intimidating the nuns into hysteria. (That scene is also staged anachronistically – the reference here being a firing squad in a forest,[59] in particular the kind of scenes in WW2 movies where dissidents or Jews have been rounded up and then shot).

The Devils is one of those movies that's *meant* to be exhausting and an assault on the senses and mind. It's like *The Texas Chainsaw Massacre* or *The Exorcist* or *Straw Dogs* or *A*

---

59 Filmed in Blackwood Park, near Pinewood Studios, used in zillions of movies.

Clockwork Orange,[60] to mention films of the same era (the latter two were released the same year as *The Devils*). It's *supposed* to be grim and overwhelming. Yet it is also, like *The Exorcist* or *Texas Chainsaw Massacre* and *Straw Dogs* and *A Clockwork Orange*, flamboyant and supremely confident film-making, from filmmakers who were pushing at the confines of acceptability and taste. It's not meant to be a walk in the park followed by a cup of tea and a snooze in front of the fire.

✞

The torture of Urbain Grandier is truly relentless; if it's meant to be camp and comic, then this's very black humour (but Ken Russell conceived the movie as black comedy).[61] Maybe certain areas of *The Devils* have to be so intense (and serious), in order to exaggerate the black humour of the other parts. Only rarely is this level of suffering inflicted on an individual depicted in mainstream cinema, outside of horror movies. It recalls the end of *Braveheart* (1995), and films of the time like Pier Paolo Pasolini's infamous *Salò* (1975).

(There's a link between Ken Russell and Pier Paolo Pasolini: in the early 1970s Russell was offered *Gargantua and Pantaguel* (1532-52) by François Rabelais, a film which apparently Pasolini was going to do but pulled out. But when Russell saw Pasolini's version of *The Canterbury Tales*,[62] he was horrified. The director of the excesses of *The Devils* found *The Canterbury Tales* 'the most disgusting film I've ever since in my *life*!' [Bax, 229]). (It's a recurring sentiment of Ken Russell's – that he can be very put off by seeing the violence and excesses of some movies, yet he can portray that kind of thing in his pictures. It's the difference between seeing someone else do it, and doing it yourself, perhaps. I'm also reminded of Steven Spielberg finding the violence in *The Gangs of New York*

---

60 At one time Ken Russell had been interested in making *A Clockwork Orange*.
61 Similarly, some viewers can't believe that Alfred Hitchcock saw movies such as *Psycho* as black comedies. But then, Hitch had a very macabre sense of humour!
62 One of the odd things about *The Canterbury Tales* (for a British audience) was that much of it was shot in locations in England (such as Canterbury, Rye and Wells). It was curious seeing a cool, European *auteur* like Pasolini, whose films are full of images of sun-kissed, Southern Italy, or the cultured corridors of power in Rome, or the Middle East, winding up on little, English streets under overcast, English skies. The English locations, plus the appearances of British TV and film actors (such as Tom Baker, Hugh Griffith and Robin Askwith), plus the bawdy humour, linked *The Canterbury Tales* to films such as the *Carry On* or *Confessions of…* series – camp, British, sex comedies.

(2001) off-putting, and telling director Martin Scorsese that he found it difficult to watch such material, even though he did it in his own films (such as *Saving Private Ryan*).)

✞

YOU ARE WATCHING A KEN RUSSELL MOVIE!

The king, Louis XIII (Graham Armitage), who reigned from 1610 to 1643, is introduced in *The Devils* as a buffoon from the off: the 1971 film opens with King Louis appearing as the Goddess Venus in an ultra-camp dance number at a theatrical masque (no Ken Russell film is complete without a dance number).[63] He wears a silver codpiece and bra, a silver cape and high crown, while the (male) dancers're in similarly silvery and thoroughly anachronistic costumes[64] (dressed as women). The choreography (by Terry Gilbert) is deliberately camp.

It's hard to think of another serious historical movie, not a comedy, which introduces a king like this (yeah, and even comedies have to go some way to be sillier).

But it's based in fact, according to Ken Russell, who said that King Louis was

> an extravagant homosexual, a great shot, hater of Protestants, lover of shooting blackbirds and dressing as a woman and choreographing his own numbers; all are used in the film. (Bax, 206).

And, as Jack Zipes noted in 2012's *The Irresistible Fairy Tale*, the French courts really did stage shows like this:

> In all the court entertainments in Italy and France during the baroque period, the spectacle was of utmost importance, consisting of magnificent displays based on myths and fairy tales that celebrated the glory as well as the power of the court, which was likened to some kind of enchanted fairy realm. Those ballets, masquerades and operas were taken seriously in various European courts; they often were made up of ten to fifteen tableaux of scenes: the stories were danced and sung by gifted actors and acrobats, machines and traps were invented and used to create illusions; and characters such as fairies, witches, wizards, gnomes, gods, ghosts, devils, and noble protagonists

---

63 The costumes are outrageously anachronistic, employing plenty of shiny silver – very early 1970s, very glam rock. Another anachronism has *Dies Irae* by Hector Berlioz being played during the funeral procession.
64 Shirley Kingdon once again drew on pop culture – glam rock – for the anachronisms.

were involved in plots that demanded the intervention of some
good higher power, either a fairy, god, or goddess. (26)

A filmmaker devoted to the magic of theatre like Ken
Russell is not going to pass up an opportunity like this, especially when backed up by the historical evidence for such spec-
tacles, festivals and extravagance (one imagines that Russell
would be quite happy organizing royal festivities in the French
court of the 1600s!).

The opening of *The Devils* demonstrates the total confidence of Ken Russell and his team, to be bold enough to open a
historical drama like this: there is no slow, ponderous scene-
setting, no long shots of castles or towns, no reams of captions
to wade thru, no expositional dialogue, no ponderous Charlton
Heston or Orson Welles voiceover... Instead, the King of
France appears as the Goddess Venus wearing nothing but a
bra and silver shell codpiece... and indulging in some *outré*
choreography!

The scene's a 'fuck you' to the historical movie genre, but
not to the audience. The scene also announces to the viewer:
'YOU ARE WATCHING A KEN RUSSELL MOVIE!' (as if
they didn't know: in 1971, Russell had no less than *three
movies* playing in first-run theatres in London – and three *big*
movies, not shot-in-two-weekends indie flicks).

The portrayal of the king and the cardinal in *The Devils*
are very different from their usual portraits in movies – think of
any *Three Musketeers* movie, for instance (two *Musketeer* flicks
were made not long after *The Devils* in Britain and Spain,
helmed by Dick Lester, and starring, incidentally, Ollie Reed
and Richard Chamberlain).

Cardinal Richelieu (1585-1642, played by Christopher
Logue), humours and indulges the king like a child, but is the
real power in France (Richelieu took over the government of
France in 1624: 'his main aim was the establishment of
absolute royal power in France, and also of French supremacy
in Europe').[65] Richelieu dismisses the King's performance with
a single reference to Venus – as if Venus (i.e., mythology, or
love) is completely off the point: for Richelieu, life is about
politics and power, and dressing up and pretending to be the

---

65 I. Robertson, *Blue Guide: France*, A & C Black, 1997, 37.

Goddess of Love is a frightful bore (Richelieu's shown yawning at the King's performance, which marks Richelieu out as superior and dismissive; it may also be a taunt to the audience: in this show, the movie says, you won't yawn, you won't be bored! Yes, but some of those real, French, 17th century *masques, ballet comiques* and operas went on for five hours!). Notice that it's the king who kisses Richelieu's hand at the end of the scene (emphasizing the power relationship). The title credits run over Richelieu and the King in close-up.

It's the power-behind-the-throne scenario, but *The Devils* exaggerates that cliché by making Louis XIII an over-dressed (and cross-dressed) superficial dilettante, a dabbler and fashion plate who's only really interested, it seems, in having a good time.[66] While Cardinal Richelieu puts forward the case for breaking down the fortifications of France's towns, for example, in the blackbird scene, the king is more concerned with firing at the Protestants in bird costumes.[67] (That's the single scene in *The Devils* which doesn't work so well for me: the satire or comedy or whatever it's meant to be jars with the rest of the movie. And it seems to come from a different picture. But Russell liked to include satire like that from time to time, and it does make its ideological and thematic point well).

⚜

There are some impressive montages in *The Devils* – such as the one when Urbain Grandier is giving his speech to the towns-people, which's intercut with King Louis and Cardinal Richelieu talking in a garden (it's the scene where the king shoots at Protestants dressed as blackbirds, among the silliest scenes in Ken Russell's cinema).[68] Another montage follows Sister Jeanne's story and cuts between the Mother Superior masturbating in her cell – and whipping herself afterwards (she

---

66 Yet Richelieu is also crossdressing, in the Catholic manner of clergy in red dresses; the characterization of Richelieu being pushed about by two nuns also emphasizes his oddness. Not quite a cripple, Richelieu's characterization is the familiar cinematic one of the disabled bad guy who has the most power in the movie.

67 However, the king isn't wholly a fool who can be manipulated by Richelieu; he has the measure of the hysteria erupting in Loudun, when he visits the town and exposes the trickery (in Aldous Huxley's book it's a nobleman who performs this act; the king also combines the character from the novel of the debauched royal prince Henri de Condé).

68 The cross-cutting pattern was already established in the script, Russell and Bradsell said, not discovered during post-production.

has lots of gruesome, steel, flagellation devices, sex toys for the extreme S/M of Catholicism) – and Grandier and Madelyn de Brou having their secret, night-time, marriage ceremony (a 'blasphemous nuptial mass') in the church. (In terms of the controversy of these scenes, and *The Devils* as a whole, there isn't that much that's shown – much of it is implied but offscreen. For instance, when the film depicts Jeanne masturbating, it occurs in a long shot with the camera soon dollying back and panning, to reveal one of the nuns – Sister Agnes – watching (and loving it); and the flagellation with the whip is done offscreen, on a C.U. of Sister Jeanne's hand clutching yet another crucifix, with sound effects.[69] Compare that to thirty years later and the endless flagellation on-screen in 2004's *The Passion of the Christ*).

Again, much of the criticism surrounding Ken Russell's work draws attention to his visuals, but often it's the editing that really brings out the impact of those visuals. The montages are one example in *The Devils*, as well as some of the shock cuts (the opening cut from the King and Richelieu to the C.U. of maggot-ridden corpse is one shock cut – another is the cut from the chaotic Cathedral scene, where Urbain Grandier is arrested, to the close-up of his tongue being pierced which begins the torture sequence). Much of the credit must go to Russell's regular editor Mike Bradsell, whose editing and pacing adds so much to *The Devils* (Bradsell recalled that editing *The Devils* had been relatively easy, and shots had fallen into place organically and naturally; it wasn't a picture where the editors had to struggle to complete the movie. However, preparing re-edited versions for the censors and the studio wasn't so easy).

The plague scenes in *The Devils* were also highly exaggerated: Urbain Grandier walks through a devastated Loudun, with fires burning and plague victims gasping, staring wide-eyed, being winched down from houses above, and expiring. Cue close-ups of extras with revolting, decaying faces.

In one scene, Urbain Grandier enters the home of a dying woman who's being administered quack cures by the two

---

69 It's a standard tactic in cinema – to show the effect of something nasty or explicit, you use someone else's reaction to it, and let the audience imagine the real thing for themselves. It gets around the censor, but it also provides a commentary on the act (and also emphasizes the act of looking).

doctors (Ibert and Adam) who become instrumental in Grandier's torture. The woman's naked body's covered with glass jars containing leeches and a wasp. Fire flickers in the background from an oven (the lighting, by cinematographer David Watkin and his team, is stunning in this sequence).

There's also a large plague pit full of bodies, which Urbain Grandier visits the following morning. And corpses being piled onto a cart and a guy yelling, 'bring out your dead!' The *Monty Python* team were probably thinking of *The Devils* when they sent up plague scenes in *Monty Python and the Holy Grail* (they had satirized Russellania in their TV show, in a piece called 'Ken Russell's Gardening Club, 1958'). The plague doesn't feature in either Aldous Huxley's book or John Whiting's play, according to Russell: the fact was discovered by a French scholar (Bax, 223). So the 1971 movie used it: why? because it enhanced the already crazy goings-on, and played into the themes of the corruption and decay underneath the surface of the life of the community.[70] (Depicting big plague scenes was also Russell's chance for scenery like that in *The Seventh Seal*, or the popular Biblical epics of the 1950s and 1960s, where scenes involving lepers were mandatory. But in those sword 'n' sandal epics, Jesus was on hand to cure the lepers. In the helhole that is Loudun in *The Devils*, there's nobody around with such a miraculous touch).

But the most controversial scene in *The Devils* was cut out of the film, a decision made by Warner Brothers and the censor. It featured the so-called 'rape of Christ', the climax of the convent possession sequence, where the naked nuns cavort crazily around and on top of a wooden Cross and a figure of Christ in the Cathedral (meanwhile, Father Mignon watches from above and masturbates, as any self-respecting Catholic priest would!).[71]

It was an over-the-top scene, as Ken Russell and his team intended, combining nudity and religion, sexuality and Christ-

---

70 Russell certainly does have a fascination 'with the decayed, the used, the soiled, the defective, and eventually with the grotesque', as Jack Fisher remarked (42).
71 Ken Russell played *The Fiery Angel* by Sergei Prokofiev and *The Rite of Spring* during the 'rape of Christ' scenes, to help his actors get in the mood. As Aldous Huxley put it in *Along the Road*, 'since Mozart's day composers have learned the art of making music throatily and palpitatingly sexual'.

ianity,[72] but it was, for Russell, the central scene of *The Devils*. Russell intended the 'rape of Christ' to be intercut with a scene of Urbain Grandier alone in the mountains, a very quiet, reverential scene:

> The naked nuns tear down a wooden figure of Christ and throw themselves on it, having it in every possible way... Both Warner Brothers and the censors thought it was too strong so I took it out... But it was really central to the whole thing, intercut as it was with Grandier finding himself and God in the solitary simplicity of Nature. Over-ripe, perverted religion going as bad and wrong as it can possibly become, with the eternal truth of the bread and the wine and the brotherhood of man and God in the universe. (Bax, 210)

Some of the 'rape of Christ' images survived in *The Devils*: nuns stroked phallic candles; women masturbated, and writhed around on the floor, eyes rolling and tongues lolling out;[73] they whipped themselves, fell on top of each other, danced, shook and shrieked. The scene involves many elements – not only naked nuns, for instance, but also the townspeople who've come into the Cathedral to watch, gape and laugh. The background action is brilliantly chaotic and animated, and the scene also includes Barré and Sister Jeanne in prominent roles (Jeanne performs the hysteric's arc, for example, in a disturbing moment). And into it all comes King Louis XIII and his entourage.[74] You can appreciate that it was a nightmare to shoot – definitely one of the most challenging scenes in Russell's whole career.

For the actors playing the nuns, the rape of Christ scenes required not only nudity but plenty of physical acting. Not easy. On top of that, the actresses were required to have their heads shaved. To persuade some of the more reluctant actors (plenty of actresses would refuse), the production offered them 150

---

[72] Again, in Aldous Huxley's book it was based on eye witness accounts: in a letter to Walter Montague, Thomas Killigrew related how he was invited to hold the limbs of the nuns in order feel how the Devil was possessing them. Other Britishers visited Loudun and described what they saw, including Lady Purbeck and Sir George Courthop. For Huxley, the scene became like a grotesque fairground side-show, with onlookers invited to step right up and touch the nuns: 'these spouses of Christ have been turned into cabaret performers and circus freaks' (1970, 157).

[73] Apparently, some of the rape of Christ takes got out of hand, Russell recalled, and Equity (the actors' union) got involved (PF, 116-7).

[74] When the king arrives in the Cathedral, celeb couple Twiggy and Nigel Davies (a.k.a. Justin de Villeneuve) can be glimpsed in the background as fops.

quid ($225). But it certainly enhances the scene that not only are the nuns nude, and hysterical, they are also shaved, like prisoners or concentration camp inmates.

But even without all of the 'rape of Christ', *The Devils* is still *immensely* powerful. And it still does cut from the mayhem in the Cathedral to Urbain Grandier conducting his mass beside the lake.

Rarely have movies – well, British movies at least – depicted such chaotic, intensely hysterical scenes with so much nudity (albeit female nudity – priest Barré strips off his top). And Ken Russell was probably the only British director who could have done it, at the time (and very few filmmakers since then would dare do it; and many producers would no doubt try to persuade the director to drop it from the script).

But it's the end of the 'rape of Christ' scene that's vital: when Urbain Grandier turns up, framed in the doorway. The staging and camerawork is brilliant here, with David Watkin and his camera team producing elaborate tracking shots worthy of Orson Welles as they follow Urbain Grandier into the church, thru the chaos, past the smoking, swinging censer, and all the way up to Sister Jeanne.[75] It's the moment when Grandier and Jeanne meet face to face, and right after that momentous encounter, Grandier is arrested (when the Baron exploits the feverish atmosphere and orders Grandier's arrest).[76]

The 'rape of Christ' sequence is carefully constructed dramatically: as screenwriter (rather than as director), Ken Russell doesn't simply cut straight to the mayhem inside the Cathedral, which's such sensational material. No: the entire sequence has a narrative logic, building up from the orgy to major dramatic beats, such as Sister Jeanne being urged to confess, and finally to the two big reveals: the arrival of the King and his entourage, and the finale, Urbain Grandier appearing in the doorway.

Ignoring the out-there nature of the sequence – sex-plus-nudity-plus-violence-plus-religion – you can see how meticulously the episode has been planned and scripted. For critics who complain that Ken Russell's cinema emphasizes shocks

---

75 A grand shot that probably took hours to rehearse, set up, light and shoot.
76 Grandier entering the church consciously alludes to Christ in the temple with the money-changers, and his arrest parallels Christ in Gethsemane.

and vulgarities and over-the-topness, the 'rape of Christ' episode is solid proof that those shocks and brazen images can only work if the foundations have been laid correctly, if the context has been set properly, and if the hysteria builds in a convincing and dramatically logical manner.

And it does: Ken Russell and his team know so well how to construct a scene: that is, to literally *construct* a scene, piling it up piece by piece, shot by shot. Take away some of the beats and the shots, some of the looks and lines of dialogue, and it won't work. In short, *The Devils* is so powerful largely because it is so brilliantly staged and delivered. Yes, the material is incredibly strong on its own, but it's the way that the movie is presented to the audience with such assurance, such flair, such wit and such imagination, that makes it a true classic. (And a true one-off: there is nothing like this in all of British cinema).

✞

It is also the *complexity* of the portrayal of the characters and the issues that is so impressive in *The Devils*. Urbain Grandier is a conflicted personality; he's a hero with flaws (the movie makes sure the audience understands some of those flaws early on). His penchant for women might be understand-able or forgivable to a modern cinema audience (it was OK for James Bond and Our Man Flint in the 1960s, for instance), and not count as a fault; but the film clearly outlines the levels of sexual repression and sin that run through this community of Loudun. Vanity, the love of power and authority, arrogance and insensitivity are further flaws in Grandier's character, yet he acts at times as one of the most sensible people in the town.

The Devils is specially good at delineating the *motives* of each of the major characters. Everyone has their reasons and their goals. It's true that in some films directed by Ken Russell, narrative or dramatic elements such as motives aren't so fully developed. In *Tommy*, for example, Russell persuaded Pete Townshend to insert some backstory for Tommy's father, and *The Music Lovers* develops a marvellous use of flashbacks, but in other films he prefers to dispense with backstories.

✞

As a respite from the political and religious machinations of the plot, and the downbeat nature of much of the material in

The Devils, there is a romance, between Urbain Grandier and Madelyn de Brou (Gemma Jones[77] – another terrific performance. Jones is perfectly cast). Madelyn might be the most 'normal' character in the piece, and Grandier is probably at his most humane in the scenes he shares with her.

And although most viewers probably think of *The Devils* as being dominated by Urbain Grandier and Sister Jeanne – which it is – it's actually Madelyn de Brou who is in some ways the central figure. Introduced early on – when she begs Grandier who's passing by to look at her mother, a plague victim who's being treated with bonkers medicine by the comic pairing of Adam and Ibert – Madelyn soon develops a desire for Grandier.

It's Madelyn de Brou who further links Sister Jeanne and Urbain Grandier, when she goes to Sister Jeanne asking to join the convent (Jeanne pours scorn and bile on Madelyn from the outset of their unusual interview (conducted through the bars of the convent's window), deprecating her appearance (the down-cast eyes),[78] her pretty rosary, and her sin of pride). Jeanne despises Madelyn for possessing the quiet spirituality she pines for but can't manufacture (Madelyn is how Jeanne might've started out when she was younger and idealistic); but Jeanne is also right that Madelyn is a somewhat stuck-up, goody-two-shoes. In her negative aspects, Madelyn represents the pious religiosity that Catholicism aspires to but which too often is misdirected, or is corrupted; and Madelyn is also too 'pure' and 'innocent' to be wholly convincing (could you remain 'pure' and 'innocent' growing up in a town with crazy people like Adam and Ibert around?!).

And it's Madelyn de Brou who's the last person to be seen in the 1971 Warners production, when she walks away from the town. Yet the romance does not slow the movie down, or deflate some of its power, but enhances it (and when Ibert and Adam witness the marriage in the church at night, it becomes part of the accusations hurled at Urbain Grandier).

It's no 'walk into the sunset' image, though: at the end of this bleak, unrelenting movie, there can be no happy ending,

---

77 In recent years, Gemma Jones has appeared in Jackie Chan movies, *Harry Potter* movies and Woody Allen.
78 As if Madelyn de Brou is a caricature of a painting of a Catholic saint.

and nothing approaching a happy ending. Because what's happening in Loudun is happening across France. (Joseph Gomez compared the marvellous final shot to *The Triumph of Death* by painter Pieter Brueghel [G, 161]).

☦

The theme of the nuns spying on each other and on the world outside the convent recurs numerous times in *The Devils*. That's partly to do with dramatic necessity, to connect the worlds inside and outside the nunnery, but the evocation of paranoia is fundamental to stories of political corruption, whether it's in the White House in 2014 or London in 1592. It begins with the nuns watching the funeral procession at the beginning of the film (and fighting like kids over who gets to watch from the top of the ladder). Sister Jeanne spies on her sisters, then dismisses them – only to sneak into a basement alcove where she can ogle Urbain Grandier for herself and swoon into an erotic reverie (she also overhears the towns-people remarking of Grandier – 'he can have me any time!', and: 'there's a man worth going to Hell for!').

Later, Sister Agnes spies on Sister Jeanne masturbating then whipping herself. Sister Jeanne watches the nuns goofing around with a re-enactment of the nighttime nuptials of Urbain Grandier and Madelyn de Brou. And the nuns themselves are watched avidly by the crowd at the public trial, and during the 'rape of Christ' scene.

☦

Torture scenes run throughout *The Devils*. In the middle of the 1971 film, for instance, the denizens of Loudun are put inside giant, wooden wheels which drive ropes to pull down the fortifications. (Torture wheels on poles are one of the signature images of *The Devils* –famously in the opening sequence, lining the road to Loudun (filmed at Bamburgh Castle), and in the final shot.)

Full of Ken Russell's over-the-top imagery, with not a few comic moments ('it's not everyday baby sees daddy being burned at the stake', Max Adrian quips to Urbain Grandier's bastard child while Philippe Trincant stands beside him, joyously drinking as Grandier is burnt at the stake), *The Devils* is Russell's sustained attack on hypocrisy, obsession, religious bigotry, the manipulations of the State and politics, and mob mentality (it was his only political film, Russell sometimes remarked; but, actually, Russell has tackled politics head-on many times). It wasn't so much that Russell wanted to 'shock' (almost impossible to achieve anyway, especially today, and a dumb, limiting ambition for an artist), his project was rather to expose intolerance (religious and political).

It was mainly the manner in which Ken Russell and the team tried to achieve those aims that created the negative response to the movie: by using extravagant performances, outlandish imagery, and the irreverent treatment of religion. For some people even today, images, even if they're a fantasy, of a Christ figure sexually embracing a Mary Magdalene character, can be disturbing. *The Last Temptation of Christ* created a similar (much more widespread) controversy in 1988: in that Universal movie, a clearly signposted fantasy sequence showed Jesus and the Magdalene having sex and bearing children, the point being to show what Christ's life might have been like had he not died on the Cross. As expected, religious fundamentalists took the dream sequence at the end of *The Last Tempt-ation of Christ* literally.[79]

Besides, Ken Russell wasn't interested in so-called 'realistic' violence or shock. He was being intentionally fantastical and exaggerated:

> People are used to watching television and seeing the Korean War or the Vietnam War or Ireland. I think even that, in the end, becomes associated with fantasy. It becomes a fantasy of reality, of handheld cameras running down the street. That's why I would never do a modern film like that. People have come to expect that sort of violence. They don't stop eating while it's

---

79 The evangelical groups claimed they had over 3 million signatures on their petitions against the film. Bill Bright, of the Campus Crusade for Christ, offered Universal $10 million for the destruction of the picture. Between 7,500 and 25,000 people protested outside MCA/ Universal Studios' 'Black Tower' in the week before the film's opening on August 12, 1988. The protesters included the Eastern Orthodox Church of America, the National Catholic Conference, the Southern Baptist Convention, the Archbishops of Canterbury and Paris, and people from the American House of Representatives.
There were scenes of protest against *The Last Temptation of Christ* in New York, Washington, San Francisco, Chicago, Seattle, Toronto and L.A. Around a thousand people protested at cinemas in New York and Salt Lake City. Screens were slashed by protesters; a print was taken. In Paris, at the UGC Odéon cinema, when the film opened in September, there was a riot, with Molotov cocktails being hurled. Similar protests occurred in Marseilles, Avignon and Besançon. There was a fire at the Cinéma St Michel on October 22, 1988.

going on. I do want to shock people into a sense of awareness. (1973)

Ken Russell stressed that the material in the book by Aldous Huxley was far more horrible than anything put in the film. *The Devils* had to be harsh, because the subject was harsh (Bax, 202). The gross humour was part of Russell's project of exploring religious hypocrisy: 'designed to point out the nonsensical irony of these horrors being committed in the name of God' (ibid.). It's not supposed to be taken literally or totally seriously. Here, Russell's penchant for over-the-top drama serves the themes and material very well. It's not the sombre seriousness of Arthur Miller's *The Crucible*, or the solemn horror of *Salem's Lot*. It's deliberately camp, silly, and out-size.

At the same time, there is a real power of rage running throughout *The Devils*, which erupts most passionately in the portrayal of Urbain Grandier. Everyone in *The Devils* seems to be off-kilter or plain crazy. And the once sane folk only require a slight nudge to send them into hysterics. The sanest character is definitely the Grandier, and also his wife Madelyn de Brou. If there is a mouthpiece of Ken Russell and the team in *The Devils*, it's definitely the Grandier.

Ken Russell saw Urbain Grandier as 'the fall guy in a political conflict', whose greatness took him by surprise, who was out of step with his times but managed to effect great changes (Bax, 205). He loses the battle (his life), but wins the war. After this, no one could be burnt as a witch in France, Russell insisted, and the people must've realized that Grandier couldn't have been guilty of the 'crimes' he was charged with.

In Ken Russell's conception, Urbain Grandier doesn't take *everything* in Catholicism seriously. He acknowledges that religions are made up of human beings with all their frailties and desires. And you can't expect even a priest to be the perfect Catholic 24 hours a day. Sometimes they will be reciting the sacred words parrot fashion (as in the plague pit scene).

But it *was* important for Ken Russell to show that Urbain Grandier did take the central ritual of the Catholic religion seriously, the Eucharist, which's one reason why the film-makers placed Grandier away from Loudun, in the mountains, to perform the Mass on his own (and with Madelyn de Brou).

The rise of Urbain Grandier to greatness is depicted in a face-off with Baron de Laubardemont and his cronies, who are pulling down the walls of Loudun (with the aid of some enormous wooden wheels and ropes).[80] In that instance, Grandier wins – he arrives in the town square with a group of soldiers who train guns and arrows at de Laubardemont.

✞

The Devils alters the historical time-scale of the events in Loudun and Paris – for instance, there were more appeals, the King changed his mind about the walls, Barré left for Chinon (and was recalled), and there were much more legal wrangling (G, 163). The events in Loudun stretched on for years, but *The Devils* compresses it into maybe months or even weeks (but movies typically compress time, combine characters and events, and leave out masses of material).

But when Ken Russell was attacked for altering history, he insisted that what was depicted in *The Devils* was historically accurate. A caption opens the movie to state this: 'this film is based on historic fact. The principal characters lived and the major events depicted in the film actually took place'. Of course, there is artistic licence being employed all over the place – but that occurs with any historical movie, or play, or novel, or painting, or whatever.

The Devils is not a documentary, it's history portrayed within the context and modes (and limits) of a feature movie. And Ken Russell and his team were concerned with getting the central issues right.

✞

The final scenes of *The Devils* are a *tour-de-force* of staging, performance and wielding the whole, technical arsenal of cinema. The equal, I would say, of anything in British – or world – cinema. Really? Oh yes. Go back and have a look at the last 10 or 15 minutes of *The Devils*. It's astonishing.

The Devils is one of those movies where the hero dies. A martyr. A victim. A scapegoat. A hero. A sacrifice. (Take your pick).

No Hollywood Last Minute Rescue here. It's Death all the

---

80 The destruction of the town walls had to be filmed twice, when the cues to time the explosions went wrong. The scene was re-set ten days later.

way. The grand trajectory of the drama – that Urbain Grandier has to make his way to the stake, be tied to it and burnt alive – is all-encompassing. But along the way the filmmakers include all manner of incidents and details, such as: the use of black and white costumes, and the black masks; the sideshow of capering players on a stage in front of an enormous Mouth of Hell (who send up the story);[81] the gallery of rogues up on the balcony (Magistrate Trincant and his daughter Philippe, gleeful that justice is being done and Grandier is going to die, accompanied by the equally joyful Adam and Ibert); Grandier being hauled along behind a mule then thrown off; Grandier bound on the ground; the condemnation of Sister Jeanne and her sisters; Father Mignon's confused, ambivalent response (a look of anger then horror); the compassionate, hooded hangman, who offers to strangle the priest before the fires are started; the astonishing images of Grandier crawling in a low angle close-up while the circus cavorts behind him; Father Barré kicking Grandier's feet and Grandier's screams…

Still the State emissaries and bully boys hiss and bellow for a confession, but of course Urbain Grandier does not give anyone the pleasure. The kiss – of compassion which becomes a kiss of betrayal – is a marvellous and grotesque touch, bringing together the crowd (the idea that they sway in unison is terrific (like a rock concert audience) – and the assistant directors (Ted Morley and Nicolas Hippisley-Coxe) in a big, challenging scene like this did their work beautifully).

It's truly remarkable filmmaking, so many stages to the sequences, so many details, though of course a hero going to the stake is fantastic dramatic material to climax a story. But even if you've seen it before (in *Joan of Arc* movies, for instance), this interpretation is still riveting and heart-rending (not least for Oliver Reed's outstanding performance).

And, no, Ken Russell and his team are not going to stop at the beginning of the fire, and step away with a long shot and a fade to black… they are going to depict Urbain Grandier in different states of flamey decay. Wow – it's truly gruesome, but even in the midst of excruciating agony, Grandier still manages

81 And also demonstrate that it all amounts to nothing but fuel for a story and an entertainment, in the end. The ultimate in exploitation and cynicism. The troupe of players would become, in the 20th century, a film crew, cannibalizing history and suffering to provide entertainment.

to appeal to and sermonize the crowd (that might be unconvincing at the level of realism, but it works dramatically superbly).

But Oliver Reed in gory, fire-scarred make-up is not only what makes this scene so startling: it's the *point-of-view images* seen *through* the flames (achieved one imagines with optical super-impositions and mirror shots as well as practical effects), of every character in the movie. And also cuts to the mummers and their skeleton costumes dancing manically. (You can see why *The Devils* might play well in Italy – or in Mexico – where it comes across as a Mexican Day of the Dead carnival). The flames make the simple but important point too that the town has become Hell on Earth.

A triumph of montage editing by Michael Bradsell and the sound editors, this is Ken Russell and his team at their wildest and most incisive (certainly Russell didn't top this sequence in the rest of his career): because the point-of-view images of each character seen though the flickering flames condemns all of them, yes, but also begs them, implores them, denounces them, but doesn't expiate them.

What is being burnt here, sacrificed here, torn to shreds here, apart from poor Urbain Grandier? It's the society's faults, their obsessions, their intolerance – their sins, to use the Catholic term.[82] But also some better part of themselves. The film condemns actions and ideas which make humans less than human, when humans lose something of their humanity.

When Urbain Grandier undergoes his lengthy Cavalry – a crawl to Golgotha along the wooden scaffold – one person is conspicuously absent from the vast crowd gathered to witness the event. Everyone else is present, the complete cast of crazy characters in this Christian circus – except for Madelyn de Brou. During the whole torture and court trial sequence, Madelyn is kept off the screen. Though it might have been tempting to cut to her shocked expression as she watched the idiocy of the trial or the utter horror of seeing her husband being burned alive at the stake, *The Devils* doesn't need it. The imagery is already so sensational (and Madelyn is being saved

82 One of Grandier's final cries is to implore the people to look to themselves, to their town, to their *country*. He might have finished with saying to their *world*. The implication is the modern world, too.

for the final scene).

✿

The *dénouement* of *The Devils* involving Sister Jeanne and Baron de Laubardemont, which follows the stake scene, is brilliantly modest and small-scale, which only heightens the total cynicism of the Baron (and by implication the government of France). At the start of the scene, Sister Jeanne has her back to the camera and seems about to plunge a hot poker into her vulva, to drive out those sexy demons (Christianity has some of the most bizarre self-harming practices in history). By now, we've seen so much craziness, this scene doesn't startle.[83]

But when the Baron appears, all of Sister Jeanne's craziness disappears, and she seems quite normal and lucid. The matter-of-fact tone of the Baron's appraisal of events, and what will happen next, enhances the attitude of the State: all of this madness has simply been an excuse for exercising power. That's all it was: a way of the State gaining control of the provinces. And now that Sister Jeanne[84] has ceased to be useful, she can, as far as the government is concerned, fade away into oblivion.

✿

So the final shot of *The Devils*, which ironically employs the classic crane shot of the Hollywood ending, is not much of a way out or a sop or a means of finding something positive to express in amongst all of the madness of the preceding two hours. It's a symbolic ending, however: Madelyn de Brou, one of the only sane people left in Loudun (or one of the only people who don't go along with the lunacy that grips the denizens of the town), decides she's had enough and flees the town, scrambling over the broken walls.[85]

At least someone gets out alive, you might say. But what sort of life will Madelyn de Brou have now (assuming she's not traumatized by what she's witnessed)? The cut from the chaos

---

83 There was more to this scene, with Sister Jeanne using the bone that the Baron gives her (part of Grandier's remains) as a dildo (of course the bone looks like a cock and balls – the dick's gotta be the bit of Grandier that Jeanne receives after his death!).

84 When Sister Jeanne tells the Baron that she has wronged an innocent man, it is not what the Baron or the State want to hear.

85 Of course, Madelyn de Brou would have stayed for Grandier's burial and funeral service, and in reality would also have taken some other belongings, food and maybe a friend or relative or two (this is not the time to be wandering around France unaccompanied).

of the apocalyptic execution scene to the utter banality and nothingness of the man shovelling black ashes and bones says it all: all of this terror and horror has amounted to... a heap of ashes.[86] To nothing. And the cut from the ashes below the stake to Madelyn's reaction also speaks volumes: she is beyond tears, beyond feeling anything. She just knows she's got to get out of there.

✞

Was *The Devils* worth making? Ken Russell wondered. 'To me, yes, *The Devils* was a political statement worth making' (BP, 193). And it has resonances that were very much of the present moment – and Aldous Huxley had inevitably made comparisons with France in the 17th century and the contemporary era in *The Devils of Loudun*

> Though frequently Manichaean in practice, Christianity was never Manichaean in dogmas. In this respect it differs from our modern idolatries of communism and nationalism, which are Manichaean not only in action, but also in creed and theory. Today it is everywhere self-evident that *we* are on the side of Light, *they* on the side of Darkness, they deserve to be punished and must be liquidated (since *our* divinity justifies everything) by the most fiendish means at our disposal. (1970, 192)

Ken Russell resolutely stood by his film, throughout the period when it was attacked as blasphemous and flopped in North America (though it was 'an all-time hit in Italy where the Doge of Venice was burnt in effigy when he tried to ban it', Russell claimed [BP, 193-4]).[87] 'They said *The Devils* was blasphemous,' Russell told *SFX Magazine* in August, 1999, 'whereas I see it as being about abuses within the Church. It's a very moral tale.'

The Devils is a movie of now, of course (or 1970-71, when it made, but also of now (like all classics), because it still resonates big time). As Joe Gomez put it, *The Devils* is 'not merely a supercharged historical recreation of the last years of Urban Grandier; it is also an æsthetically exciting, visionary

---

86 'In terms of pictorial qualities alone the ending is triumphant cinema' (Jack Fisher, 59).
87 Apparently, the Vatican criticized *The Devils* as 'the perverted marriage of sex, violence and blasphemy'. It was banned but then shown in Italy (and *Women In Love* was allowed to be released, too). According to Robert Sellers, reaction to *The Devils* helped to change the out-dated censorship laws in Italy.

film about our own time' (1976, 70). Of course, *all* movies are *at least* about the time when they made (because they are always that, no matter what else they might be). But some historical movies pretend to ignore the present day, as if you can have a 'pure' re-enactment of the past, as if you can re-create history from scratch, in a 'pure' form. You can't. *The Devils* in fact is very conscious of the contemporary period of the late 1960s and the early 1970s.

☦

I've not bothered with extensive theoretical explorations in my study of *The Devils* (because I want to focus on the movie as much as possible, without veering off the subject), but it's worth noting that there is a huge amount of theoretical writing about the links between insanity, hysteria and altered states of consciousness and the relation to religion. Contemporary feminism, for instance, has studied mediæval religious hysteria, which relates directly to *The Devils*.

Instead of using the usual approach of Sigmund Freud, the writings of French feminism are useful in thinking about the depiction of the nuns and the religious communities in *The Devils*. The French feminist Luce Irigaray, for instance, has been concerned with the notion of women as 'outsiders', of the otherness and outsideness of women in a patriarchal regime. Irigaray is interested in those women who have been 'outsiders' in history – the hysteric, the witch, the mediæval mystic, those people who 'stand outside' culture, using the techniques of ecstasy ('ex-stase', Irigaray spells it, 'ecstasy' meaning, from the Greek, 'stand outside'). Both Irigaray and Julia Kristeva spoke of the special, creative positionality of the mediæval women mystics, who occupied the maternal, liminal place of the mother, where the object of devotion became less fixed, more open, less dogmatic, more 'feminine'.

For Julia Kristeva, Christianity offers a limited number of ways in which women can participate in the 'symbolic Christian order': for women who are not virgins or nuns, who have orgasms and give birth

> her only means of gaining access to the symbolic paternal order is by engaging in an endless struggle between the orgasmic maternal body and the symbolic prohibition – a struggle that

will take the form of guilt and mortification, and culminate in masochistic *jouissance*. For a woman who has not easily repressed her relationship with her mother, participation in the symbolic paternal order as Christianity defines it can only be masochistic. (*Tales of Love*, 147)

Two of the classic ways in which women have been allowed to participate in Christianity is the '*ecstatic* and the *melancholy*' (ib.). According to Elizabeth Grosz in "Lesbian Fetishism?" (1991), women can disavow their own castration (*contra* Sigmund Freud) through hysteria – women phallicizing part of their bodies; the 'masculine complex' – women taking the phallus as their love object; and narcissism – women turning their bodies into the phallus.

Even at the most simplistic and childish level, *The Devils* activates some of these concerns – with phallic imagery, a favourite with Ken Russell, with the eruption of sexual and religious repression in the 'rape of Christ' orgy, and with the twisted sadomasochism of Catholicism. And it's not only the community of the convent and the nuns, it's also the community of Urbain Grandier, the priests and their Church which's explored for its repression, extremity, S/M, hypocrisy and hysteria. (You could also link the evocations of witchcraft in *The Devils* with the rise in popularity of occultism, paganism and wicca in the late 1960s/ early 1970s, figures such as Aleister Crowley (a perfect subject for a Ken Russell movie!), books like *The Occult* by Colin Wilson, and popularized in the dabbling with satanic themes in rock bands like Led Zeppelin, Black Sabbath and the Rolling Stones).

☩

Video and DVD versions of *The Devils* have been the focus of much contention, with critics and fans hoping for a full, uncut version, and the distributor (Warners) reluctant to deliver (the 117 minute restored version remains unavailable on home entertainment formats – the longest cuts are 108/ 11 minutes). *The Devils* has been screened in restored versions (including with the director presented for Q & A afterwards – in Southampton in 2007 and in Montréal, Toronto and L.A. in 2010, and in London in 2011, for instance).

Inevitably, *The Devils* was a problematic film for the censors (ironic, too, because it was partly about State censorship). In Britain, that meant John Trevelyan (out-going censor), new censor Stephen Murphy, Lord Harlech and the British Board of Film Censorship; in the U.S. of A., the film was given an 'X' rating[88] by the M.P.A.A.[89] *The Devils* was banned in Ken Russell's hometown of Southampton, and 16 other local councils. In the Land of the Free, 2 minutes were cut out of *The Devils*, including some of the shorter, more graphic images (G, 163). According to Mark Kermode, the movie was trimmed of the 3-4 minute 'rape of Christ' scene before being submitted to the censors in Feb, 1971 (on the advice of Trevelyan).

The Festival of Light (led by Peter Thompson) protested against *The Devils* outside theatres (however, compared to some movies, such as *The Last Temptation of Christ, Hail Mary*[90] or *The Passion of the Christ*, the protests against *The Devils* were much milder).

Censor John Trevelyan had drawn the line at allowing the word *cunt* in *The Devils*, however: the script had included a line where Sister Agnes says cunt, but as Trevelyan told Russell, 'I'm afraid we can't have Vanessa saying 'cunt'. It's taken me ten years of fighting just to get 'fuck' accepted. I'm afraid the British public isn't ready yet for 'cunt'" (Bax, 211). And for the next forty years or more, it was still rare for movies to include the word cunt. (Other language was also trimmed. Russell remarked that Trevelyan had been more helpful on *Women In Love* than *The Devils*).

In Blighty, local administrations can prevent the screening

88 No studio wanted to receive an 'X' rating from the MPAA, because distributors and exhibitors didn't want to show 'Xs'; they wanted 'Rs'.

89 Warners re-cut the movie to gain an 'R' rating in 1973, when they saw their own movie *The Exorcist* doing incredibly well, and released *The Devils* to cash in.

90 From the outset, even before the cameras had rolled, *Je Vous Salue, Marie* (Jean-Luc Godard, 1985) was a controversial film. A range of institutions, organizations and individuals protested against the film (as usual, many of these hadn't seen it, or had misunderstood it). The controversy surrounding *Hail Mary* resulted in the film being banned, or withdrawn, and theatres being picketed; in North America some 5,000 people demonstrated against the film at its premiere at the New York Film Festival, at the Lincoln Center. (Thirty years later, I'm sure many people still haven't seen the film).

Hail Mary created controversy when it depicted the Blessed Virgin as a gas station attendant. There were bomb threats, 5,000 protesters reciting the rosary to cinema queues, and the 'film bears the distinction of being the first ever condemned by a pope (Pope John Paul II), and being the first instance in 400 years that a pope directly intervened in the suppression of a work of art' (Steven Dubin, 93).

of a movie if they wish, even if the BBFC has passed it. And local councils have done so – with pictures such as *Monty Python's Life of Brian*,[91] *9 1/2 Weeks, Salò,* or *120 Days of Sodom* and *The Last Temptation of Christ* There have been films that the BBFC has banned but which have been shown (such as *The Texas Chainsaw Massacre*, which the Greater London Council gave an 'X', so it could only be seen in London).

The Devils proved a difficult movie to re-cut to suit the censors and Warners, because the requested cuts damaged the movie dramatically. Both Ken Russell and editor Mike Bradsell have recounted how satisfying the censors (and Warner Brothers) drove them nuts. Warners, for instance, wanted to cut back on the nudity – on the pubic hair ('public hairs get you an automatic X', a sales rep at Warners told Russell [PF, 122]). Nudity was pruned, as was Sister Jeanne masturbating, the enema/ exorcism scene, Grandier's torture, and the 'rape of Christ'. But even after the censors had wielded their scissors, *The Devils* was 'still without doubt the most savage film ever released in Britain', noted Robert Sellers in *Oliver Reed*(203).

In one of Ken Russell's many run-ins with the press, he bopped newspaper critic Alexander Walker over the head on BBC TV with a copy of the newspaper (the *Evening Standard*) in which *The Devils* had been denounced ('the masturbatory fantasies of a Catholic boyhood').[92] That has become one of the infamous Russell events: it's surely something that many film-makers would love to do – bash a film critic over the head (preferrably with a loaded Magnum that accidentally fires into the schlub's skull).

91 In the case of *Monty Python's Life of Brian,* despite being rated 'AA' (14 and over), 11 local councils banned it, 62 enforced the classification, and 28 reclassified the film 'X'.
92 It was also the use of the Dread Word *fuck* that viewers objected to. In those quaint days of the Sixties an' Seventies, a word could drive audiences nuts. Like the moment when theatre critic Kenneth Tynan said 'fuck' on television in the Sixties, and 20 million people rioted, or when the Sex Pistols were interviewed by Bill Grundy on British TV in 1976. The following day, the *Daily Mirror* yelped 'a pop group shocked million of viewers last night with the filthiest language heard on British television'. The newspaper headlines became famous: 'THE FILTH AND THE FURY', 'ROCK CULT FILTH' and 'PUNK? CALL IT FILTHY LUCRE'.
A truck driver, James Holmes, had apparently kicked in his TV set, outraged that his 8 year-old son had heard the bad language. 'It blew up and I was knocked backwards. But I was so angry and disgusted with this filth that I took a swing with my boot' (*Daily Mirror*).

At the time, Alexander Walker was one of the premier film critics in Blighty – and Ken Russell was by then a major name not only in the British cinema, but internationally. Many other critics came out against *The Devils*. George Melly, the camp jazz dandy, dubbed it 'vulgar, camp and hysterical' and 'a hideous pantomime'. Judith Crist admitted in *New York*: 'we can't recall in our relatively broad experience (400 movies a year for perhaps too many years) a fouler film'.[93] For the *Christian Science Monitor* it was 'an offensive mockery of Christianity'. Vincent Canby called Russell 'a hobbyist determined to reproduce *The Last Supper* in bottle tops'. *Variety* reckoned that Russell had 'gone berserk'. For Paul D. Zimmermann, 'Russell has gone beyond extravagance to insanity'. And in the *L.A. Times*, Charles Champlin said *The Devils* was 'a degenerate and despicable piece of art' (G, 114-5).

They were all wrong.

The critics were all *wrong*.

The Devils is a masterpiece.

✟ ✟ ✟

---

93 Oliver Reed challenged Judith Crist to a showdown on a chat show on TV. Of course she declined!

This page and over: images from The Devils,
Ken Russell's 1971 masterpiece.

Above: Ken Russell on the set of The Devils with the two stars,
Oliver Reed and Vanessa Redgrave.

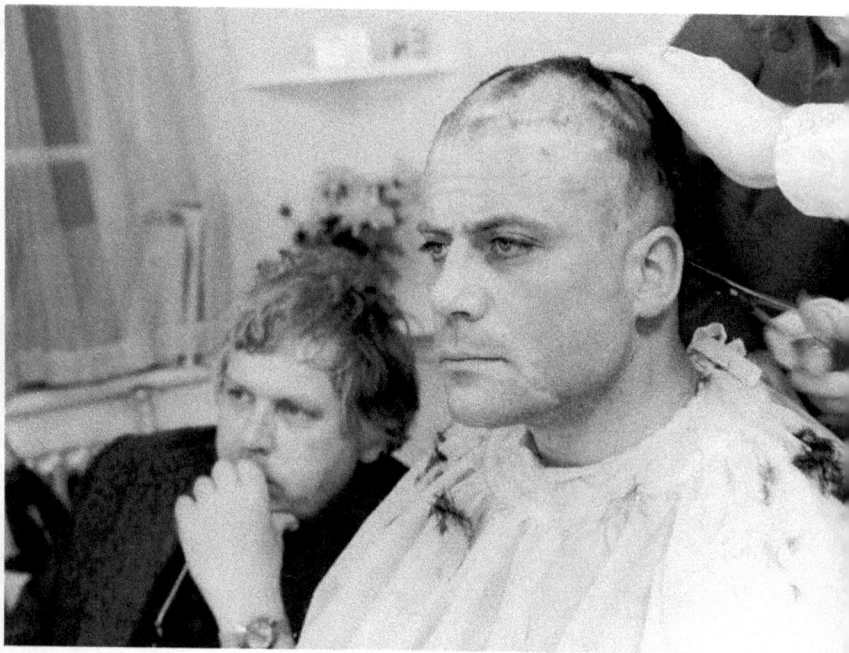

The Devils' director and the actor in the make-up chair

WARNER BROS

VANESSA REDGRAVE / OLIVER REED

dans

Un film de KEN RUSSELL

LES DIABLES

Une production ROBERT H. SOLO / KEN RUSSELL

Scénario de KEN RUSSELL

D'après la pièce de JOHN WHITING

et "The Devils of London" de ALDOUS HUXLEY

Mise en scène de

KEN RUSSELL

PANAVISION   TECHNICOLOR

WB

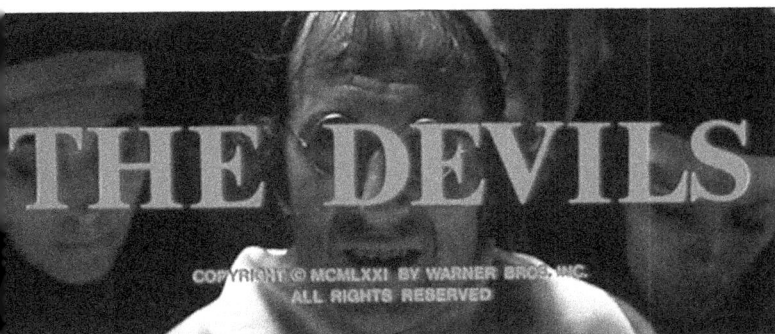

The Devils tell us where the real evil resides in the main title –
in the State and the Church (above), and politics and corruption
leads to one end… death (below).

URBANVS GRANDERIVS
IVLIODVNENSIS ECCLESIÆ
RECTOR . MDCXXVII.

Urbain Grandier

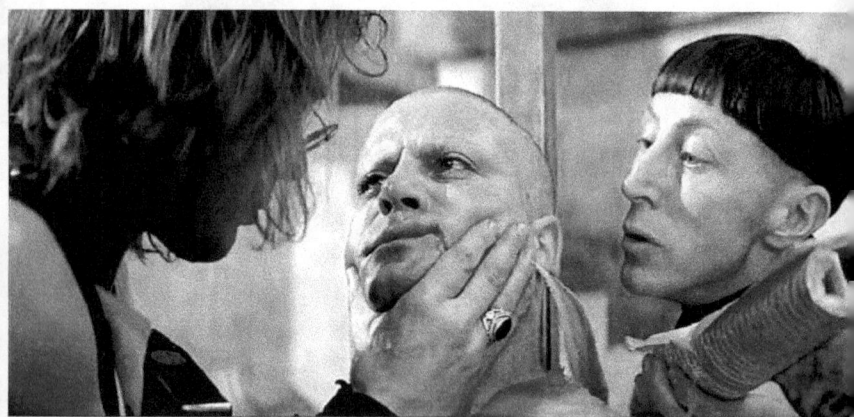

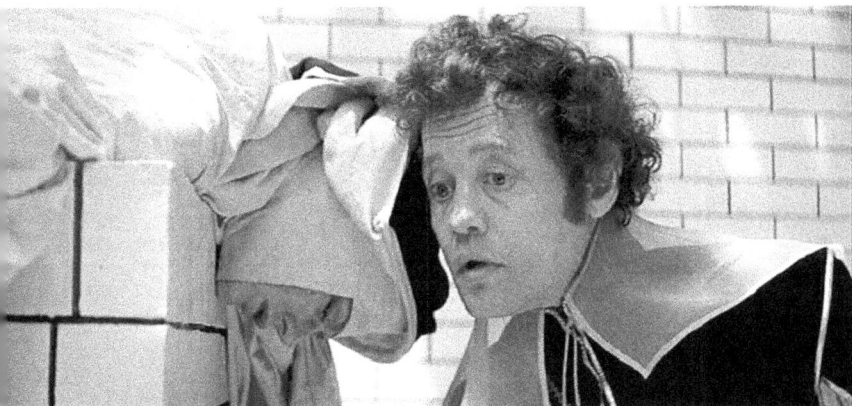

Dudley Sutton as the Baron in The Devils,
a masterful embodiment of the cool, efficient,
indifferent, bored and utterly ruthless aspects
of the State and the military.

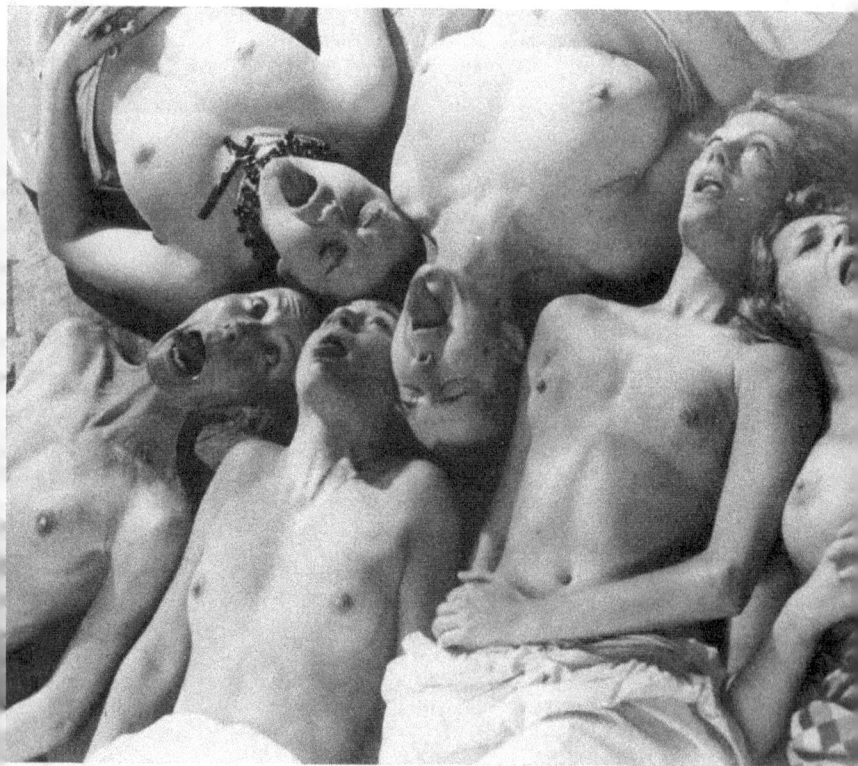

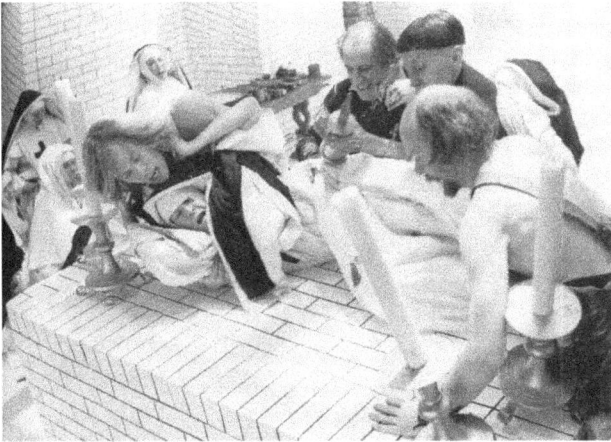

'A rape in a public lavatory' –
Ken Russell's conception of The Devils

The final shot of The Devils.

It's no 'walk into the sunset' image, though: at the end of this bleak, unrelenting movie, there can be no happy ending, and nothing approaching a happy ending.

The last shot of The Devils, which ironically employs the classic crane shot of the Hollywood ending, is not much of a way out or a sop or a means of finding something positive to express in amongst all of the madness of the preceding two hours. It's a symbolic ending, however: Madelyn, one of the only sane people in Loudun (or one of the only people who don't go along with craziness that grips the denizens of the town), decides she's had enough and flees the town, scrambling over the broken walls.

2

✝

INTRODUCTION TO KEN RUSSELL

WHY DO I LOVE KEN RUSSELL?

*For me, Ken Russell is the greatest living filmmaker
in Britain. Even though he died on November 27,
2011, he's still somehow very much alive. After the
death of Michael Powell in 1990, who else was
there? As an image-maker, Russell is not only a total
natural, he has very few peers among filmmakers –
not only in Britain, but also around the globe.
Russell's inventiveness seems to know no bounds, and
his films are cascades of images, so much so that it
can't all be taken in on the first viewing of a picture.
Russell does everything a great director and a great
artist should do, and then he does so much more.*

Why do I love Ken Russell's movies so much? For many
reasons: the spirituality, such a rare commodity in recent
British cinema: Russell's films are not afraid of addressing
spiritual issues. ✝ The poetry. ✝ The music – no other filmmaker of the same era in Britain has been such a tireless and
enthusiastic promoter of music. ✝ The dancing – no other
British film director has included so much dance in their
output (and *very few* directors anywhere!).[1] ✝ The British
popular culture elements. ✝ The English landscape.[2] ✝ The
romance and romantic sensibility. ✝ His stories of artists and
creativity. ✝ His interviews and public persona, appearing on
everything from websites and YouTube to trash like British
TV's *Big Brother*. ✝ His encouragement of young filmmakers

[1] Yep, there ain't a lotta dancing in the flicks of James Cameron, Ridley Scott,
Michael Bay, Jerry Bruckheimer, Wolfgang Petersen, Roland Emmerich *et al*.
[2] Ken Russell's Britain is much more *England* than it is Scotland, Ireland of
Wales.

and his teaching.[3]

England... Britain... Wouldn't it be wonderful if British or English movies could be made about England or Britain that were as awe-inspiring as recent Japanese movies made about Japan, like *Princess Mononoke* or *Spirited Away*? Or wild, flamboyant, enormously imaginative *animé* series such as *Fullmetal Alchemist, Escaflowne, Ghost In the Shell: Stand Alone Complex, Moribito: Guardian of the Spirit* or *Mushishi*? Why can't Brit filmmakers produce anything close to that? Britain has the history, the mythology, the eccentricity, the art. Instead, what do we get? Crappy heritage movies, horrible and vicious gangster movies, smug, self-satisfied rom-coms, and dull-as-shit soap operas!

Where are the great filmmakers who can make mythical, visionary works about Britain?

Ken Russell has got closer than most.

✣ Why isn't there a Ken Russell Film Festival every year? (in the New Forest or Southampton, naturally – come as your favourite Ken Russell character! Dress up as a nun or a Nazi or a hooker or a WW1 soldier or a Decadent dandy!).

✣ Why aren't the BAFTAs re-named the Russells?

✣ Why isn't the Royal Albert Hall re-dubbed the Imperial Russell Palace of Music?

✣ Why isn't there a Ken Russell radio station, playing Russell's beloved classical composers and folk songs (but without the inane blather of BBC Radio 3 and Classic FM)?

✣ Why isn't there a Ken Russell chain of cinemas, show-ing German Expressionist masterpieces, British naval WW2 pictures, MGM musicals and Charlie Chaplin shorts? (And why is every friggin' movie released in Britain today on a wide scale in a first-run cinema North American?).

✳

Ken Russell has been dubbed 'the *enfant terrible* of British cinema', 'the Wild Man of the BBC' and 'a fish and chips Fellini' (no, no, it's vice versa – Fellini is a 'pasta and pizza Russell'!). I've been calling him The Greatest Living

---

3 Ken Russell has contributed to many educational courses and film courses. He has been happy to give lectures or help out with workshops. He has been a visit-ing tutor at Newport Film School and the University of Southampton.

British Filmmaker for ages.[4]

We all have our favourites. For me, Ken Russell's cinema ranges from the completely stupendous and spell-binding – *The Devils, Tommy, The Music Lovers, Dante's Inferno, The Debussy Film, Delius: Song of Summer, Isadora Duncan, The Dance of the Seven Veils*– to the sheer fun – *Crimes of Passion, Women In Love, Billion Dollar Brain* – to the flawed but majestic – *Lisztomania, Altered States*– to the flawed and disappointing – *The Rainbow, Lady Chatterley, Gothic, Valentino, The Lair of the White Worm*– to pieces I just find flat – *Always On Sunday* and *The Fall of the Louse of Usher*.

Part of problem of assessing the works of Ken Russell is availability and accessibility (a topic we will return to). *The Devils* of course continued to be a movie which was *not* available in the form the filmakers intended.

If you mention Ken Russell, many people will have seen *Women In Love* and *Tommy* and maybe one or two other flicks, such as *The Music Lovers* or *Billion Dollar Brain* (but they likely won't realize that *Billion Dollar Brain* was directed by Russell). If they're older, they might have seen some of the pieces for television, including the *Monitor* programmes, and will talk fondly of *Elgar*. But that's about it.

Which's better than some filmmakers – at least many viewers will have some idea who Ken Russell is, or they will link Ken Russell to particular movies or TV shows. Most film directors don't have that kind of recognition: *very* few film directors have a high profile media image, and are recognized by the general public (even so-called 'major' film directors still get sold as 'from the director of' on the trailers and ads, rather than being referred to by name).

But beyond that, I would guess that the general viewing public (whoever the hell they are) wouldn't have seen or know much about Ken Russell's many, many other projects.

And that is in Britain. Outside of the green, sceptred, rainy isle, Ken Russell's star will fade rapidly, I would imagine. For instance, he would be known in parts of the United States of America, and in France (where they love movies and filmmakers more than anyone), but not much beyond that.

4 One of the only other people to agree with me is critic Mark Kermode: 'Russell is Britain's greatest living director', Kermode asserted in *Hatchet Job* (34).

However, many more movies directed by Russell are available in the U.S.A. – not least because he directed most of his movies for North American producers and studios.[5]

Walerian Borowczyk, Ingmar Bergman, Andrei Tarkovsky, Rainer Werner Fassbinder, Luis Buñuel – these are European filmmakers revered by the film *cognoscenti*, but Ken Russell's name would not be placed among that company by many film critics. As Russell himself remarked, if he'd been called 'Russellini' he might be more accepted in movie circles.[6] (But no, folks, it's the *other way around*: Federico Fellini is 'the Italian Ken Russell'!).[7]

In a way, it doesn't matter... but it does if you've evaluating cinema and a particular filmmaker. There are whole books, for instance, on over-rated filmmakers who have only made three or four movies! Quentin Tarantino, Peter Jackson, Steven Soderbergh, Terry Malick, etc. By comparison with them, Russell is a major filmmaker with an incredible body of work.

Yet to fully appreciate Ken Russell's cinema, you need to have seen films such as *The Devils* and *Savage Messiah* and *Mahler* and *Delius: Song of Summer* and *Crimes of Passion* and *The Rainbow* and so on. You also need to have caught a good proportion of Russell's TV work. Russell's output is truly staggering and mind-boggling: in television and cinema, he has produced a huge number of pieces.

For instance, if you think that Ken Russell turns out brash, vulgar, self-consciously excessive and dumb movies, you must see *Delius: Song of Summer* or *Savage Messiah* or *Prisoner of Honor*. The problem is, only a handful of Russell movies are broadcast on TV, and most of Russell's TV programmes have hardly been seen at all since their original air date.[8] It's true that *Elgar* was repeated a number of times in the 1960s, but that's a film that doesn't represent Russell's work

---

5 However, filmmakers with an encyclopedic understanding of cinema, such as Martin Scorsese, wrongly believed that more of Russell's BBC work was available in Britain than the U.S.A.
6 Sometimes Russell is 'Russellini', often he's 'Russellstein' (Eisenstein) and 'Russellelles' (Welles), and sometimes he's 'Russell-lin' (Chaplin).
7 M. Kermode, 2013, 34.
8 The BBC's newer cable channel, BBC Four, has re-broadcast some of the early Russell works.

properly, and is regarded as a white-wash and PR job[9] by the director. It's more about what the audience wants to see about Edward Elgar (1857-1934). 'It's me hero-worshipping him, and it's what everyone wanted him to be like, what *I* wanted him to be like,' admitted Russell (in G, 45).[10]

It's true that most TV shows aren't usually repeated any-way.[11] Some are, but it's a tiny proportion of the whole output of television – even of a small country like Britain. It's also true that TV shows are very rarely exported. So viewers in Italy, say, or South Africa, will probably never have seen a TV show directed by Ken Russell. Similarly, most theatrical films are *not* shown outside of their country of origin. A Jean-Luc Godard movie or an Ingmar Bergman movie might travel to other European countries, or to the U.S.A., but only because they are well-known filmmakers with a very high critical standing. But most movies made in, say, Poland, will only ever be seen in Poland, and only ever on Polish TV (if they are lucky enough to be broadcast at all – many shows're made but never seen).

So a full appreciation of an important filmmaker such as Ken Russell cannot take place unless viewers have seen most of his major works. I discovered this when recently writing books on Jean-Luc Godard and Walerian Borowczyk. Andrei Tarkovsky was easy – he only helmed seven feature films, all of which are available. But many of the movies of Godard and Borowczyk (including key works) are *not* available, not on video or DVD. The advent of video, and later DVD, has cert-ainly made many works obtainable, but even then often only in particular territories or in sub-standard versions.

With Ken Russell, you'd think that, in Britain at least, his

---

9 Certainly it led to an increase in sales of Edward Elgar's music, and altered the public reception of Elgar in Blighty.

10 However, there was some ironic commentary on Elgar's music – for instance, when one of his most famous pieces was played, the *Pomp and Circumstance March*, which has become one of England's unofficial national anthems, and about as pro-British, pro-establishment and nationalistic as music can get, the *Monitor* programme included images of the First World War, taken from the archives at the Imperial War Museum in London.

11 One aspect of television that Ken Russell liked was that shows were repeated, whereas movies were released, did the rounds of the theatres, then disappeared. Sometimes they might pop up on TV. As he remarked in 1973: 'if I could feel that films I did for television were shown all over the world at frequent intervals I'd probably never make a so-called feature film again' (Bax, 138). Those views were expressed before home video and DVD, which Russell embraced, and before the rise of the internet, which Russell also embraced wholeheartedly.

films would be readily available. Many are, but many are not. There are numerous reasons for this – to do with money and sales, obviously – but also legal issues, who owns what, etc. It's probably true that if Warners or MGM or United Artists or the BBC or whoever found out that a Ken Russell movie might sell 30 million units on DVD, it would be in Wal-Mart or Tesco's this afternoon.

Some filmmakers never produce audio commentaries to DVD versions of their movies, and one wishes they would: Woody Allen, Ingmar Bergman and Steven Spielberg, for example, are some filmmakers I really wish would provide commentaries. Happily, Ken Russell does, and I highly recommend buying the DVD versions of his films for the commentaries alone. Russell is a wonderful commentator on his own movies, offering all sorts of priceless stories and snippets about the productions.[12]

The American DVD release of some of Ken Russell's 1960s BBC films (*Ken Russell At the BBC*) is absolutely indispensable: the box set includes *The Debussy Film, Isadora Duncan, Dante's Inferno* and *Delius: Song of Summer*. If you haven't seen some of these masterpieces, get this box of DVDs. You won't believe your eyes.

I have been amazed many times in writing this book about Ken Russell's cinema. He's astonishing, as we all know, but until only recently have I realized just how astonishing. *Delius: Song of Summer* has been available for some time, and it's one of Russell's finest works. But I hadn't seen three of the 1960s TV films, *The Debussy Film, Isadora Duncan* and *Dante's Inferno*, before (collected on the BBC Video DVD).

OMG, this man is a genius! I simply can't believe how Ken Russell achieved it all. The level of imagination and flair is just astounding. Russell proves for all to see that with a group of dedicated actors and film crew, a masterpiece can be attained on a tiny budget (and you need a ton of ideas, a strong screenplay and lots of food – plus a tipple or two).

✳

Ken Russell has never been establishment as a film director like, say, Alfred Hitchcock, David Lean, Carol Reed

<hr>

12 On the internet, the Savage Messiah site is a good place to start: iainfisher.com/ Russell.

or Michael Powell, some of the film directors continually
wheeled out as the best of British talent. However, one of
Russell's films made it into the Top 100 British movies coll-
ated by the British Film Institute (the guardians of Brit film
culture) in 1999 (guess which one? Yeah, *Women in Love*
Let's ignore the fact that the studio was North American
(United Artists), that the money was American, that the co-
writer and producer and originator of the project (Larry
Kramer) was also American.)

But, as this book insists, Ken Russell as a filmmaker is
every bit as fascinating, as talented, as stylish, or as crazy as
Hitch, Lean, Reed or Powell & Pressburger. And his pictures
are just as extraordinary.

✳

Quite a few film critics as well as film fans criticize Ken
Russell's later work in the light of his earlier work. It's unfair,
but it's difficult not to do it. Thus, *Mindbender* or *Dogboys* will
be compared with *The Devils* or *Tommy*. It's unfair because
the context and conditions of each project are different: the
production of, say, *Altered States*, was pretty tough, and
Women in Love for instance, was produced in a different cultural as well as cinematic context from, say, *Prisoner of Honor*
or *The Fall of the Louse of Usher*

And we should always remember that it's *extremely difficult* to make films as good as the finest of Ken Russell's movies
– *The Devils*, *Tommy*, or *The Music Lovers*.To demonstrate
that, you could have a go yourself. Assuming you can raise the
finance for a movie about nuns and priests in Loudun or a
classical composer, you'd have to tackle by far the toughest
task on any movie: developing a script that did everything you
wanted to do (also within a particular budget, also satisfying
your backers, also something filmable).

Which's why some movies – including the best of Ken
Russell – seem miraculous. How did they get the money and
resources and actors to produce *The Devils*?! Or other filmmakers' work, like *The Wind Rises*! Or *Chimes At Midnight*!
Or Akira Kurosawa's *Ran*?! It's completely remarkable.

The best movies seem as if they have always already
existed. As if they came from nowhere but should always have

been there. As if you have always known them, to the point where you seem a part of them (almost as if you had made them yourself).

But not every movie can be that miraculous (if only!). And so not every Ken Russell picture can be *Savage Messiah* or *Mahler* or *Delius*.

The vitriol that Ken Russell has personally attracted from critics is striking, as if he's become the whipping boy for whatever is pissing off the critics. But a large number of 'major' film directors have produced turkeys. Watch more'n five or ten movies on general release, and you will turn up at least one turd.

Recent turkeys include:

Steven Spielberg, *Tin-Tin* (some would add *Hook* and *1941*)

Ridley Scott, *Hannibal*,[13] *Kingdom of Heaven, G.I. Jane, Black Hawk Down*

Sam Raimi, *Spider-man 3*

Peter Greenaway, *8 1/2 Women*

Peter Jackson, *The Hobbit, King Kong, The Frighteners*

Alan Parker, *Evita*

Brian de Palma, *The Bonfire of the Vanities, Snake Eyes, Mission To Mars*

Terry Gilliam, *The Brothers Grimm, Fear and Loathing In Las Vegas*

Quentin Tarantino, *Kill Bill*

Paul Thomas Anderson, *Punch-Drunk Love*

(Of course, one wouldn't class Jackson, Raimi, de Palma, Parker, Tarantino, etc, as 'major' film directors).

And how about these duds? –

The Lion, the Witch and The Wardrobe (cost: $180m),

---

13 *Hannibal* (2001), part of the *Silence of the Lambs* Thomas Harris franchise, was overseen by film legend Dino de Laurentiis (1919-2010). *Hannibal* was a pitifully bad thriller, woefully misjudged in tone and substance. It's difficult to believe that Ridley Scott directed it, and that David Mamet and Steve Zallian worked on the screenplay (*Steve Zallian!* He wrote *Schindler's List!* Much-celebrated playwright *David Mamet!*). Some critics agree with me: 'very likely the worst film of this year and quite possibly the next', commented Charles Taylor in Salon.com, while Ella Taylor in *L.A. Weekly* called it 'the flabbiest of cop-outs'. Mick LaSalle in the *San Francisco Chronicle* found *Hannibal* 'wilfully gross, fundamentally stupid and in no way worth the discomfit of watching it.' According to Wikipedia, the budget for *Hannibal* was $87 million. 87,000,000 bucks! You have GOT to be kidding! For a routine thriller that would cost less than a million on TV! And what could Ken Russell have done with $87 million?!

Prince Caspian (cost: $200m), *Voyage of the Dawn Treader*, *Spider-man 3* (cost: $300 million), *Home On the Range* (cost $110 million), *Snow White and the Huntsman* (cost: $170 million!), the *Bourne* series, *Quantum of Solace*, *Casino Royale*, *The Hunger Games*, *Batman Begins*, *The Beach*, *8MM*, *Alien vs. Predator*, *Chocolat*, *Vanilla Sky*, *Amélie*, *About a Boy*, *Billy Elliot*, *The Hulk*, *Oceans 11*, the *Charlie's Angels* movies, *Unbreakable*, *Jungle Book 2*, *Lemony Snicket*, *Sin City*, *Lara Croft*, *King Arthur*, *The Village*, **The Da Vinci Code**, **Speed 2**, **Lolita**, **X-Men Origins:** *Wolver-ine*, the *Bridget Jones* films and *Where the Wild Things Are*.

So, sure, Ken Russell has directed some financial flops, and some very disappointing pictures, but many of the bombs I've noted above (there are *plenty* more! – as we all know!) are shockingly inept and misconceived (and *very* expensive): *Snow White and the Huntsman*, a rancid travesty of a movie,[14] *Casino Royale*, the 2006 *James Bond* re-boot which had the sophistic-ated, world-weary super-spy acting like a ditzy, love-sick teenager, *Where the Wild Things Are*, Universal's cretinous movie-as-psychotherapy, offensive on every possible level, *Alien vs. Predator*, a shockingly awful devaluation of a once-entertaining horror franchise, *The Hulk*, simply dreadful and woefully misjudged (despite the high-calibre talent involved), *X-Men Origins: Wolverine*, a deeply disturbing cesspit of a movie, and *Chocolat*, a gruelling two hours of insipid shit.[15]

Some of those movies are truly abysmal (some are even offensively bad, with their insidious pro-military, pro-war, pro-American ideology). And the sum total of the budgets and P & A (prints and advertizing) and marketing of just this handful of movies amounts to – $4 billion? $5 billion? $10 billion? (Just *one* of those crappy movies would've paid for *all* of Ken Russell's unmade projects! Ack!).

✳

14 A complete flop, *Snow White and the Huntsman* (Universal, 2012), was… a series of empty shots, a fairy tale eviscerated of all magic. There's literally *nothing here*, nothing going on. I wait and wait for *something* to happen. But it doesn't.

What a waste of money! *Snow White* isn't 'bloated' or over-done or OTT (some of the usual accusations against current blockbuster flicks), it's not 'done' at all (it's uncooked). It's just empty. There really is nothing there at all. And it cost $170 million!!

15 Despite starring two gorgeous actors, Johnny Depp and Juliette Binoche.

In one respect Ken Russell is far ahead of the critics, and that is in the realm of music. No *major* film critic, alive or dead, has the anything like the knowledge that Russell has about music. Thus, they simply *can't* assess the depictions of music and composers accurately. (Music critics, tho', have taken Russell to task for his representations of composers and music, particularly, of course, the assassinations. But even they would also have to (grudgingly) admit that Russell contributed towards the dissemination of classical music in popular culture).

✳

I have refrained from quoting too many critics who dislike Ken Russell's cinema: you know who they are, and you know what they've written. There's no point really in bringing those complaints and attacks back to life. Russell's films polarize people as few other British filmmakers' works do. It does seem that people either love his movies or hate 'em. (*The Devils*, such a strong statement, on many levels, generated especially intense reactions, across the spectrum).

If you've bought this book or are reading it, I'm guessing you like Ken Russell's films, and *The Devils*, a lot. So we don't need to spend time going over what Pauline Kael or Vincent Canby or Judith Crist or George Melly or Alexander Walker said about this or that Russell movie.

Besides, Ken Russell himself has found the sheer number of critics who have come out against him daunting and upsetting. In his review of Joseph Lanza's 2008 study of himself, Russell said that when Lanza piles up so many negative reviews, it has the effect of depressing the hell out of the director. And Russell wondered if the sheer number of bad reviews might influence the undiscerning reader.[16]

I'm reminded of England's greatest painter, J.M.W. Turner. *Every* major art critic of the day came out against Turner's art: William Hazlitt, John Taylor, James Boaden, Richard Westmacott, William Thackeray, Leigh Hunt, *The Times*, *The*

---

16 Ken Russell stated in the London *Times* in 2008: 'But because Lanza feels compelled to reprint the worst of every bad review my films have received as a coda to each chapter, I can only surmise that I'm damned on every page. It has taken some nerve for me just to keep reading. More than once the temptation to retire to bed with the covers over my head reared up like a phantom holiday in the park. Did I do that? Did I say that? And more to the point, did they say that?'

Athenaeum, Tatler, etc. It deeply distressed the painter (though he was a tough character, a working class Cockney).

But all of the critics of Joseph William Mallord Turner were *wrong. WRONG.* And no one remembers what Hazlitt or Thackeray said (except the animosity between, say, James Whistler and Turner). But no one can forget Turner's extraordinary paintings. I've been to exhibitions in New York City of Turner's art which have been packed with punters, and lectures on Turner which fill a giant auditorium at the Met.

J.M.W. Turner's art lives on... But the critics fade into *utter oblivion.*

3

✝

KEN RUSSELL: ENGLAND'S GREAT VISIONARY FILMMAKER

We do live on a magic island, without doubt, but so far as British films are concerned there is precious little evidence of this. By and large, contemporary filmmakers seem to revel in squalor, glorify ignorance and extol violence. There is another kind of life outside of this which many people in this country would like to celebrate, if only they were given the opportunity and not made to feel guilty about it. It has nothing to do with religion; it is to do with the spirit of the land in which we live, that elusive quality touched on by the music of VW (Vaughan Williams) and his contemporaries such as Arnold Bax, Frank Bridge and John Ireland: music expressing the majesty of nature, forgotten rituals, pagan goddesses and ancient heroes.

Ken Russell, *A British Picture* (238-8)

ENGLAND'S GREATEST LIVING FILMMAKER.

Ken Russell is England's greatest living filmmaker; I've been saying this for years, and even now he's staging musicals featuring angels and great artists on heavenly clouds,[17] it's still true. Russell seemed to have always been around.

After the deaths of Michael Powell and David Lean, Ken Russell was The Man.

Who else was there? Oh, yes, there are many other British film directors who have become more successful, commercially, than Ken Russell: Ridley Scott, Tony Scott, Alan Parker, Adrian Lyne, Mike Newell, *et al.* And there are the 'important' or 'serious' Brit filmmakers, like Mike Leigh or

---

17 Nothing's changed there then! – Ken Russell would be right at home in heaven (chatting with his favourite classical composers, for instance) – but he'd probably ask for a transfer to somewhere hotter and wilder!

Ken Loach or Alan Clarke. And the mavericks, like Peter Greenaway and Derek Jarman.

It's true that filmmakers like the Scotts, the Parkers, the Hudsons and the Lynes can make big, glossy movies with tons of action and pretty people and all, and it's true that I love many of the films of the above film directors...

...But there's something about Ken Russell's films that makes him, ultimately, a more fascinating filmmaker than pretty much *all* other British filmmakers of recent times. It's do with, I think, the subjects that he's chosen and how his movies seem to be reaching for something. Often they don't reach it; often they don't deliver on their promise or their goals. That happened more with the later pieces... But the group of movies that Ken Russell produced from the late 1960s to the end of the 1970s are remarkable on so many levels. Part of it is to do with the sheer *joy* of making cinema, which the films of that period are full of. And then there is the enormous *ambition* of those subjects (even more extraordinary bearing in mind that these works were mainly made for low budgets). And there's the way that Russell tackled those subjects and themes and stories. Visually, they are stunning. The muse of music has no superior in British cinema. And there are some outstanding performances. [18] It's all quite remarkable.

✳

Henry Kenneth Alfred Russell was born in Southampton in Southern England on July 3, 1927;[19] he grew up in Southampton. He died in Lymington, Hampshire, on November 27, 2011. As well as being associated with Southern England, where he lived (in the New Forest), and where many of his movies have been filmed (all along the South Coast), and with London and the Home Counties (where Britain's film production is centred), Russell also has strong links to the Lake District in Northern England.[20]

---

18 For a film director often derided for emphasizing visuals and spectacle too much (unfairly and mistakenly, I think), Russell managed to provide the creative context on set for numerous great performances in his movies.

19 Ken Russell is of the generation of Stanley Kubrick (b. 1928), Jean-Luc Godard (b. 1930), Bryan Forbes (b. 1926), Kenneth Anger (b. 1927), Andrzej Wajda (b. 1927) and Andy Warhol (b. 1928).

20 For many years Russell had a place in the New Forest, and also a bungalow near the ocean. A fire in recent years burnt up numerous belongings. Russell has also lived in his beloved Lake District, and in London.

Ken Russell studied at Pangbourne, as a cadet at the
Royal Naval College, from 1941; and later at Walthamstow
(the Technical College and School of Art, where he met
Shirley Kingdon, his first wife). He spent time in the Merchant
Navy[21] and the Royal Air Force. He worked in an art gallery
(Lefèvre Art Gallery) in Bond Street, London. In the 1950s, he
was a stills photographer, for magazines such as *Picture Post*
and *Illustrated*. He became fascinated by ballet, and studied
evenings in Hampstead, at the International Ballet School.[22] He
toured with dance companies (both photography and choreography would feature prominently in his movies).[23] By the late
1950s, Russell was working for the BBC, making arts documentaries (the first was in 1959 – having impressed the BBC
with his home-made movies).

Ken Russell was married four times – to Shirley Kingdon
(married between 1956-78), Vivian Jolly (1983-91),[24] Hetty
Baynes (1992-99) and Elize Tribble (2001-2011). Jolly,
Russell's second wife, was a film student and assistant on
Savage Messiah. Russell met his fourth wife, actress Baynes,
when he was casting a *South Bank Show* documentary. Russell
met his fourth wife Tribble when she answered a lonely hearts
ad he placed in *The Times*: 'Unbankable film director Ken
Russell seeks soul mate – mad about movies, music, and Moët
and Chandon champagne'.

Every biography, autobiography, interview and study of
Ken Russell agrees that in his youth movies played a huge role.
Russell consumed thousands and thousands of movies in his
childhood. He has cited so many cinematic influences, so
many film icons he worshipped, so many movies he saw, some
repeatedly: William Boyd Westerns... *The Fleet's Inn* ('drool-
ing over Dorothy Lamour' a dozen times)... Betty Grable in
Spring-time In the Rockies('lots of Grable musicals')... giant,

21 He left the Navy, according to Joseph Gomez, due to a nervous breakdown
(1976, 18).
22 Ken Russell acknowledged that he wasn't the greatest of dancers, and dancers
were some of his (many) heroes.
23 Ken Russell has written at length in his autobiographies and interviews of his
time in the Merchant Navy, his tours with dance companies, and his early
attempts at amateur filmmaking.
24 Anthony Perkins officiated at Ken Russell's wedding to Vivian Jolly – the
ceremony took place on the *Queen Mary*, included extracts from Thomas Hardy
and William Wordsworth, and doubled as a wrap party for *Crimes of Passion*.

German Expressionist epics like *Metropolis* and *Die Niebel-ungen* and of course the crazy, abstract *Cabinet of Dr Cali-gari*... Andy Clyde, Old Mother Reilly... *The Secret of the Loch*... *Citizen Kane*...Mickey Mouse... Charlie Chaplin... Felix the Cat... Snub Pollard... Betty Boop... *Of Mice and Men*... *The Westerner*...and 'almost every Warner Brothers film'...

Going to the movies was not just every week, but several times a week for Ken Russell (often with his mom or aunts or relatives). Sometimes 2 or 3 times a day. As he recalled: even when he was stationed out of town in the military, he 'still managed to see almost every film released in the early Forties', and sometimes would bicycle 30 miles to Salisbury to catch a movie (which gives an idea of his passion for cinema, which never left him).

CLASSIC RUSSELL.

The two periods of 'classic' Ken Russell work would be the TV documentaries of the early-to-late 1960s (with 1962's *Elgar* as the highpoint that everyone remembers), and the feature films of the late 1960s to late 1970s (with *Women in Love* and *Tommy* being the high watermarks among audiences if not critics).

Certainly, it's with *Women in Love*[5] that Ken Russell begins that extraordinary run of feature-length movies: *Women In Love* thus helped Russell's career enormously (enabling him to stage something as challenging and as ambitious as *The Devils*): *Women in Love* was followed by *The Music Lovers* (his favourite movie), which was followed by *The Devils*, which was followed by *The Boy Friend*, which was followed by *Savage Messiah*, which was followed by *Mahler*, which was followed by *Tommy*, which was followed by *Lisztomania*. That's a run of eight amazing movies. You could add *Valentino* and *Altered States* (many wouldn't).

'OUTRAGEOUS', 'VULGAR', 'ENFANT TERRIBLE'.

Over the course of his film career, Ken Russell has been asked the same questions again and again. Like Alfred Hitch-

---

25 D.H. Lawrence himself had not been opposed to the idea of making *Women in Love* into a movie, when it was suggested back in the 1920s.

cock or Charlie Chaplin, Russell is one of the very few film directors that the general public might have heard of and who also has a recognizable media persona. As he put it in *A British Picture*:

> Am I difficult to work with? Do I hate actors? Am I a miso-gynist? Do I set out to shock just for the sake of it? Do I distort facts? Does it bother me that many of my films are flops? Is it true that I never go to the cinema? What does it feel like to be the oldest *enfant terrible* in the business? (BP, 161)

In short, people – film critics too, who should know better – believe and endorse the legend (and Ken Russell, like Orson Welles or Werner Herzog or Michael Powell, certainly helps along the legend with his anecdotes and chat show stories).[26] But maybe he recounts those stories because it's expected of him, and it's what people want, and it's easier than sitting in silence.

Ken Russell was known as an 'outrageous' filmmaker, delighting in 'shock' tactics – as Joe Gomez succinctly put it in his excellent mid-1970s study of Russellini: 'his films are outstanding examples of the 'kick 'em in the crotch' school of overstatement' (1976, 70) – including extremes of sex,[27] temp-erament, behaviour and violence;[28] his style employed flam-boyant camerawork, rapid cutting, anti-naturalism, and extrava-gance; he preferred out-size acting, often camp[29] and self-mocking; his themes were art, sex, death and the individual (usually the artist) in society; his films seemed to be apolitical, far more interested in depicting the many strands of an artist's life than social comment or ideology. If Russell had any political views, they were formed in the middle of the 20th century (Existentialism, bohemia, the artist as rebel, psycho-

---

26 Ken Russell is the film director as 'Mr De Thrill', the director in *The Boy Friend*.
27 Glenda Jackson defended the depiction of sex in a Ken Russell movie: it wasn't exploitative, she affirmed, it was part of the characters and the drama. And eroticism is so personal anyway.
28 Later filmmakers, such as Peter Greenaway or Derek Jarman, were sometimes dubbed 'controversial' by the media. But how tame the works of Greenaway and Jarman appear beside those of Ken Russell!
29 Ken Russell is so camp he out-camps many gay filmmakers, as Raymond Murray pointed out in his guide to gay and lesbian cinema. Critics have noticed that homosexuality is sometimes sent up or denounced in Russell's cinema. This campest and gayest of heterosexual filmmakers often portrays homosexuality negatively.

analysis, and a profound 18-19th century Romanticism), and rounded off by the hippy ideals of the 1960s. Russell's one overriding theme or driving philosophy was Romanticism, and the myth of the Romantic artist informed most of his work (meaning Romanticism in the 18th and 19th centuries, with its tenets of infinity, going to extremes, the sublime, subjectivity, emotionalism, ecstasy, paganism, mythology, poetry and art, mysticism and spirituality, unity, idealism, the individual over/ against society, and so on). 'He's a very romantic man', Glenda Jackson said (1972).

The psychology that Ken Russell employs in his cinema is of the Freudian school, as if Russell picked up a book on Sigmund Freud in the 1950s, and applied it to everything he did after that (mid-century philosophy informs *The Devils,*a s it does Aldous Huxley's book – Huxley is a quintessential mind of the mid-20th century). Russell's philosophy and approach is very much of the mid-20th century, of the 1940s and the 1950s, *not* the 1960s (he was 33 when the Sixties began). That is the mid-20th century of Existential philosophy (with its emphasis on outsiderness, alienation and the individual), the Surrealism, psychoanalysis, Parisian *avant garde*, the American Beat Generation, jazz and early rock 'n' roll (tho' classical music has always been Uncle Ken's rock music). Over that all, World War Two dominates.

Ken Russell's films were just as often set in rural landscapes, including the wild reaches of Cumbria, as in towns and cities; his pictures were not London or Home Counties-biased, like so much of British cinema; Russell's cinema enshrined the myth and dream of England/ Britain, like the work of Derek Jarman, John Boorman and Michael Powell, a place rich in history, poetry, art and culture.

What is a filmmaker, in the realm of commercial, entertainment cinema? A storyteller. *A filmmaker is a storyteller* (among many other things). And I guess I like the stories that Ken Russell tells, and I like most of his characters. It ain't the same with many contemporary filmmakers – I don't like (and don't want, and don't need) their stories or their characters.

Yes, the *way* that Ken Russell tells his stories and presents his characters is wild, unusual, flamboyant, colourful –

and sometimes crude and hysterical. But I still much prefer his stories and characters to so many of contemporary Western cinema's stories and characters. Who cares about violent gangsters and drug dealers and the banal, stupid, smug, arrogant, vain white heroes and heroines of so many contemporary Hollywood or British movies? Not I.

Luis Buñuel is a useful comparison in terms of the critical reception with Ken Russell: quite a few of Buñuel's movies were satires and comedies about religious or social topics (often with Catholicism as the target – chiming with *The Devils*). Yet although Buñuel is revered by many critics, some of his satires aren't particularly funny, and certainly not as successful as some of Russell's satires. A late 'comedy' of Buñuel's like *The Milky Way* (1969), for instance, is a series of feeble, anti-clerical skits (and filmed in a flabby, indifferent manner, too). And not a patch on *Dance of the Seven Veils* which Russell directed a year later.

Anti-Russell critics are many; some critics just can't get on with Ken Russell's form of cinema. British critics especially don't seem to know what to make of him. David Shipman said in *The Story of Cinema* that while Russell is 'capable of spectacular and *outré* images on the screen... he has no gift for character, situation, pacing, rhythm, tension or tone' (1130).

That is *rubbish!*

Critics saw Ken Russell's cinema as self-indulgent, excessive, pretentious, boorish, coarse, and simplistic. D.H. Lawrence's champion, the (over-rated but influential) critic F.R. Leavis, hated Russell's interpretation of Lawrence (*Women in Love*), calling it an outrage and 'an obscene undertaking'. Russell's movies are not what critics expect, or want: and they don't offer a pretext for the things that critics like to write about. As Jack Fisher put it, 'the critics, confronted with work which doesn't stimulate what they are prepared to say, flounder and react negatively'.[30]

'The cult of Ken Russell really depends on an act of faith, a willingness to believe in the master's integrity in what he does,' remarked Peter Webb in *The Erotic Arts* (290). That applies to virtually any artist. You have to go along with what they're doing. Otherwise there's no exchange at all.

30 J. Fisher, in T. Atkins, 40.

Asked about the notion of being 'indulgent' in movies, a critique often hurled at Ken Russell, the filmmaker replied:

> Films are hard to make and I think the word indulge really leads one to believe that it's an easy sort of business and it's really extremely difficult. You'll be standing out there in the rain thinking that it's not an easy job being a film director. But the director is the director and if he feels for whatever reason, perhaps under great delusion, that he wants that scene and he can get away with it even though it might be questionable in terms of taste then he should be allowed to do it. It's his movie. But if the committee steps in and says you can't do that because we're going to cut it out then it's a waste of time.

Excessive? Well, *duh*, of course Ken Russell's cinema can be excessive. As Michael Gallagher pointed out, in reference to *The Devils* and *Lisztomania* (in the *Catholic Film Newsletter* of all places), 'to accuse Russell of excess when he is working in this area, however, is very much like accusing Rubens of sensuality'.[31] Yes – being excessive is what Russell does for a living.

Like Federico Fellini and Kenneth Anger, Ken Russell's is a pagan, earthy, visionary form of cinema: Camille Paglia in *Sexual Personae* calls Hollywood the modern Rome, with its depictions of

> pagan sex and violence that have flowered so vividly in our mass media. The camera has unbound daemonic western imagination. Cinema is a *sexual showing*, a pagan flaunting. Plot and dialogue are obsolete word-baggage. Cinema, the most eye-intense of genres, has restored pagan antiquity's cultic exhibitionism. Spectacle is a pagan cult of the eye. (33)

Huw Wheldon on Ken Russell:

> Ken needs a strong producer or a strong script-writer, or both, because without them his own powers of invention and imagination are so enormous that he's like a bird being driven along on a huge gale. It was this gale that made him such a marvellous colleague. Most of my colleagues in those days were drivers but Ken was like a team of stallions. He had a leaping imagination and, as frequently happens with people of this kind, great tenacity and determination. He would go through a stone wall to get the proper location. If it's necessary to be on the 54th floor then you go to the 54th floor, and *certainly* you walk up the

---

31 Quoted in PF, 7.

stairs. (Bax, 123)

Entertainment came first in movie-making for Ken Russell: 'to entertain first, and the preaching comes second. Most of my films are based on that premise'. Russell said that he made his films for himself, and hoped that someone else was entertained (RC, 247).

There are times when you're watching a Ken Russell work and you think, oh crap, he's not going to do *that*! And he does. Yep, Russell delights in delivering some really simplistic symbolism or gestures, stuff that a fifth grader or 14 year-old kid getting hold of a video camera might think was really cool.

✳

Ken Russell's public persona was also larger-than-life, and often threatened to undermine the attention given to his movies. He had run-ins with censors and film critics (famously attacking Alexander Walker with a newspaper on television in 1971 on the late night discussion programme *24 Hours*); he was a regular (and entertaining) guest on TV chat shows and documentaries (talking about Oliver Reed, for instance, or Keith Moon, or the current state of the British film industry). He was on TV and radio and in print so often his stories, such as one about how the naked wrestling scene was shot in *Women in Love* became very familiar (Russell has discussed that scene so many times, it would make a movie longer than ten *Women In Love*). He often appeared in his films (*Lady Chatterley, Whore, Gothic, Valentino, Tommy* and so on), and presented TV documentaries (part of Russell's personality is definitely the frustrated actor).

Approaching someone from the outside as a subject for a movie, from the media, from books and magazines and news-papers, would all be lies, Ken Russell asserted: he didn't want the everyday facts about someone, what time they woke up, but the spirit of their work: 'the spirit of music, the spirit of Mahler, the spirit of D.H. Lawrence, that's what I'm into. That's the truth, the artistic truth' (RC, 245).

No one had really got to grips with the real Ken Russell, the director complained: 'nobody knows the real me and I've never seen the real me written about' (RC, 245).

His reputation as the Bad Boy of British Cinema, a rebel,

an iconoclast, etc, was ill-founded, said Ken Russell. In person, he said he was quite mild-mannered and shy, which disappointed and upset people when they met him (BP, 156). That Russell is shy and quiet is attested by numerous colleagues: Huw Wheldon recalled that when he met Russell in the late 1950s, he was 'shy and quiet... A little watchful, but silent and extremely modest' (in PF, 36). The abrasive Russell emerged after he left the Beeb, Wheldon remarked: but although 'singularly quiet, gentle and modest', Russell was also very confident from the beginning, knew what he wanted, and would walk through walls to get it (Bax, 121). Of course: only someone with incredible drive, energy and ambition could've produced that huge amount of work. You don't make movies and TV shows by sitting on your ass at home complaining that nobody returns your calls or reads your scripts! Russell is the classic filmmaker as self-taught artist, where the philosophy is: *fuck it, let's grab a camera and go do it already!*

The more flamboyant, dandy and outspoken aspects of Ken Russell's media persona developed in the late 1960s. Before that, Russell was often seen as introvert: as his stature increased with the successes of *Women in Love* and *The Music Lovers*, the familiar Ken Russell – camp, loud, OTT – came to the fore in media appearances. In John Baxter's priceless book *An Appalling Talent*, Russell is described thus:

> He is wearing a grey flannel suit, additions to which include a black sweater decorated with a jewelled semiquaver, a lapel badge of a ferret with the caption "Deviate Today", silver rings showing on one an Egyptian *ankh* and on the other Mickey Mouse, black shoes with white kid tops and a blue cloth cap whose badge is embossed with a double-decker tram and the word "Leeds". (Bax, 95)

And when Joseph Gomez visited the set of *Tommy*, he found Russell:

> Sporting an unkempt silver-grey beard, longish hair, sunglasses, and a candy-striped suit and resembling a cross between Sam Peckinpah and Edmund Gwenn (Kris Kringle in *Miracle On 34th Street*). (1976, 91)

As well as shy and reserved, Ken Russell has also been

described as temperamental and mercurial, occasionally given to outbursts of anger on set. But also very generous, and a lot of fun – there can be a lot of laughs on a Russell set.

John Baxter described Ken Russell in the familiar terms of an emotional, volatile personality: those whom he discovers to be enemies are resented, but loyalty and friendship and devotion are rewarded – with loyalty, friendship and devotion (Bax, 124).

Despite occasionally falling out with some people on his crews, and one or two actors, and the odd writer or producer, during the most successful times of his career, Ken Russell had plenty of people eager to work on his movies. There was a regular bunch of filmmakers and actors, for instance, who would turn up to work on each subsequent production. If a Ken Russell movie really was a tough experience, with the director overly demanding and given to prima donna outbursts, and the hours long, and the pay low (and the food terrible), many performers and crew wouldn't come back. But they did.

One thing was sure with a Ken Russell movie: you got to do stuff, in front of or behind the camera, that you hardly did anywhere else. (There are things that actors have done on a Russell movie/ TV show that they will only have done that once: running along a field waving the Czech flag while naked, dressing up as a combination of Wagner, Hitler and a storm-trooper and mowing down Jews in the street with a machine gun, being burnt alive at the stake, and of course wrestling in the nude!).

THE FILM CAREER.

Writing this book, I am struck again and again by the sheer amount of work that Ken Russell has produced, by the quality of it, by the breadth of subjects in it, by the number of genres he has tackled, and by the torrent of images he has created. 'Putting pictures to music has always been a pleasure,' Russell wrote, 'like being paid to screw your favourite film star' (BP, 268-9).

Simply to consider Ken Russell's television work would require a hefty book in itself. Russell is probably always thought of a film director first, but he has actually produced many more TV shows than feature films.

In 2000, Ken Russell (aged 73) ventured into the world of very low budget filmmaking, a return to home movies, based in his New Forest home, edited on computers, with friends and helpers working for next-to-nothing (Russell embarked on an ambitious interpretation of *The Fall of the House of Usher*, and hoped to sell his movies on the internet). Other short films of the 2000s included *A Kitten for Hitler*(2007), *Hot Pants* (2006) and *Boudicca Bites Back*(2009). *Hot Pants* comprised 'three sexy shorts': *Revenge of the Elephant Man*(2004), *The Mystery of Mata Hari* (2004) and *The Good Ship Venus*(2005). That Russell couldn't obtain backing for his later projects was awful, Glenda Jackson complained after his death, for a film-maker with his incredible talent and body of work.

The 23 feature films directed by Ken Russell and released theatrically are:

French Dressing
Billion Dollar Brain
Women In Love
The Music Lovers
The Devils
The Boy Friend
Savage Messiah
Mahler
Tommy
Lisztomania
Valentino
Altered States
Crimes of Passion
Gothic
Aria (segment)
Salome's Last Dance
The Lair of the White Worm
The Rainbow
Whore
Mindbender
The Lion's Mouth
The Fall of the Louse of Usher

The films directed for television include:

Isadora Duncan
Dante's Inferno
The Debussy Film
Delius: Song of Summer
The Dance of the Seven Veils
Clouds of Glory
The Planets
A British Picture
Road to Mandalay
The Strange Affliction of Anton Bruckner
The Insatiable Mrs Kirsch (from *Tales of Erotica*)
The Mystery of Dr Martinu
The Secret Life of Arnold Bax
Prisoner of Honor
Lady Chatterley
Ken Russell's Treasure Island
Alice in Russialand
Classic Widows
In Search of the English Folk Song
Dogboys
Elgar: Fantasy of a Composer On a Bicycle
Brighton Belles

Ken Russell favoured films about classical composers (Tchaikovsky, Mahler, Strauss, Prokofiev, Debussy, Delius, Elgar, Liszt, Sir Arnold Bax, Bruckner), and artists (Gaudier-Brzeska, Byron, Shelley, Wordsworth, Coleridge, Rossetti, Valentino),[32] and literary adaptions and allusions (D.H. Lawrence, Lord Byron, Percy Bysshe Shelley, Oscar Wilde, Dr Polidori, Aldous Huxley, H.S. Ede, Bram Stoker, Edgar Allan Poe and Len Deighton). Most of Russell's films have been based on novels or biographies[33] (as with many film directors, including the greats): *The Music Lovers Savage Messiah, The*

---

32 Ken Russell said he might like and revere artists, but he also recognized that they were people too, and he saw their flaws (RC, 246).
33 The biopic is one of Russell's key forms – but fictionalized, highly theatrical versions of biographies.

Lair of the White Worm, Valentino,The Rainbow, Women in Love and *Lady Chatterley*. Plays have also been favoured by Russell: *Whore, Salomé's Last Dance,The Devils, The Boy Friend*, and the musical *Tommy*. Ken Russell filmed three D.H. Lawrence novels (*Women in Love, The Rainbow* and *Lady Chatterley's Lover*) – something, I think, no other director has done.

The most celebrated of Ken Russell's early films, made for the BBC (where his mentor was Huw Wheldon), were about classical composers (Edward Elgar, Claude Debussy, Sergei Prokofiev, Béla Bartók, Richard Strauss, Frederick Delius). He also directed films about Antonio Gaudi, James Lloyd, Dante Gabriel Rossetti, Lotte Lenya, Isadora Duncan, Marie Rambert, Shelagh Delaney, Gordon Jacob, and painters Robert McBryde and Robert Coquhoun.

Ken Russell called his film on Richard Strauss, *The Dance of the Seven Veils,*'an irreverent comic strip, as lurid as his music' (1993, 101). Russell wanted to pop Strauss's pompous ego, but the resultant film was controversial, with questions being asked in the House of Commons. Russell noted that he wasn't employed by the BBC after the Strauss film for 21 years (until *Lady Chatterley*). It was only screened once, and never since. What a shame! It's *wild*!

An early trip to Haworth, centre of the Brontë cult, when Ken and Shirley Russell were newly-weds in 1957 (Russell was 30), resulted in a series of b/w photographs of Kingdon impersonating the Brontë sisters in costumes she'd made. For Russell, it was

> the beginning of a lot of things I still attempt on films. I still
> enjoy location, for instance. The recce trip is one of the most
> enjoyable things about filmmaking. And the do-it-yourself
> approach has carried on. We still beg, borrow and steal props
> and make do and mend and improvize a lot. It might be rough
> and ready but it pays off in a kind of intangible authenticity.
> (Bax, 92)

Ken Russell's *Monitor* and *Omnibus* documentaries of the late 1950s and 1960s included *Bartók, London Moods, Mr Chester's Traction Engines, Old Battersea House, Architecture of Entertainment, Cranks At Work, The Light Fantastic, Marie*

Rambert Remembers, The Miner's Picnic, Shelagh Delaney's
Salford, Gordon Jacob, Guitar Craze, McBryde and Coquhoun:
Two Scottish Painters, Poet's London, Portrait of a Goon, Vari-
ations On a Mechanical Theme, The Debussy Film, Elgar,
Lotte Lenya Sings Kurt Weill, Dante's Inferno, Always On
Sunday, Diary of a Nobody, The Dotty World of James Lloyd,
Lonely Shore, Watch the Birdie, Pop Goes the Easel, Preserv-
ation Man, Antonio Gaudi, Don't Shoot the Composer, Song of
Summer and *Dance of the Seven Veils* (Remember that many
of the *Monitor* and TV pieces were only ten or fifteen minutes
long).

Ken Russell had a long-standing friendship with Melvyn
Bragg, presenter of ITV's *South Bank Show* in England. Russell
made a few documentaries for *South Bank Show*, and other TV
slots, in the 1980s and 1990s. Bragg (b. 1939 – now Lord
Bragg) is one of Russell's most important collaborators – not
only has he been one of Russell's strongest supporters, he has,
with the London Weekend Television/ *South Bank Show* team,
given Russell many opportunities to present documentaries and
film essays on national television.

And Melvyn Bragg[34] wrote one of Ken Russell's most
significant movies: *The Music Lovers,* the one Russell regards
as a masterpiece, a long-cherished project which he wouldn't
change at all. And Bragg also co-wrote TV films such as
Always On Sunday,[35] *Clouds of Glory,* and *The Debussy Film.*
(It must be significant, too, that Bragg shares with Russell a
passion for British Romantic poets and artists, and also for the
Lake District – for a while they were neighbours up in
Cumbria).[36] Following his early film scripts, Bragg worked
chiefly in televison and radio (a pity, because his movie scripts
are excellent).

Ken Russell produced a documentary on Georges Delerue
in 1966, who had scored his first feature film, *French Dressing*
(and went on to compose the music for *Women In Love)*
Delerue (1924-92), along with Henry Mancini and Michel

---

34 Bragg's movie credits include *Jesus Christ Superstar, The Music Lovers,*
Isadora, Play Dirty, Orion and *A Time To Dance.*
35 With Melvyn Bragg, Ken Russell wrote a portrait of the French painter Henri
Rousseau, the misunderstood 'primitivist' – *Always On Sunday* (1965).
36 Bragg has included the Lakes in his fiction, with Thomas Hardy as an obvious
touchstone.

Legrand, was one of the chief composers of the French New Wave films (he wrote the scores for *Don't Shoot the Piano Player, Contempt, Hiroshima Mon Amour, La Peu Douce, Day For Night, The Conformist, Anne and Muriel, A Man For All Seasons* and *Anne of the Thousand Days*, for example. Many of those movies are regarded as classics).

Joseph Gomez identified two traditions of filmmaking that were forerunners of Ken Russell's cinema: the film biography, such as those about Émile Zola or Louis Pasteur or Abraham Lincoln or Glenn Miller or General George Patton or Sir Thomas Becket. Russell has made the biopic his own genre. Russell's films draw on the biographical filmic tradition but depart from it radically. They might begin with research and facts, but they don't bother with historical contextualization,[37] for instance, or with achronology.[38] And they reserve the right to veer off into fantasy, nightmare, dream and more fantasy: Russell has never let anything hold him back when he wants to explore the inner life of his subjects. If they're hankering after sex, or fame, or spiritual oneness in their dreams, Russell will show that, rather than have 'em talk about it to someone else, or muse wistfully in voiceover.

The other tradition is the British documentary – first on film, then, from the 1950s onwards, for television. But the British documentary tradition is closely linked with socialist-realist approaches, of which the 'kitchen sink' dramas of the 1960s are an off-shoot. Ken Russell, needless to say, is *not* part of the left-wing or left-liberal political school of filmmaking in Britain, the Mike Leighs and Ken Loachs. (For instance, altho' Russell has included scenes of hard labour such as mining (in *Women In Love*), or scraping a living in poverty (in *Savage Messiah*), it is not in the naturalistic/ realistic mode of the 'kitchen sink' brigade).

Focussing on an individual in the biopics cleverly combines two strands in Ken Russell's *œuvre*: documentary/ history and fantasy/ fiction. A point that Russell has made time and

---

37 But the first question for everybody (cast and crew) in the team would be: 'what year is this?'
38 Some of Ken Russell's historical films simply dispense with many of the conventions of the genre. For instance, bustling street scenes or long shots or cities, to set the scene. There are none at all in *Lisztomania*, and very few in *Mahler*.

time again is that reality is always more fantastical and unbelievable than fantasy. It's true: real life is *far stranger* than anything anyone can imagine. Any time critics or studio executives have questioned whether this or that crazy event really occurred, Russell has responded with photographs and written evidence to say, yes, that crazee stuff *did* happen. 'People are always saying my films are bizarre,' Russell said, 'but they pale beside reality'.[39]

Ken Russell is among the most accomplished filmmakers at stretching budgets. [40] Many of his films were made in the region of $400,000-$1,500,000. And, considering many were historical films, that meant that Russell and his production team had to find all manner of ways of enhancing the movie within strict limits. Working in the same arena of historical films on very low budgets (and in the same era) were filmmakers such as Werner Herzog, Luis Buñuel and Pier Paolo Pasolini.

Although Ken Russell disliked historical films for their romanticized, nostalgic look, he wasn't against doing lots of historical research. For pictures such as *The Devils* and *Savage Messiah*, Russell said he conducted tons of research. Russell remarked that it was impossible to use every bit of information that research turned up, 'so you may as well use the ones that suit your concept best' (Bax, 223). Russell smarted from critics attacking his historical films for something that was actually accurate (often it was the things that seemed the more ludicrous that were actually true).

One of Ken Russell's notions was a kind of cinematic simulacrum, a re-animation of the dead and of the past: to use the real locations if possible,[41] and to use the dialogue that people really said, and to cast actors who looked like the originals. Then 'there is a chance that one will get some resonance, capture the elusive, ghostly moment when it all happened' (Bax, 134). At the same time, Russell also acknowledges that the idea of dressing modern actors up in old

39 Quoted in J. Baxter, 1976, 22
40 Ken Russell enjoyed having a high budget on *Altered States*– his biggest (RC, 249).
41 Over the course of his career, Ken Russell must've filmed in more of Britain's country mansions and churches, as well as 100s of picturesque spots in the landscape, than almost any other film director.

costumes and having them pretend to be real, historical people was also bogus – and he sent up that way of making document-aries in his wild, OTT *The Dance of the Seven Veils*(*The Devils* also sends up its characters, including the Grandier, for instance, drawing attention to his vanity, his selfishness, his arrogance, and his pomposity).

One could extend the study of Ken Russell's films into areas like Russell's cinema in the international marketplace, and how they have fared at the box office. If Russell's films had been huge hits, he probably would've been given more money to spend on his films. At the same time, there would have more studio (and producer) interference. One of the advantages of low budget filmmaking is the independence. It's all about balances: even with their modest budgets, Russell had many run-ins with studios and producers who disagreed with how he'd put his movies together.

Part of the context of Ken Russell's work of the late 1960s and early 1970s, for instance, which's the golden age of Russell's cinema, is that North American studios were still investing in European (and British) film production (that is, timing played a significant role in Russell's career: had he entered feature film production 7-10 years later, it would have been a different story).[42]

Sometimes the American film studios got more than they bargained for from some of their British productions (such as *The Devils*, *Performance* and *The Music Lover*). Ken Russell remarked that American film studios wanted to have it both ways: they wanted to come to Great Britain and produce movies – which they did more of in the 1960s than any other time (and the British film industry never really recovered when they pulled out) – but they also wanted them to conform to their conservative values. And when they saw the more out-there movies they'd paid for, such as *The Devils* or *Perform-ance* (both funded by Warners), they reacted badly.

And when Hollywood pulled out of Albion, partly due to its own crisis, around 1970-71, bang went the backing of studios like United Artists and Warner Brothers. For some

---

42 For instance, you can only make a series of stupendous movies like those of Ken Russell's if you have decent financial backing, the resources of a fully-equipped studio, a terrific crew, amazing performers, and talented collaborators.

commentators, including me, the British film industry has never really recovered from that collapse.[43] It was certainly much more of a struggle for many British filmmakers after the early Seventies, including Ken Russell. His films *Mahler* and *Savage Messiah*, for instance, were made on much smaller budgets ($268,000) than *The Devils*, *Women in Love* or *The Music Lovers* which were backed by Warners and UA. (Would *The Devils* have been made at the same scale in, say, 1975? Perhaps. But not in 1981-82, when British cinema was at one of its lowest ebbs).

One of the striking things is that, although most of his productions were financed with North American money, the casts were usually all-Brits (one or two Americans were cast in the earlier movies, such as *Billion Dollar Brain*, and increasingly from *Tommy* onwards; but Ken Russell's movies avoid token Americans or international casts). Not only that, but many of the key roles were taken up by relatively unknown British actors: nobody in the U.S.A. would've heard of Dudley Sutton, Georgina Hale, Christopher Gable, Judith Paris, Max Adrian or others in the Russell Repertory Company, all of whom appear in *The Devils*). If *The Devils* or *The Music Lovers* or another historical movie of the 1960s and 1970s were made today, roles such as Baron de Laubardemont and Father Barré in *The Devils* Count Chiluvsky in *The Music Lovers*, would definitely be cast using prominent American or international performers.

Ken Russell had a deal with the small, North American company Vestron in the 1980s which allowed him to make lower budget films without interference (Dan Ireland, Vice President at Vestron in acquisitions, was a big fan of Russell's work).[44] The budgets were very low – 'so tight it hurts', complained Russell (BP, 274). However, Russell was a wayward talent, and even when he was given free rein, he still occasionally produced low quality films. His movies of this

43 Yeah – when was the last time you saw a British movie about a British subject in a first-run British movie house? I don't mean *James Bond, Harry Potter* or something filmed in Britain, or using British actors and crew, and I don't mean on television, DVD, Blu-ray, video or online, I mean a properly, fully *British* theme and subject in a British cinema.
44 The Vestron deal of 3 movies came about partly due to the success on video of *Gothic* (released in the U.S.A. on Vestron Video), according to Joseph Lanza (PF, 272).

1980s period – *The Rainbow, Gothic, The Lair of the White Worm* and *Salomé's Last Dance* were for some critics low-power pictures. Many had literary origins (Bram Stoker, John Polidori, Mary Shelley, Oscar Wilde and D.H. Lawrence).

I have to admit, each of the four pictures of 1986-1989, from *Gothic* to *The Rainbow*, failed to amaze me in the same way as *The Devils* or *Tommy* or *The Music Lovers* did. They are not in the same class, I reckon. However, repeated viewings uncover all sorts of treasures in those four movies: the most significant aspects are that they are all about *British* subjects, they were based on material that was British, they were made in Britain, they were produced by a (mainly) British cast and crew, they were directed by a Brit, and, perhaps most important-antly, they were in a *British* style of filmmaking (OK, the finance was North American – but the money is American for most of the 'British' movies you've seen or heard of. And, sad to say, any movie that appears to be 'British' that you've seen in a first-run theatre will be backed by American or foreign money).

Disregarding the $$$$$, this is the 'British picture' of Ken Russell's ideal philosophy: movies made about British subjects. But they weren't bleedin' gangsters in white Jags, not silly heritage melodramas, and not 'realistic' dramas about miser-able lives on housing estates.

COMMERCIALS AND CAPITALISM.

Selling your soul to commercial television, commercials made for television, is one of Ken Russell's *bête noires* He reckoned he produced about 20[45] in the early to mid 1960s:

> Black Magic chocolates; that was a bad one. Half a dozen for Galaxy chocolate bars, all slow-motion things shot in Rome. I did Horlicks, baked beans, though I drew the line at cancer-killing cigarettes. But I thought that even the apparently harm-less ones were immoral and doing me as much harm as everyone else, so I stopped. (Bax)

Everybody remembers the famous and amazing scene in *Tommy* where Ann-Margret rolls around in a sea of baked

---

[45] Meanwhile, Ridley Scott was happy to boast that he had made about 2,000 commercials before he went into features.

beans, washing powder and chocolate (it was altered form its original conception in the script). It's a send-up of mass advertizing, which is a recurring theme in Ken Russell's cinema: he distrusts the idealizations of advertizing, and reckons that they create gulfs between desire and attainment in Western society. The ad men show one thing, but the consumer can never attain it.

Commercials for Ken Russell are

> fantasies on life which promise a romantic solution but which can only lead to disillusionment, disappointment – death! To me, commercials are the twentieth century's greatest crime against man. I hate the insidious brain-washing effect they are having on our society. (Bax, 192)

The flood of chocolate and soap powder out of the television set in *Tommy* is also an ironic comment upon Ken Russell's own work within the advertizing industry. Like many of his contemporaries, Russell has made some TV commercials. That bitterness was originally going to be stronger in *Tommy* – in the script, Nora wouldn't have enjoyed it so much, and there would have been an ironic compilation of music from Peter Tchaikovsky, Sergei Rachmaninoff and Liberace. (Even so, the scene is still over-the-top, but it works partly because of the intense anger fuelling it).

For Ken Russell, the core of *The Music Lovers* was really the 'destructive force of dreams', how dreaming can disrupt lives, rather than simply a story about Peter Tchaikovsky. *The Music Lovers* was 'a black comedy about the decadence of romanticism'. Russell linked this to the rapacious consumerism of a late capitalist society:

> The television adman's trick of passing off his dream as an attainable and desirable reality is to my mind the great tragedy of our age.

American painter Ad Reinhardt remarked:

> The ugliest spectacle is that of artists selling themselves. Art as a commodity is an ugly idea… The artist as businessman is uglier than the businessman as artist.

One of the over-arching themes of *The Devils* is disillus-
ionment – the movie charts a continuous, seemingly inevitable
descent from idealism to cynicism, from morality to debase-
ment, from the dream of religion to the corruption of politics.

HUMOUR AND SATIRE.

There is a *lot more* satire and irony and send-up, some of
it vicious and unmerciful, in Ken Russell's cinema than many
critics as well as many audiences realize. There is an anger,
too, especially in the films of the 1968-1975 period (I am
reminded of friends of Jean-Luc Godard, including Anna
Karina, who were shocked sometimes by just how angry
Godard was – at everything, not only America and capitalism –
but most of all at himself. The rage erupted in movies such as
Weekend La Chinoise and *Masculine Feminine*). Ken Russell's
cinema is sometimes as caustic and vitriolic as Godard's: *The
Devils*, most especially, but also *The Music Lovers,Women in
Love, Savage Messiah* and *Mahler*. The anger certainly gives
those pictures a tremendous energy, as with Godard's work.
(Anger is also a key element in the work of Ingmar Bergman,
Oliver Stone and Hayao Miyazaki).

The *Monty Python* team satirized Ken Russell's films a
number of times (their famous TV shows were first broadcast
between 1969 and 1974, the time of Russell's 'golden age' of
filmmaking). In one send-up, entitled *Ken Russell's Garden
Club, 1958* (1971), a bunch of people in silly costumes (including a pantomime goose), a Gumby and a naked woman cavort
in a tangle of bodies on a flower bed (part of the Pythons'
series 3, programme 1, *The Money Programme*). In another
sketch (in series 3, programme 9, *The All-England Summarize
Proust Competition*), a group of language students (wearing
headphones, in booths) do a dance routine, Sandy Wilson's
version of *The Devils*. And in the blindingly brilliant comedy
Monty Python and the Holy Grail, they took on the plague
scenes in *The Devils* – 'bring out your dead!'

Ken Russell's kind of cinema has always been easy to
parody, because it's extravagant, over-the-top and ambitious
(and *distinctive*, which makes it easier to parody). Actually, it's
already parodying itself. No one can out-Russell Russell,

because his movies satirize their subjects ruthlessly. (Really, it wasn't the Pythons spoofing Russell's movies so much as loving that kind of filmmaking themselves – the Pythons weren't averse to having people dressed in animal costumes or doing silly dances in their sketches).

RELIGION

✟

One aspect of Ken Russell's cinema is so potent and pervasive it's impossible to miss, but it's not uppermost in many appraisals of his output by critics and viewers: *religion*.

What are the major themes in Ken Russell's cinema?

Art and artists, yes.

Classical music, yes.

19th and 20th century culture, yes.

Sex and love and relationships, yes.

Nature and pantheism, yes.

Death, suicide, loss, yes.

And a stylistic approach which's typically parodic or camp as well as reverential – an approach that simultaneously sends up and celebrates its subject matter, yes.

But there is one theme that often pushes aside all of those themes: religion.

Religion is a major component of the following pieces: *The Dance of the Seven Veils* (Richard Strauss's Catholicism), *Mahler* (Gustav Mahler's conversion to Catholicism), *Lisztomania* (in which the superstar composer lives in Rome (in/ near the Vatican), and hobnobs with the Pope, and Nazism as a new religion), *Faust* and *Méphistophélès* (bargains with the Devil), *Salomé* (Strauss's opera, and Oscar Wilde's play), *Tommy* (a rock messiah with a cult of followers), *Altered States* (religious guilt and drug-taking as self-transcendence), *The Lair of the White Worm* (all about an ancient snake cult), *Crimes of Passion* (featuring a manic priest), and of course *The Devils* (which acts as a summary/ crystallization of Russell's views on religion). There are many other examples.

No other major British filmmaker in the history of British

cinema has put religion to the forefront in so many films and
TV shows. It's a concern so fundamental to Ken Russell's
cinema, it places him in the same company as Ingmar Bergman, Pier Paolo Pasolini, Andrei Tarkovsky and Carl-Theodor
Dreyer.[46]

And *no* other filmmaker in recent times has staged so
many crucifixions. Not Martin Scorsese, not Piero Paolo Pasolini, not Abel Ferrara, not Paul Verhoeven, not even the many
directors of made-for-TV religious specials and mini-series.[47]

Nope, when it comes to crucifixions, Ken Russell is king:
they occur in *The Lair of the White Worm, The Dance of the
Seven Veils, Mahler, Altered States, The Debussy Film* and of
course *The Devils* (there may be others I've forgotten about).
So many crucifixions! – to the point where it must have
become routine for Russell's film crews:

> 1st A.D.: 'What're we filming today, boss?'
> Russell: 'A crucifixion'.
> 1st A.D. 'Right you are, guv. Bill! Fetch the dummy nails[48]
> and the blood!'

✟

Ken Russell converted to Catholicism around the time he
was making his first film, *Peepshow*, in 1956. As Russell told it
in 1973:

> During a lunch break one day on *Peepshow* I had been talking
> with this North Country friend of mine [Norman Dewhurst]
> about the Mass. He mentioned the phrase "Take of my body and
> eat", and I suddenly realized that, as far as he was concerned, it
> was the living body of Christ he ate in the communion service.
> That was the most mind-shattering thing that had ever struck
> me. I don't think I ever thought of anything again in quite the
> same way. I was ripe for conversion. (Bax, 101)

Catholicism fed most of Ken Russell's subsequent movies,

---

46 Needless to say, Ken Russell did not like *The Passion of the Christ*, he felt
that Mel Gibson and co. had misinterpreted the *Bible*.
47 Had Ken Russell been born thirty years earlier, and had be gone to Hollywood, he might have been one of the great filmmakers of religious epics in the
Cecil B. De Mille and William Wyler manner in the 1950s and 1960s.
48 Director Norman Jewison recalled that when they shot the Crucifixion scene
in *Jesus Christ Superstar*, an extra playing one of the soldiers was going to
hammer a real nail through Ted Neeley's palm b4 someone stopped him.

and his movies wouldn't be the same without his conversion:

> All my films have been Catholic films, films about love, faith,
> sin, guilt, forgiveness, redemption. Films that could only have
> been made by a Catholic.[49]

What are the views expressed about religion in Ken
Russell's cinema? They are very easy to see (you can find them
vividly staged in *The Devils*):

✞ Organized religion has its uses, can be æsthetically
pretty, but is all too often corrupt and dangerous.

✞ Individual spiritual feeling and transcendence can occur
within organized religions, but often flourishes best outside of
them.

✞ The means to self-transcendence and spirituality are
many: in Russell's cinema, they might include:

(1) art,

(2) sex and love,

(3) drugs,

(4) music,

(5) nature mysticism.

KEN RUSSELL AND BRITISH CINEMA

> Art is never expressing anything but itself.
>
> Oscar Wilde, *The Decay of Lying*

Ken Russell isn't usually placed with the European New Wave
filmmakers by critics. Some filmmakers working in Blighty,
such as Dick Lester, Lindsay Anderson and Ken Loach, had
consciously taken up some of the French New Wave's techniques. You can see the influence of the New Wave on
Russell's films, though. And there are direct links to the
French *nouvelle vague*: Russell had Georges Delerue compose

---

49 And the conversion to Catholicism helped his addiction to snuff, Ken Russell
admitted. He was taking snuff (Dr Rumney's Mentholyptus) to the point where it
became a problem (PF, 31). Being Catholic added a new irony to his worldview,
Russell said, and helped to get rid of easy sentimentality – because Catholicism
taught him that there was no easy way out.

the music for *French Dressing* and *Women in Love* (he scored
New Wave classics like *Jules et Jim*, *Shoot the Pianist*,
Hiroshima Mon Amour and *Contempt*); and Jeanne Moreau was
Russell's first choice for *Savage Messiah*.

British cinema – both François Truffaut and Jean-Luc
Godard denounced British cinema, claiming that it didn't even
exist. Those bastards! Well, OK, they do have a point. But to
counter their oh-so French sneering, their oh-so arrogant
denunciations, I would put forward some names:

Alfred Hitchcock

Charlie Chaplin

David Lean

Michael Powell

and Ken Russell

Oh, for certain, Truffaut and Godard (and all of the Parisian film *cogniscenti*) would dismiss David Lean as lightweight
and populist, and Michael Powell as too fey, arch, self-
conscious and pretentious, but they couldn't ignore Alfred
Hitchcock or Charlie Chaplin – oh no, they are two filmmakers that French ciné culture absolutely reveres (along with
Tsui Hark, Jerry Lewis, Woody Allen *et al*). And, *no*, Hitchcock was *not* American, even though many of his most famous
and celebrated movies were made (and set and financed) in the
Land of the Free. Nope, Hitch is *British* through and through
(and he didn't even go to make movies in the U.S. of A. until
he was 40!).

I've added Ken Russell to that list. Why not?

In the 1960s and the 1970s, when Ken Russell was at the
height of his power as a filmmaker in the theatrical release
arena, his series of films (and TV shows) could certainly hold
up well against *anything* that continental Europe or North
America was turning out. True, Godard, Rohmer, Chabrol,
Truffaut and their ilk in the Nouvelle Vague have been the
darlings of film critics, and Russell has never had a similar
solid, gushy critical following.

Of all the countries of the world, it is *Italian* filmmakers
that I think of most often in connection with Ken Russell. And

three Italian filmmakers in particular: Federico Fellini,[50]
Luchino Visconti and Pier Paolo Pasolini (you can certainly
spot the influence of Fellini on Russell, though Russell is virtually anti-Pasolinian; yet the poetics of cinema, which Pasolini
continually evoked, are fundamental to Russell's movies. And
anybody can see that parts of *The Devils* explore the same
territory as Pasolini's cinema, and in similar ways).

Closely followed by Germans such as Fritz Lang and F.W.
Murnau (there are 100s of links between Ken Russell's cinema
and the great German filmmakers – but that's also true of just
about anybody, as their influence has been almost universal.
Whatever you see today in movies, well, the Germans had
already done it in the 1920s). And of course Hollywood:
Vincente Minnelli, Gene Kelly and MGM musicals, but also
Busby Berkeley musicals of the 1930s, and RKO Fred Astaire
musicals of the 1930s and 1940s. Orson Welles, always
(*Citizen Kane* in particular). Among fellow Brits, Michael
Powell above all, but also Charlie Chaplin, and maybe a little
Alfred Hitchcock from time to time (but not much).

But although Ken Russell is one of the very few international filmmakers who evoke an authentic 'British' culture
and society, who has been devoted to aspects of art and culture
in Britain, he is not really a 'British' filmmaker. Neither is he
American, or international: he is his own genre and category:
Russellian. Just like Orson Welles or Alfred Hitchcock created
their own niches within world cinema – watch two or three
successive shots from Hitch or Welles, and you can tell it's
them, out of 1000s of movies. It's the same with Russell.

In short, Ken Russell has always been an outsider figure (a
maverick, an oddball, an individualist, an eccentric even), in
many respects.[51] From the kind of movies (the subjects, the
approach) he makes… to the way of working.

> Maybe I was born in the wrong country. I'm not into small-time
> no-hopers and the dull and boring things that seem to interest

50 Ken Russell liked Federico Fellini's movies, and wrote in 2007 in praise of
Fellini's classic 1954 picture *La Strada*, which 'features the director's wife,
Giulietta Masina, in a heartrending performance as a female clown, Gelsomina,
who partners a hard-hearted strongman in his act after her mother sells her to a
carnival'. In turn, Fellini enjoyed *The Devils*.
51 'I've never played the game. I have my own game and I'm very happy playing
that', Ken Russell said in 2009.

English film directors. I don't see any point in making films about people painting electricity pylons in northern England. It's ludicrous, and that's the British film industry. (2009)

Similarly, within the British film industry, Ken Russell has not been one of the establishment figures: in 2009 he commented:

I don't really consider myself part of the industry here, and never have, because all my films but one have been financed by Americans.

That's a point worth considering, but it's true of many of the most celebrated filmmakers in Britain or born in Britain: many of their movies are financed by North American companies (certainly that's true of filmmakers like Ridley and Tony Scott, Mike Newell, Alan Parker, Paul S. Anderson, etc).[52]

Often thought of as a *British* film director making *British* movies about *British* subjects, Ken Russell has actually directed most of his movies for North American film studios and North American film producers, with, crucially, *North American* money, and most of his feature-length movies have been about non-British subjects. *The Devils* is of course about France and French history.

It's not just about finance, though: take *Harry Potter* and *James Bond*, two of the most well-known and financially successful movie franchises associated with the United Kingdom. Put aside that those films are North American-financed (which includes marketing, PR, distribution, etc, as well as the negative cost and the rights); the *form* of the *Harry Potter* and *James Bond* movies is entirely American.

Even though *Harry Potter* and *James Bond* contain British characters and settings, are made or based in Britain, and include British crews and performers, they are wholly *American* movies.[53]

---

52 That most of Ken Russell's features are North American-financed is part of the reason why his movies are much more available in the Land of the Free than in many other territories. As Russell says, there are shelves devoted to his films in the U.S.A., but not in Blighty.

53 It's the same with *Star Wars* and *Indiana Jones*: although they were based in film studios in Britain, employed many people from Britain in the crew, and in front of the camera, no one thinks of them as 'British'.

MICHAEL POWELL AND KEN RUSSELL.

In *Fire Over England*, Ken Russell expressed his admiration for Michael Powell's movies, such as *The Red Shoes* ('the best film on classical ballet ever made'), *I Know Where I'm Going!* ('the most magical romantic comedy ever made in England'), *Black Narcissus,A Canterbury Tale* and others. Russell said he saw *The Red Shoes* twice at the Odeon, Haymarket, when it opened in 1946;[54] although *The Red Shoes* was melodramatic, with the sets looking like 'chocolate box surrealism', the ballet had 'many imaginative touches' (1993, 33). Russell admired Powell's talent for bringing out the British landscape, in films such as *Gone To Earth*, *I Know Where I'm Going!* and *A Canterbury Tale* (Powell and Pressburger were very unusual in this respect, among the very few to get to grips with what the world of Britain really was).

But Ken Russell also makes some waspish swipes at Mickey Powell, such as the comment that the last time he saw Powell the elder director was working as a teaboy for Francis Coppola at Zeotrope in the early 1980s (not true of course).[55] Russell was dismissive of *Peeping Tom*[56] (along with many critics and audiences – at the time, but since then the 1960 picture has been re-evaluated as a cult classic. However, Powell didn't write *Peeping Tom* – Leo Marks did).[57]

It's ironic seeing Ken Russell lay into Michael Powell, because Russell has made his fair share of turkeys in his time – or what crrritics have perceived as turkeys (*Whore*, *The Lair of the White Worm*, *Gothic,Lady Chatterley*, etc). Also, Russell

54 Where I saw Russell's own *Crimes of Passion* in its first run, forty years later.
55 Powell was working at Zeotrope Studios, which Coppola had relocated from 'Frisco to Hollywood General Studios (where, incidentally, part of *The Thief of Bagdad* had been filmed, which Powell had co-directed).
56 Ken Russell was bemused by Powell's decision to make *Peeping Tom*, in which 'he engineered his own suicide... Has any other director in the history of the cinema been buried by one of his own movies?' (1993). I don't agree with Uncle Ken: and if it was 'suicide', it was a helluva way to go! It was more complicated, more ambiguous than that.
57 *Peeping Tom* has rightly been reconsidered and reinstated as a Powell classic after its initial critical drubbing (whereas many films deserve to die a thousand deaths). And *Peeping Tom* was bound to be appreciated by filmmakers and critics, especially the late modernists and postmodernists. Like *Psycho, Peeping Tom* lends itself well to a rigorous filmic deconstruction with its dramatic exploration of the relation between desire and looking, desire and death, desire and women, desire and cinema, desire and art. *Peeping Tom* is one of those films that becomes an endlessly discussed 'text' in critical cinema studies, a film almost tailor-made for critics to bring in Sigmund Freud, Jacques Lacan, voyeurism, scopophilia, the mirror image, narcissism and intertextuality.

had only one film that has definitely entered 'classic' status as far as movie critics and film fans are concerned (*Women in Love*, though *The Devils*, *The Music Lovers* and *Tommy* are definitely masterpieces, and *Delius: Song of Summer* and *The Dance of the Seven Veils* are very high quality works, not to mention *Lisztomania* or *Mahler* or *Savage Messiah*), while Powell had at least four accepted masterworks (*The Red Shoes*, *A Matter of Life and Death*, *Colonel Blimp* and *Black Narcissus*; many would also include *Gone To Earth*, *I Know Where I'm Going!*, *Tales of Hoffman* and *Peeping Tom*).

Mickey Powell and Ken Russell share many things in common: both absolutely *love* dance and movement; they tend to prefer using cinema visually, not verbally; they love to cut to music (cinema as a multi-media form); they love excess – in performance, *mise-en-scène* melodrama, sets, costumes, light-ing; they use literary sources, and employ many high cultural allusions; they operated at times as mavericks, on the edges of the British film industry; they had problematic relations with the studios; they fiercely fought for their independent status; they have been much misunderstood, slated by critics, and controversial; they are Romantic poets of cinema, deeply conscious of British literary history, the Romantics, nature poetry, and the inspiration of the British landscape. And both found it difficult to get the films they wanted to make off the ground in their later years: Powell's last decades were espec-ially sad in terms of high quality film production (*viz.* the longed-for interpretation of *The Tempest*, the one 'lost' Powell project many would dearly love to see, like Orson Welles' unmade but much discussed version of *King Lear*), while Russell hadn't done anything really significant in years and years, since the 1980s.

Is Ken Russell an *auteur*? I don't know for sure, but I bet he
doesn't like the term or the concept – and I don't know of *any*
major filmmaker who does. It's entirely an idea cooked up by
film critics, many of whom haven't much of a clue about what
really goes into making a movie (indeed, film critics, who are
presumably *professional* writers, have very poor knowledge
about movie production, marketing and distribution. For
example, they continually emphasize dialogue, the easiest
thing to put into a film review (like the lyrics of a pop song –
you just quote them), and also the easiest thing to denigrate.
But all major filmmakers stress that dialogue is a very small
part of the overall scheme and impact of a movie. Screenwriters, for example, emphasize the importance of structure
and form – and characters – far more than dialogue).

To the extent of conceiving, writing, producing and directing his own films, Ken Russell is only partially an *auteur*; he
does not write all of his own films, for instance. But in the
sense of exercising a huge amount of control over most of the
stages of production, yes (down to operating the camera (those
distinctive tilted, kinetic, handheld camera moves come
directly from the way that Russell wields the camera),[58] sometimes lighting scenes, and being closely involved with all of the
other principal aspects of filmmaking).

In the sense of producing *as well as* directing his films –
yes (and that is absolutely vital: Orson Welles, for instance,
also acted as a producer on most of his twelve completed feature films he directed, and that makes a huge difference). Being
his own producer meant that Russell was able to exercise more
control over the pre-production – such as casting, and com-
missioning writers to create a script. (However, Russell, like
just about *all* major filmmakers, has rarely had final cut on his
films, and has also had to trim back movies due to censorship
– for instance, *The Devils* and *Crimes of Passion*).

In the sense of having particular themes, concerns, and
even images, Ken Russell is definitely an *auteur*. At the level of

---

58 Ken Russell likes to operate the camera on his films (unions and DPs
permitting). Like filmmakers such as David Lean, Steven Spielberg and Walerian
Borowczyk, Russell works very closely with the cinematographers of his films.

the æsthetic, the visual, the aural, and the technical, Russell is most definitely an *auteur*, a filmmaker whose imprint is all over his films. Let's face it, there are *very few filmmakers* that you can look at and say, yep, that was definitely made by so-and-so. And you can do that with A Ken Russell Film – and you can recognize A Ken Russell Picture from very early on in the proceedings, too. Very few filmmakers would begin a film with a scene of a man kissing a woman's tits back-and-forth, faster and faster, speeding up a metronome and music, and following it rapidly by a semi-naked sword fight (and without a title, credits or explanation).

Ken Russell explained in 1973 how he worked with screenwriters:

> I usually tell [writers] how I would like the story. We discuss it; they will say why they don't like something or how they think something can be improved or come up with their own idea. They read it to me, and we revise as we go along. Usually, when I'm shooting, I revise yet again according to the necessities of the day. I believe in using what is available, and when I've changed my mind, I rewrite the whole thing.[59]

It's very significant that Ken Russell has co-written many of his movies and TV programmes, and has also had sole writing credit on many of them. Although the general view seems to be that film directors do everything on a movie – it's the *auteur* theory plus laziness (it's just easier to talk about one artist instead of 100s) – most directors do *not* write their movies (and I maintain that the writing, the concept, the creation of the characters, and the structure, are things the *screenwriter* does, *not* the director, the producer, the studio executives or the second unit clapper loader's cat).

Ken Russell acknowledged that he couldn't write as well as his writers, certainly when it came to dialogue.[60] But I'd say when it comes to getting across ideas in written form so they can be translated into images and sounds and music, Russell did just fine.

✳

Alain Robbe-Grillet's comments (made at the time of 1962's *Last Year At Marienbad*) summarize the position of Ken

59 In T. Fox, 102.
60 In J. Walker, 1974.

Russell perfectly:

> I don't think either the cinema or the novel is for explaining the
> world. Some people believe there's a certain definite reality and
> all that a work of art has to do is pursue it and try to describe
> it... I don't think believe a work of art has reference to anything
> outside itself. In a film there's no reality except that of the film,
> no time except that of the film... The only reality is the film's,
> and as for the criterion of that reality, for the author it's his
> vision, what he feels. For the spectator, the only test is whether
> he accepts.[61]

Movies, as Josef von Sternberg explained in *The Parade's
Gone By*, are about making stuff up:

> When I made *Underworld* I was not a gangster, nor did I know
> anything about gangsters. I knew nothing about China when I
> made *Shanghai Express*. These are not authentic. I do not value
> fetish for authenticity. I have no regard for it.[62]

KEN RUSSELL AND THE CENSORS

It's tempting to get into a lengthy discussion of movie censorship and ratings, but there are good studies elsewhere which
do so.[63] Ken Russell is one of those film directors who have
become well-known for their run-ins with the film censors (and
not only censors, but also media watchdogs, such as the
National Viewers and Listeners Association and the Festival of
Light in Great Britain (and their most prominent spokesman,
Mary Whitehouse), and right-wing and religious groups in
North America).

The number of filmmakers whose works were censored,
banned or shelved is vast. In the postwar-1975 period, they
include Andrej Wajda, Pier Paolo Pasolini, Bernardo Bertolucci, Robert Aldrich, Bob Rafelson, Stanley Kubrick, John
Huston, Orson Welles, Sam Peckinpah, Arthur Penn, Frank
Perry, René Clement, François Truffaut, Joseph Losey and of

61 A. Robbe-Grillet, *The Observer*, Nov 18, 1962.
62 *The Parade's Gone By*, New York, 1968.
63 M. Barker, 1984, M. Barker & J. Petley, 1997, E. De Grazia & R.K. Newman.
Banned Films: Movies, Censors and the First Amendment, Bowker, New York,
NY, 1982, T. Matthews, 1994, P. Keough, 1995, G. Phelps, 1975, and J. Lewis,
2000.

course Ken Russell.

As well as run-ins with the censors on movies such as *The Devils* and *Crimes of Passion* (or the British government with *Dance of the Seven Veils*), some of Ken Russell's films have been re-cut by the studios: *The Boy Friend* had fifteen minutes taken out of it for the U.S.A. release by the studio (MGM). And Warners re-cut *The Devils*, and that was after the parts had been lopped off it by the censors.

On the Hollywood practice of re-editing movies after the filmmakers have delivered them to the studio, Ken Russell hated the butchery:

> They're handed over to some Hollywood "cutter" who does a quick hatchet job on something I've slaved long and lovingly over for months. One company who didn't have an editor actually got their lawyer and the projectionist to cut one of my movies. (BP, 103-4)

Very few filmmakers have 'final cut', even among film directors one would regard as masters, and even among film directors who have helped generate billions. Once a movie's been shot, control over it is given over to studios and executives (a movie, for example, will be edited on the studio lot). And it's the *studios* who *own* the film – a director might write and direct (and co-produce) a movie, but it's the studio who owns it and its rights.

One of the chief benefits of making movies on a low budget is that the filmmaker can retain (more) control of the project throughout its production. And filmmakers such as Ken Russell are so individual and unusual, it requires a good deal of sensitivity to re-cut their movies. They are simply not your average factory products churned out by mainstream, commercial film industries. So to cut a Ken Russell movie, you really have to be in tune with what the filmmakers were trying to achieve. And clearly some film studios weren't. (Film editors are thus sometimes caught in the middle of a struggle between the film directors, the producers, the censors and the studios. No wonder that many film studios take away a movie from the producers and director, and assign their own editors to projects. Some studio editors are loathed by filmmakers because they're butchering their babies).

Ken Russell's movies have often been positioned on the borders of the 'X' classification, particularly in the early 1970s. It's where Russell likes to operate – in the 'R' or 'X' zone (this is the realm of *The Devils*, of course – and this time it's not gratuitous: the 'R' rated violence, torture and nudity is absolutely central to the piece). Adopting the 'R' rating and moving away from the 'X' classification, which occurred in the early 1970s, helped Hollywood reposition itself in the marketplace (distancing itself from the negative connotations of the 'X' certificate); it also meant that those who were criticizing Hollywood for turning out sleaze, violence or porn could be assured that Hollywood was producing fewer 'X' rated films.

The new 'NC-17' rating of the early 1990s was intended (again) to diffuse the stigma attached to 'X' rated movies: it was meant for movies which went beyond 'R' but which wouldn't be classed as porn (or 'R-18'). However, the entire ratings system is all about money: it's about categorizing movies for the marketplace: who pays for the MPAA (Motion Picture Association of America) and the ratings and censorship boards around the world? The film studios do. (At this time, in the 1990s and after, the members of the MPAA were seven: Sony, MGM, Universal, Paramount, Fox, Warners and Disney).

Henry and June (Philip Kaufman, 1990) – an art movie with sex scenes released by Universal, exploring similar territory of love, sex, art and relationships in the mid-20th century of *Women in Love* and *The Music Lovers* – was the first film to be awarded an NC-17 rating from the MPAA's Classification and Ratings Administration.[64] When 1991's *Whore* was given an 'NC-17' rating, Ken Russell protested, and compared his movie to the previous year's Disney blockbuster *Pretty Woman*, which he insisted glorified prostitution (*Whore* was partly an answer to *Pretty Woman*; an 'R' rated version was duly produced).

For some critics, the 'NC-17' rating was effectively a form of censorship. It was a kind of economic censorship, because a

64 On *Henry and June*, see J. Matthews: "Henry Miller Meets the MPAA", *Los Angeles Times*, 27 Aug, 1990 and "Sell-Out Crowds for *Henry and June*", *Los Angeles Times*, 8 Oct, 1990; L. Rother: "A 'No Children' Category to Replace the 'X' Rating", *New York Times*, 27 Sept, 1990; J. Voland: "Valenti: *Henry* Ban Like 'Dark Ages'", *Hollywood Reporter*, 8 Oct, 1990; S. Farber: "A Major Studio Plans to Test the Rating System", *New York Times*, 4 Sept, 1990; D. Kissinger: "X-Rated *June* Could Ignite Major Revolt Against MPAA", *Variety*, 10 Sept, 1990.

studio wouldn't promote an 'NC-17' rated film the same way they would an 'R' rated picture (the studios, anyway, demand an 'R' rated product in the contract. Agreeing on a movie's rating is absolutely essential in positioning it in the market-place). Indeed, between 1990 and 2002, the major Hollywood distributors had only released two American movies with an 'NC-17' rating: *Henry and June* and *Showgirls* (foreign movies were occasionally distributed under 'NC-17').

The line between an 'R' rating and an 'X' or 'NC-17' rating is continually changing, but it has to be seen as a fixed bound-ary as far as the industry, the distributors and exhibitors were concerned. The line between 'R' and 'NC-17' had to be formal-ized by everyone in the industry so that business could be con-ducted without the threat of films being perceived as 'porno-graphy' or 'offensive'. Hence the decision across Hollywood to move away from the problematic 'NC-17' rating (and the old 'X' rating). With the rise of DVD, laser discs and home video, different versions of a film could be released, as well as the theatrical version and the broadcast version. Unrated cuts and 'director's cuts' could be found alongside the approved studio cuts. Even so, some of Ken Russell's movies, including and most famously *The Devils*, had not been released in the version the filmmakers intended (in Russell's lifetime).

ACTING AND PERFORMANCES

> He's not doing it, thinking, "This'll bring 'em in, this'll make more money." He's exorcising demons of some kind.
>
> Glenda Jackson (1972)

Ken Russell isn't known as an 'actor's director' like Ingmar Bergman or Robert Altman. But he sure did coax some great performances from his cast: Ann-Margaret was nominated for an Oscar for *Tommy*, Glenda Jackson won an Oscar for *Women In Love*, and Oliver Reed delivered his career best in *The Devils* (and was also incredible in *The Debussy Film, Women In Love* and *Dante's Inferno*). There are sensational performances throughout Russell's work: Christopher Gable in the Richard Strauss satire, Kathleen Turner and Anthony Perkins in *Crimes of Passion*, Vanessa Redgrave in *The Devils*, Scott Anthony in *Savage Messiah*, Roger Daltrey in *Lisztomania* and *Tommy*, Twiggy in *The Boy Friend*, Stratford Johns in *Salome's Last Dance*, Amanda Donohue in *The Lair of the White Worm*, Robert Powell in *Mahler*, Max Adrian in, well, everything (but *Delius* especially), and of course an astonishing, incendiary performance by Richard Chamberlain (and Jackson again) in *The Music Lovers*

Ken Russell acknowledged that he wasn't an 'actor's director', and didn't really know how to direct actors (I think he was being too modest). Instead, he said, he aimed to cast the film as well as he could, and to establish a creative atmosphere[65] on set. Many directors have said similar things:

> I don't know how to direct actors. I can talk to them and tell them what *I* think it's all about but I can't *make* them act and I'm not interested in doing so. That's up to them. What I *can* do is choose people and put them in an atmosphere that brings something out of them they didn't think they had. (Bax, 189)

Ken Russell could create a wonderful environment on the set, Richard Chamberlain said, in which actors were encouraged to experiment. Alan Bates remarked: 'I don't think Ken would listen to anything an actor said'. Glenda Jackson maintained that Russell could not direct actors much; instead, he would focus all his attention on some minor visual detail. Certainly Russell found working with Jackson 'a very great experience'. He discovered that she was so good he didn't need to say much to her about direction (Bax, 189). (But he was furious that Jackson declined to appear in *The Devils*).

What Ken Russell did best, Glenda Jackson remarked, was 'intensely emotional scenes', and for those he would create a strong atmosphere for the actors (1972). Rather than great acting, Russell said he was often after atmospheres. It wasn't about great speeches or dramatic ability. He has remarked that

---

65 'In a lot of my films it's the atmosphere I'm after and acting ability doesn't have a lot to do with that', Russell remarked (Bax, 190). Sometimes Russell would deliberately deflect attention from the scene or the actors or ramp up the tension by focussing on some minor detail, like a chair, or a costume, in order to 'create a tension, an atmosphere, a charge of electricity' (Bax, 189).

the initial discussion with an actor is where it all happens, is the really crucial meeting, where he lays out the story and the character.

The performances in Ken Russell's films have the appearance of improvization and spontaneity. But no: as with many another film director (Jean-Luc Godard, Ingmar Bergman and Francis Coppola come to mind), it's all actually carefully orchestrated. There might be suggestions from the actors, but the moves, the lines, the gestures, the blocking and so on are all worked out beforehand (and then rehearsed). The result may *look* effortless and spontaneous, and to viewers and to (too many) critics it can *look* as if it's 'just happening' there and then, but that's great art.

Sammi Davis, the star of *The Rainbow*, told me:

> Mostly if a scene didn't flow, Ken would say, 'Do it better', and I would say, 'You're right, I'll do it better'. He was fun to me in that way, he just said it like it was. In the film business there are many ways to inspire or gain a reaction or connection. With Ken, his ability to always just be himself is his key form of inspiration.[66]

I don't know for sure,[67] but I imagine that being an actor in a Ken Russell movie means throwing yourself into it wholeheartedly and trusting the director. If he tells you to take off your clothes and act as hysterical nun, you do it. I bet Russell isn't the kind of director who's going to get into a two-hour discussion about your motivations for being nude in this particular scene.[68]

> I don't talk to my actors too much. I explain as much as I can to them but life isn't to do with explaining or manipulating. There's a danger of killing an instinct by analysing it. (Bax, 128)

And again, Ken Russell explained that often it was on his first meeting that everything about the character was laid out for the actor:

I really direct an actor's performance during that first hour when

66 S. Davis, letter to the author, 2007.
67 But I have chatted to Sammi Davis about it.
68 Actress Diana Laurie (in *The Lion's Mouth*) remarked of working with Ken Russell: 'He is a mix, he's such a mix of generous and stingy, relaxed and control freak, warm and then at times quite suspicious or untrusting of you, and comfortable and uncomfortable with himself.'

I explode my concept of the character into his head for good and all. That is the moment of the creation of the character – the rest is rhubarb. (Bax, 184)

If Ken Russell has a reputation for being tough sometimes on his performers, so have other directors: Stanley Kubrick, Jean-Luc Godard and Federico Fellini, among many others, are also known for pushing their actors.

Ken Russell could be 'very demanding', 'very headstrong' and 'emotionally exhausting to work with', remarked DP Billy Williams.[69] Dorothy Tutin commented, as many actors have done, on Russell's eagle eye for detail, for the visuals.

Somehow Ken was the eye. He worked like a sculptor, using film as his material. The crew felt this too. I've never known a crew so on the ball. They had to be. Ken has an eye like a hawk. (Bax, 196)

And Dorothy Tutin also recalled, *pace Savage Messiah*, that the actors felt like they were performing not for the camera, but for the director. It's a common attitude among actors: they love to get a response from directors, to make them laugh or cry.

He knows *exactly* what the film will be like, and we weren't doing it for the camera – we were doing it for *him*. It was often a question of catching up with Ken and his conception of the film. (Bax, 196)

Ken Russell has said he can talk to the actors about the characters and the story, but after that it's up to them. Sometimes he will deliberately keep an actor uninformed about aspects of a role (a common tactic).

Ken Russell has also employed psychological techniques that some would regard as harsh, tactics where a director will secretly manipulate a performer in order to obtain a particular result. For instance, not allowing Dorothy Tutin to have pins in her hat on a windy day, and also telling the crew that nobody was to help with her hat. Or making actors wear undergarments even if they won't show up on camera (a common gripe among actors). And you would have to accept that, going

69 B. Williams, in D. Schaefer, 1984, 271.

in, knowing it was a Ken Russell movie.

In *An Appalling Talent,* Ken Russell was very critical of the extras on some of his movies – on *The Devils*, *The Music Lovers* and *The Boy Friend*, for instance, some of the extras mocked the principal performers during takes, asked for more money, disrupted filming, and behaved badly in the rape of Christ scenes (Bax, 208f). There was a dispute between Equity and Russell's production over the use of extras. (Subsequent Russell productions had run-ins with Equity: *Valentino* and *Moll Flanders*).

SEX AND NUDITY.

I'm sure that many actors would have not even bothered to go to a casting session if a role was advertized in the trade papers thus: 'this role will require full nudity'. And in Holly-wood there are clauses in some actors' contracts about which bits of the body can be shown. That can be worked out by agents and producers months beforehand – much better than getting cold feet the day before filming.

But there's a starchy, British nervousness about nudity and sex in cinema, isn't there? Somehow, it's OK for Jean-Luc Godard or Pier Paolo Pasolini to ask for actors to go nude or simulate tupping in their movies, 'cos they are masters of the Euro art film, right? They're bleedin' *French* and *Italian*, ain't they? Intellectual and arty and oh-so sophisticated.

But for a British film director, it seems, well, just not done, old boy. Fine for porn, or stag reels, or a saucy seaside postcard (one of many bizarre British traditions), but not for a movie that you and your maiden aunt might go and see at the local fleapit of a Friday evenin'.

But a Ken Russell movie doesn't think like that – it's not that Russell was setting out to upset or shock the bourgeoisie (though there is an element of flaunting bad taste in his movies) – rather, it's what was required for the piece. I'm sure it was not the filmmakers thinking along the lines of, 'shit, this is going to really *annoy* people, isn't it?', but, 'you get your clothes off for this scene, dear.'[70]

That's all it is. It's a body, it's a bit of fooling around, it's people fucking (like they have to do for there to be people at all: no sex = no humans). As Spike Milligan put it: 'People like to fuck'. The fuss about sex and nudity and 'bad language' and 'bad taste' comes from film critics, media watchdogs, broadcasters, and one or two irate people who live in Tunbridge Wells in England and read the *Times* (i.e., arch conservatives, who usually happen to be white and middle-aged and middle-class, too).

There's plenty of gay and lesbian material in Ken Russell's cinema too, from lesbianism in *The Devils*, *The Rainbow* and *Dante's Inferno* (but cut from the final show), to homosexuality in *The Music Lovers*, *Women In Love*, and *Salomé's Last Dance*. Russell has also worked with gay writers such as Barry Sandler and Larry Kramer. As Russell has quipped, maybe he is gay. 'I don't think anyone knows themselves. We can all pretend, but I have no idea what I am. I'm me!'

RUSSELL'S WOMEN.

Ken Russell's cinema is full of beautiful women – so many amazing people have appeared in his movies and TV shows, including models Gala Mitchell and Twiggy, and actresses Fiona Lewis, Annette Robertson, Kathleen Turner, Françoise Dorléac, Ann-Margret, Tina Turner, Michelle Phillips, Nell Campbell, Blair Brown, Leslie Caron, Sammi Davis, Amanda Donohue, Helen Mirren, Theresa Russell, Vanessa Redgrave, Natasha and Joely Richardson.

Compared to all of his contemporaries, Ken Russell's cinema has offered more significant roles for women. The above list is just a small selection of the actresses who have worked for Russell. And let's recall again that Russell's works feature once-in-a-lifetime roles for actors: *The Devils*, *Dante's Inferno*, *The Debussy Film*, *Isadora Duncan*, *The Dance of the Seven Veils*, *Delius: Song of Summer*, *Women in Love*, *The Music Lovers*, *Savage Messiah*, *Mahler*, *Tommy*, *Lisztomania*,

---

70 Rick Wakeman relates an amusing anecdote about the filming of the Rheingold scene in *Lisztomania* with its naked maidens: it was supposed to be a closed set with a minimal crew for the actresses who would be nude, but on the day the stage was heaving with 300 guys, hardly any of which had anything to do with the movie (2010, 113).

Valentino, Altered States, Crimes of Passion, The Rainbow, and *Lady Chatterley*. Those kind of ultra-challenging star roles don't come along very often.

OLIVER REED.

If there's an actor who's most associated with playing Ken Russell's alter-egos on film, it is probably Oliver Reed (1938-99).[71] An actor with a dark, bullish, glowering look[72] (like a British Brando), and a cult following, Reed has appeared in leading roles in *The Devils* (probably his finest role), *The Debussy Film, Dante's Inferno, Women In Love* and *Tommy* (as well as having cameos in other Russell movies, such as *Lisztomania, Mahler* and *Prisoner of Honor*. Some filmmakers have actors who act as lucky charms in their movies, and they like to include them in every film, if they can; Reed in one of those lucky charms for Russell). Reed was an instinctive actor, who took his work seriously, and learnt his lines,[73] and who preferred to capture scenes in one or two takes.

Meeting Ken Russell was a turning-point in his career, Oliver Reed acknowledged. 'Working with Russell nearly always produced Ollie's best acting, and the reason for that was simple: Ollie believed in Ken' (R. Sellers, 288). Russell was very important to Reed's career. They liked each other, shared a similar sense of humour (and a taste for recklessness). As Glenda Jackson put it, 'there was real affection and real respect, I think, on both sides. Oliver would have done anything for Ken, absolutely anything'.[74]

Stories about Oliver Reed are many, some legendary, and many humourous. Ken Russell has often told the story of visiting Reed and getting into a drunken sword fight (Reed had wanted to do a film about Sir Thomas Becket, and launched into a rehearsal at his home with real swords). And everybody knows the showbiz story of preparing for and filming the nude wrestling scene in *Women In Love* Really good parts for Reed

71 One of Ollie Reed's nicknames for Ken Russell was Jesus – Russell often wore sandals, had a beard and long hair.
72 Oliver Reed's voice was not a loud, shouty voice, but soft and often a whisper ('the whispering giant', he was called). When Reed played villains, he did it with a low, quiet voice, because a bad guy didn't have to storm about and shout.
73 Many have attested to Ollie's drunken nights, only for him to turn up on set sober and well-prepared.
74 Quoted in R. Sellers, 180.

dried up in his later career (*Castaway*, 1987, was a notable role, tho' a weedy movie), and in the 1970s and 1980s he appeared in many, many truly dreadful movies (purely for the $$$$$). Reed famously made a great come-back with *Gladiator* (2000), as the gladiator manager Proximo, but he died during the last part of filming (and even his demise – arm-wrestling with a bunch of sailors in Malta – became part of the Ollie Legend).[75]

As well as being a well-known 'hell-raiser' and drinker, the Oliver Reed Legend also included flashing: he 'would take little persuading to produce his penis', according to biographer Cliff Goodwin.[76] Sometimes Reed's desperate need to play, to perform pranks and tricks on victims, seems not only childish but pathetic and occasionally violent (even more so when he teamed up with Keith Moon, another prankster who wore everyone out with his restless need to act the clown).

✳

CHRISTOPHR GABLE.

Much less revered than Oliver Reed, and without his star status, but also important for Ken Russell's cinema, was Christopher Gable (1940-98) – Russell's dancing alter-ego, you might say (Gable can dance on screen what Russell would love to be able to do).[77] Gable apparently gave up his dance career to be in Russell's films. Gable appeared in *Delius: Song of Summer, The Music Lovers, Women In Love, The Boy Friend,*[78] *The Dance of the Seven Veils, and The Rainbow.* Certainly in a piece such as *Dance of the Seven Veils,* Gable is absolutely wonderful: it's a star part, of course, but only one which could have been performed by a professional dancer. Gable throws himself wholeheartedly into this once-in-a-lifetime role – where else would you get to play a god, a famous classical composer (from youth to old age), stumble thru a WW1 battlefield, enjoy an Alpine picnic, drink champagne from a lady's shoe, be teased by a dominatrix, and cavort with Nazis,

---

75 As was the rewriting of the Proximo character, and the use of doubles and even digital visual effects to complete Reed's role.
76 C. Goodwin, 2001.
77 Some among Ken Russell's regular actors were first dancers: Christopher Gable, Hannah King and Judith Paris. And of course the biggest diva in the dance world starred in *Valentino*.
78 Twiggy might get all of the press attention for her role in *The Boy Friend*, but Gable is an essential part of the mix. And he can *really* dance!

carrying Adolf Hitler on your shoulders? – Only in a Ken
Russell movie!

✳

ACTORS.

Other regular actors in Ken Russell's films and TV shows
were members of the 'Russell Repertory Company': they included: Georgina Hale, Vladek Sheybal, Judith Paris, Catherine Wilmer, Iza Teller, Ben Aris, Max Adrian, Glenda Jackson, John Justin, Fiona Lewis, Andrew Reilly, Antonia Ellis,
David Collings, Peter Vaughan, Imogen Claire, Ken Colley,
Murray Melvin, Dudley Sutton and Andrew Faulds (many are in
The Devils). And most of his children have appeared in many
of his films (as well as working on them as crew – Victoria,
Xavier, Alex, James, Toby, etc).

Among the actresses who appeared in Ken Russell's
movies, the stars receive the most comment – Glenda Jackson,
Vanessa Redgrave, Ann-Margret, Kathleen Turner, etc. But
there's a group of actresses who have been essential to the
success of Russell's cinema – such as Georgina Hale, Judith
Paris, Imogen Claire, and Fiona Lewis. They are less well-
known or praised, but they form a key group in Russell's work
(many of them are in *The Devils*).

Ken Russell has often taken cameos in his movies, sometimes reluctantly, when no one else was available (or the actor
cast turned out to be unsuitable or unco-operative, as in
Valentino),[79] and sometimes joyfully, as in *Lady Chatterley*.
And in the more recent, low budget movies, such as *Hot Pants*
and *The Fall of the Louse of Usher*, Russell seems to be
enjoying himself hamming it up in front of the camera (as well
as behind it).

Ken Russell has also appeared in other people's films – in
The Russia House (1990) and *Brothers of the Head* (2006). And
on TV shows such as *Marple, Color Me Kubrick, Waking the
Dead, Celebrity Naked Ambition, Big Brother, Open House,
Carry On Darkly, Legends, Great Composers, Light Lunch, A
History of British Art, Masterchef, Denton, Without Walls, The
Last Resort*, and numerous news shows, chat shows and docu-
mentaries.

---

79 One of Russell's best cameos was as the legendary film director Rex Ingram
in *Valentino*, shooting in the California desert.

A few of Ken Russell's film influences: clockwise from top right:
Betty Grable. Leni Riefenstahl. Metropolis. The Fleet's In.
The Cabinet of Dr Caligari. Die Nibelungen.

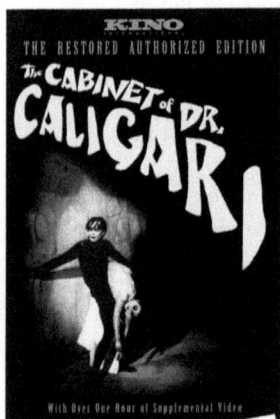

Some of Ken Russell's favourite composers: clockwise from top right: Claude Debussy. Franz Liszt. Dimitri Shostakovitch. Ralph Vaughan Williams. Gustav Mahler. Igor Stravinsky.

Ken Russell on set
(This page and over)

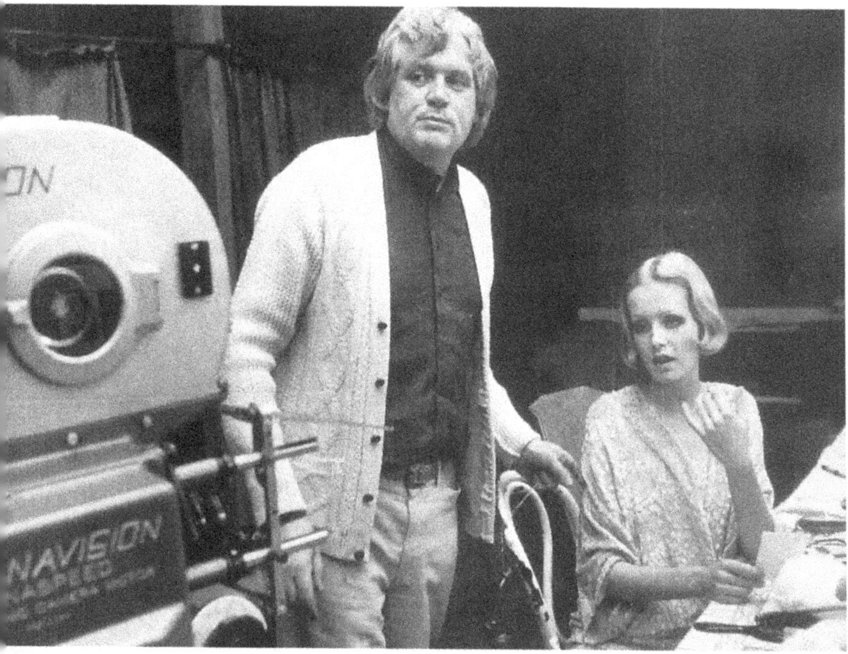
ON
NAVISION

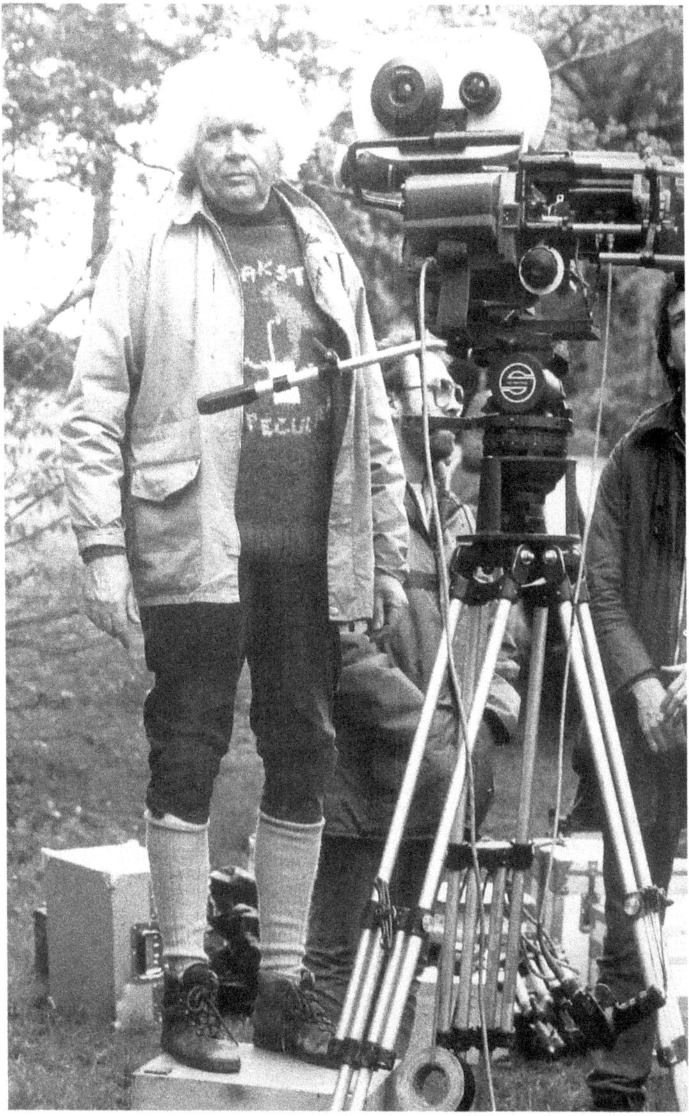

KEN RUSSELL AND THE CRITICS

> Pay no attention to what the critics say. No statue has ever been
> put up to a critic.

Jean Sibelius

Ken Russell has been well served by the writers who've written
book-length studies of his cinema: John Baxter, Joseph
Gomez, Ken Hanke, and Gene Phillips. All excellent, all
highly recommended. Other supporters of Russell's cinema
include Stephen Farber, Mark Kermode and Paul Joyce. (More
recent books include: Kevin Flanagan, Joseph Lanza, and
Richard Crouse).

The first full-length study of Ken Russell was by John
Baxter (it appeared in 1973).[80] Highly recommended (like
Baxter's other books), it is an invaluable portrait of Russell at
work, and includes many of his views and comments. It was
held back from being published because producer Harry
Saltzman threatened the book with a lawsuit.[81]

Ken Russell has written books about cinema – *Fire Over
England: The British Cinema Comes Under Friendly Fire*[82] and
Directing Film – as well as his memoirs. His autobiography –
essential reading – is *A British Picture* (a.k.a. *Altered States*).
Russell's books are to be treasured, even if some folk might
disagree about how he remembered some of the famous
stories. What comes over strongly is his passion for movies
(note, for instance, how many movies he cites seeing in his
childhood, and where, and when. Like Jean-Luc Godard,
Ingmar Bergman and Martin Scorsese, Russell has an insatiable
love of cinema).

Joseph Gomez in his 1970s book study has suggested that
Ken Russell's films have a 'tripartite structure', which incorpor-

---

80 Unfortunately, John Baxter's book is out of print. I engaged in lengthy discussions about re-publishing it, but sadly the project fizzled out. I'm not sure
why.

81 Extracts from the earlier manuscript of John Baxter's book are included in
Joseph Gomez's study. But the book is still critical of Saltzman – particularly
his treatment of filmmakers.

82 *Fire Over England* (a.k.a. *The Lion Roars*, 1993) is another idiosyncratic
installment of Ken Russell's view of the movies mixed with autobiography
(which rehashes most of the material from Russell's *A British Picture*), and
skips over films of Russell's such as *Altered States, Crimes of Passion* and
Whore (his three Hollywood films).

ates: (1) facts, research, history; (2) the characters' view of themselves; and (3) Russell's own views of the subject (205). For Gomez, Russell's films combine these three elements in varying degrees, so that a film such as *Delius: Song of Summer* sticks closely to the facts and research (such as Eric Fenby's account of living with Delius), and minimizes Russell's and his team's views of Delius.

But movies like *Mahler* or *The Music Lovers*contain much more of the subjects' self-image, as well as much more of Ken Russell's interpretations of these people and their work. Which makes them confusing to viewers expecting a regular biopic of the composers.

The biopics helmed by Ken Russell are not your average biographical movie. They don't take the same approach as the usual biopic, so can't really be judged in the same manner. They are also dealing with highly creative people, artists, not ordinary people, or 'ordinary people in extraordinary circum-stances' (the Steven Spielberg model). Which means their approach is different again.

One of the ways in which the different approach is indicated is by the opening sequences: Ken Russell's films announce from the beginning that they are *not* going to be traditional movies, with conventional narratives and drama-turgy. They are not going to move from A to B to C method-ically, or chronologically, or with full motivations for each character and event. They are not going to contain regular characters or characterizations. They are not going to adhere to traditional conventions of realism, naturalism, believability, etc. And they are not always going to take themselves so seriously, or their subjects so seriously (they will thus simul-taneously mock and celebrate their characters).

The viewer needs to take all of that into consideration, and mustn't apply all of the usual conventions of cinema to the movies of Ken Russell. And that is where so many of the mis-understandings occur: viewers come to Russell's films expect-ing, say, a conventional biopic of a classical music composer, but Russell and his team don't want to deliver that.

And so much of the negative criticism of Ken Russell's movies is about these conflicting expectations: the critics want one thing, but Russell and his team deliver another thing. If you want a conventional narrative and regular characters and a traditional movie, look elsewhere. There are plenty of movies around like that. Russell simply doesn't want to do that, and it frustrates some viewers and critics who only want that.

I'm reminded of Jean-Luc Godard, who said that he couldn't make an ordinary film; he tried, he said, but he just couldn't do it. Somehow, his movies always came out like Godard movies, with unconventional narrative structures, characters that stop and turn to the camera and declaim on Marxist politics, with self-consciously silly moments, and montages of flashing, word game captions.

Entries on Ken Russell appear in most of the main film reference books. Nearly always critics assess Russell by praising some of his finer moments, but they always end by stressing his limitations, his deficiencies, and his vulgarities. A typical critical view occurs in *The Oxford Companion To Film*:

> Russell's flair for deliberate sensationalism has perhaps obscured his considerable originality and flair. His excursions into the psychology of artists have become increasingly exaggerated: at the same time his work provides acute comments on the cruelties arising from sexual inadequacies. (L. Bawden, 610)

Halliwell's Film and Video Guide, one of the standard film guides in Britain, denigrates most of Ken Russell's movies. But what does *Halliwell's Guide* know? Here's what Leslie Halliwell said about *Summer With Monika* (1952), one of the sexiest, most sublimely wonderful movies ever made: 'Probably truthful but rather glum and unsophisticated drama of young love; not among Bergman's most interesting films.' (2000) 'Unsophisticated'?! Ingmar Bergman?! Bergman's about the most sophisticated filmmaker ever! Culturally, artistically, technically, cinematically, politically, socially, and definitely psychologically!

I would guess that pretty much every major critic in Europe and North America came out *against* Ken Russell at some time or other. There are bad reviews of his films by Judith Crist, Vincent Canby, Charles Champlin, William Wolf, Paul Zimmerman, Richard Schickel, George Melly, Robert Hughes, Gary Arnold, Alexander Walker and Pauline Kael (no surprise there).

Both Alexander Walker and Pauline Kael, two of the most prominent critics in the U.K. and the U.S. of A., were well-known for their dislike of Ken Russell's movies. Kael was sometimes extreme in her vitriol. The feelings were usually mutual: Russell called Kael a 'shrilling, screaming gossip', and famously whacked Walker with a newspaper on TV.[83] Kael attacked *Savage Messiah* savagely (why didn't Kael drink a case of champagne before reviewing Russell?!):

> now it's all random buffoonery... [he] is always turning something from the artists' lives into something else – a whopping irony, a phallic joke, a plushy big scene.[84]

I don't know if that affected Ken Russell, but he has referred from time to time to the negative responses his films have garnered. It's got to rankle just a little when you've spent a long time working away at something and along come some newspaper people and rip it to shreds. (However, I'm sure after a swig of champers and a shrug, Russell just got on with living and working).[85]

But Ken Russell's pictures have attracted much more violent negative reviews than those of many another filmmaker (and very few among British directors). Russell, it seems, became one of those filmmakers that critics love to hate – like Michael Winner or James Cameron. A punchbag for journos: 'let's beat up Russell again'... 'yeah, why not?!'

In short, Ken Russell has never had the glowing adoration of film critics that Akira Kurosawa or Billy Wilder or François Truffaut have enjoyed. He has never been the darling of movie criticism.

Not that it means anything – far more significant, as far as the film industry itself goes, is ticket sales. And in that respect, Ken Russell has not had the mega-hits of contemporaries such as Ridley Scott or Paul Verhoeven (with rentals of $100/ $200

83 Russell came out better from the fracas with Walker, in terms of public perception.
84 P. Kael, "Hyperbole and Narcissus", 1972.
85 Mark Kermode noted in 2013 that 'there's no indication that Russell was ever hampered or confined by the snipings of those who accused him of being an unruly and excessive filmmaker; such claims merely seemed to light a fire under him, encouraging him to be more adventurous, more risk taking, even more contrary' (60).

million). But box office counts for nothing for film viewers –
who cares what a film cost to make or generated on its release?
Box office receipts are routinely employed in marketing these
days – '*Sluts of the Caribbean – On Acid! In 3-D!* grossed
$100m in its first week!', as *Variety* puts it – but it's a numbers
game, pure business, capitalism and more capitalism.

In 2008 (in the London *Times*), Ken Russell said:

> Although I've read all the critics' best shots in their time, I must
> reiterate, with all the fervour of a novice's vow, that not one word
> of criticism written has ever altered in any way my scripts or
> my next project. I believe in what I'm doing wholeheartedly,
> passionately, and what's more, I simply go about my business. I
> suppose such a thing can be annoying to some people.

I don't think that Ken Russell's cinema has been served
well by critics in the general media. Of course, his films have
had their admirers, but when it comes to full-length critical
studies, there are far fewer than one would expect (or hope
for). And most of those books are out of print. Compared to
contemporaries such as David Lean or Jean-Luc Godard,
Russell has not only received far less excellent critical attention, he has also been widely misunderstood and mis-inter-
preted.

✳

Some critics may have found it difficult to write about Ken
Russell's cinema because so much of it is exploring a world
beyond words and beyond stories. It's about music, and images,
and movements. It's cinema coming close to the condition of
music.

Ever tried to describe music?

I mean, what music *actually is*? What music *is* as a sound,
and as an experience? I don't mean who composed it, who
performed it, what the musicians looked like. I don't mean the
friggin' lyrics, what sappy story the lyrics tell. I mean the
actual sounds of the music. Not the instruments. Not the tech-
nology involved in creating it or recording it.

The music itself.

Not easy. It's the same with Ken Russell's cinema – or
any of the great filmmakers. How can you describe the sight
and sound and experience of Pier Paolo Pasolini's mother

Susanna kneeling on the ground and weeping as she plays the aged Virgin Mary at the climax of *The Gospel According To Matthew* (1964), to the sound of Johann Sebastian Bach? You can't.

As Thomas Atkins put it:

> Russell's complex, combustible mixture of sacred and profane elements, high and low art, makes his films popular with audiences but difficult to analyze verbally or categorize. His best work combines the graphic immediacy and simplicity of the comic strip with the subtlety and suggestiveness of music. (1976, xi)

KEN RUSSELL'S CINEMATIC STYLE

> The whole idea of making art is to be open, to be generous, and absorb the viewer and absorb yourself, to let them go into it. I have to go into all those places in order to make it work.

> Frank Stella

THE CAMERA.

When it comes to shooting a scene, in terms of camera angles and movement, Ken Russell in his audio commentary to *Delius: Song of Summer* said there was only one way to shoot a scene, and he never had any hesitation about it. Steven Spielberg and Orson Welles have made the same remarks: they just *know* where to put the camera, and how to move it. Stanley Kubrick commented that choosing the camera angles and such like was relatively easy compared to the rehearsals.

Thus, Ken Russell does not walk onto the set and run through the standard master shot, medium shot, close-up, over-the-shoulder shot, etc, that film students are taught and that so many filmmakers persist in employing. Instead, Russell tended to shoot in single master shots, covering a scene from one, main viewpoint, sometimes adding close-ups or reaction shots. Of course, if a scene required a simple set-up of two close-ups or two medium shots, of two actors, Russell would do that (and some of Russell's later work for TV does resort to conventional shooting, partly no doubt because the schedules for TV are *much* tighter than for movies. You won't find a television production shoot running a 100 days for a two-hour movie! Or 18 months for 1980's *The Shining* and even more for 1963's *Cleopatra*! Shit, TV would've nailed *Heaven's Gate* in three weeks!).

At its best, though, Ken Russell's cinema is not a jog through standard camera angles and movements. Russell used the comparison with choreography – if the actors weren't moving, then the camera would be.

This has an effect on the editing, of course: it means that many scenes in Ken Russell's pictures are not shots of three or four seconds in a standard shot-reverse-shot pattern. It means that scenes are often broken down into single, mobile shots, sometimes peppered with reaction shots or insert shots. Although sometimes Russell and his editors will employ rapid-fire montages, much more often they will allow the master shots to run on, so that some shots are quite long.

Actors love that, allowing them time and space to get into a scene, instead of lots of short shots (but they have to be good actors to concentrate over a lengthy take). However, Ken Russell's cinema is not known for *very* long takes, such as the films of Andrei Tarkovsky, Orson Welles, Jean-Luc Godard or Theo Angelopoulos.[86]

Ken Russell enjoys actors looking into the camera, in particular moments where actors turn to wink at the camera or glance at it in fun. Another aspect of Russell's style is self-conscious anachronisms, particularly the ones which pop out of the screen in the historical movies. Some viewers find them jarring, taking them out of the moment. For instance, while he found the anachronisms in *Dante's Inferno* jarring and in dubious taste, critic Richard Schickel also praised Russell for trying to push the medium of television.[87]

---

86 What would happen if Russell had filmed in long, ten-minute takes, like Theo Angelopoulos, or Hitch's *Rope*? Instead of people meandering and staring for-lornly into space, as in Angelopoulos's eternally downbeat, Euro-Greek cinema, actors wouldn't be able to stop themselves breaking out into a Busby Berkeley dance routine, or getting freaky.
87 R. Schickel, "Great Lives On TV", *Harper's*, Jan, 1971.

EDITING.

Ken Russell likened editing to composing music, inevitably. It was a case of mixing scenes with different tempos and moods, so the result was like a classical symphony, moving through a variety of moods. Getting the flow of scenes right, and the structure of a film, was very important for Russell (one of the delights of *The Devils* is the pacing and the flow of scenes and sequences. You look at two or three scenes of it, and you can feel how it flows).

Editing is always an aspect of filmmaking that film critics tend to miss. With a filmmaker of eye-popping visuals, as with Oliver Stone or Pier Paolo Pasolini or whoever, it's easy to be distracted by the other technical aspects of the filmmaking. But it's clear with Russell, as with Stone or Pasolini or whoever, that editing is absolutely central. Because if the editing is wrong, the other elements won't work so well either.

I have drawn attention to editing many times in this study of Ken Russell's cinema, because it is *so important.* Yes, the visuals are extraordinary, and the sets, the costumes, the performances, and all the rest. But it's editing that puts all of this together. 'I like editing,' admitted Russell; 'it's very much a hands-on process' (DF, 98). *The Devils* was easy to edit.

Like Orson Welles, Ken Russell doesn't like to hang about: his movies cut rapidly from one scene to another, once the point has been made. Welles hated those s-l-o-w movies (i.e., Michelangelo Antonioni), which showed someone walking right to the end of a road. No. Welles would *cut, cut, cut!* Dorothy Tutin remarked of *Savage Messiah* that it would have benefitted from a slower, quieter scene (which she was expecting to be in there somewhere), but perhaps was better without it: 'with Ken the instant an impression's made, it's off; gone. He never dwells on *anything* and I think that's right' (Bax, 195).

PUTTING ON A SHOW.

Many of Ken Russell's films contain scenes of theatricality and putting on a show. You could hire Russell to stage the Oscars or Grammy's, for instance, and I bet it'd be fab television (there would be *loads* of dancing, for example, and glittery costumes, and at least two or three orchestras on stage as well as in the pit, and the climax would involve four hundred naked performers doing the tango with live snakes).

There are shows-within-shows too, and films-within-films. *Valentino*, for instance, contains numerous examples, ranging from informal dances to big, theatrical performances, plus screenings of films for a couple of people or a theatre full of women. *The Devils* opens with the King of France camping it up as the Goddess Venus in a theatre. There are puppet shows. Characters dance for one person or put on shows for guests (as in *Women in Love*). Sometimes whole movies involve putting on a show (*Salomé's Last Dance* and *The Boy Friend*). Russell's movies portray backstage dramas, recreations of silent films, and plenty of painting and photography, too. Voyeurism is a constant theme, particularly the eroticism of looking, of scopophilia ('we are all voyeurs', Russell says).

MEN AND WOMEN.

Generally, the main characters in the films of Ken Russell have been men – in common with the vast majority of films, written or directed by men or women. However, some of Russell's films have featured women in the lead roles: *The Boy Friend*, *Whore*, *The Devils*, *Crimes of Passion* and *Women In Love*, for instance, as well as TV work such as *Isadora Duncan*, *Lady Chatterley* and *Shelagh Delaney's Salford*.

Ken Russell would not be regarded as a leading light in feminism, however, and sometimes his movies have been criticized for being sexist, chauvinistic or even misogynist. One could counter that the objectification of women in his films is also applied to men as many times, and there is plenty of male nudity (though more female nudity, I guess). Another defence would be that many of Russell's films are set in periods going back to the Middle Ages (in *The Devils*).

TIME AND HISTORY.

Ken Russell is very fond of using framing devices and multiple narrative layers in his movies.[88] They occur in, for instance, *The Debussy Film*, *Salomé's Last Dance*, *The Boy Friend*, *Valentino*, and *Mahler*. Russell explores the self-con-

---

[88] Russell self-consciously aped the narrative structure of *Citizen Kane* a few times.

scious, modernist device of one layer of narrative (a theatre company in *The Boy Friend* or a group of amateurs in *Salomé's Last Dance* putting on a play), commenting upon and reflecting the content of the play itself (belying the view that Russell's works are narratively simplistic).

As to time periods, Ken Russell's films long favoured the 19th century and early 20th century. That's partly because so many of his films are about classical composers: Mahler, Liszt, Bartók, Wagner, Martinu, Tchaikovsky, Debussy, Strauss, Elgar, Prokofiev, etc. *Women In Love* is set in 1920; *Savage Messiah* and *The Rainbow* in a similar First World War period; *The Boy Friend* in the 1920s; *Lady Chatterley* in the late 1920s; *Delius Song of Summer* in the 1920s; and *Gothic* in the early 1800s. *Prisoner of Honor* goes back to the late 19th century and early 20th century. *The Devils* goes furtherest back, to 1623-34 (altho' the setting might also be regarded as the High Middle Ages – certainly the movie contains plenty of mediævalisms – and Sister Jeanne's erotic fantasies go back to the era of Christ).

The movies set in the present day include *Altered States*,[89] *Crimes of Passion*, *Mindbender*, *French Dressing*, *Whore*, *The Lair of the White Worm*, *Dogboys* and *The Fall of the Louse of Usher* (*The Devils* is very much about the present day, of course). This means that Ken Russell is very at home in the 19th and early 20th centuries: that is his time period.[90] It has freed his imagination, perhaps, to be able to go back to the mid-19th century or to the period of the Great War. It also means, from a production point of view, that most of his films have been historical pieces, requiring period costumes, props, sets, vehicles, and all the rest. That also means they are going to cost a little more than films set in the contemporary world.

ROMANTIC STYLE.

A recurring motif in Ken Russell's approach to the natural world is to put a single figure in amongst the sublime beauty of the world and completely dwarf them. Often Russell will instruct his camera operator to frame the figure at the end of

89 In *Altered States*, tho', Edward Jessup goes back to the dawn of time!
90 Other filmmakers have gone back to the early part of the 20th century repeatedly: Woody Allen and Francis Coppola come to mind.

the zoom, then zoom out slowly. An apparently simple technique, yes, but immensely effective. It crops up in *The Devils*,
in *Dante's Inferno*, in *Tommy*, in *The Dance of the Seven
Veils*, in *The Debussy Film*, and in many Russell works. In *The
Debussy Film*, there's a memorable scene where the camera
frames the composer swimming in the English Channel and
holds it for a long time: the human figure is a tiny speck in the
immensity of the natural world. In *Dante's Inferno*, the camera
begins on William Morris in Iceland (actually the Lake
District), and pulls back and back, revealing the epic scenery of
mountains and lakes, dwarfing the figure. The memorable
climax to *Women In Love* features Gerald Crich trudging off
into a wilderness of snow and ice (a one-take shot).

The concept clearly draws on the Romantic artists, on
British artists such as John Martin and J.M.W. Turner, and on
German artist Caspar David Friedrich. It's about Romantic
ideas such as the Sublime, the Transcendent, the Infinite, and
Nature. Ken Russell's images are direct inheritors of Romant-
icism (and some of his images are celluloid versions of a
Friedrich painting).

VISUAL EFFECTS.

With so many fire, smoke and water effects, plus explosions and stunts, Ken Russell's movies are very much visual
effects movies. Oh, they don't have spaceships and light sabres
and Godzilla monsters, so they don't seem to be special effects
movies, but they are: fire, smoke, rain and water effects, for
instance, are classed as special effects or practical effects, and
require a dedicated team to deal with them. And Russell likes
lots of fire – bombed-out areas lit with fire, or flaming torches,
or fields on fire, for instance. Fire, water, fog, steam and smoke
all add texture, which filmmakers love, and all drive up the
budget, as producers know. (The special effects crew on
Russell's films included famous technicians such as John
Richardson and Dick Smith, people who've worked on, well,
everything. Richardson was the special effects guy on *The
Devils*).

Many of Ken Russell's movies are stuffed with visual
effects – from the opticals in *Tommy* and *Altered States* to the

fire, smoke and special make-up in *The Devils* or *The Music Lovers* (*The Devils* is a huge special effects movie). Russell also loves trick shots and gimmicky shots – he is very much of the Géorges Méliès school of cinema, where a movie is a magical performance.

OVER THE TOP.

I've mentioned how exotic and weird some of Ken Russell's movies can be, but there were many films made in the 1960s through 1980s which were just as Out There – I mean those films labelled 'mondo cinema', or 'exploitation cinema', or 'sexploitation', or 'underground cinema', or 'horror cinema' (movies which developed cult status, and had re-runs at midnight screenings, and later came back from the dead (like re-animated zombies) on video cassette, and yet again on DVD and Blu-ray and online).

Spoofing Catholic themes and imagery is a big part of those European mondo/ exploitation/ horror flicks (under-standable, being as many were made in Italy, France and Spain, and even lapsed Catholics or anti-Catholics still lerrve to exploit the imagery). There are films about Dracula, Frank-enstein, monsters, vampires, occultism, horror, Satanism, the Devil, nuns, and on and on, in 100s of pictures made in Europe between the 1960s and the 1980s, the era when Ken Russell was directing his best-known feature films. And Russell's films, with their eroticized nuns, their sex scenes and nudity and flashcuts and all, are very much part of low budget, European filmmaking of the 1960s-70s, part of the clutch of horror, sex, exploitation and *fantastique* films – the vampires, aliens, serial killers, babes and freaks.

Part of the reason is that horror, thriller and occult flicks are cheap to make. And that's also why so many of those films include nudity – all you have to do is get people to take off their clothes: instant special effects! (Even better if they possess super-gorgeous bodies). You don't have to build vast sets or have costly costumes. It's the same with porno films (and also why porn often takes up horror or sci-fi or occult genres).

So although we exalt filmmakers such as Ken Russell or

Pier Paolo Pasolini or Walerian Borowczyk or whoever – because they are 'serious' filmmakers, filmmakers who've made some 'serious' work which can be properly called 'art' – there are hundreds of other filmmakers and films of that period which contain just as much outrageous imagery. I mean filmmakers like José Bénazéraf, Jess Franco, Jean Rollin, José Larraz, Massimo Pupillo, etc. Or maybe it's because, somehow, the works of filmmakers like Pier Paolo Pasolini, Alain Robbe-Grillet and Ken Russell have survived, while so many others have been forgotten.

CATHOLIC STYLE.

Ken Russell's pictures are awash in Catholic imagery,[91] so much so it constitutes a style of its own (no other British filmmaker has produced so much Catholic and Christian material – tho' European ones have). If there's an opportunity for putting in a reference to Catholicism, Russell will take it. If there *isn't* a chance, Russell will invent one! Russell's Catholic style tends towards the extreme end of Catholicism, where sex and the sacred, sin and spirit, merge: lusty nuns (*The Devils*), Christ figures kissing nuns (*The Devils*), randy, insane priests (*Crimes of Passion*), Nazi stormtroopers writhing in front of crucifixes (*Mahler*), phallic worms sliding over crosses (*The Lair of the White Worm*), Satanic goats (*Altered States*), and so on. *The Devils* is a summary of Catholicism.

In *Tommy*, for instance, Marilyn Monroe replaced the Blessed Virgin Mary as a deity for veneration in a church: Catholicism informs everything about how that scene was staged and shot – because the scene is a religious healing rite. In an animated sequence in *Tommy*, rows of RAF bombers standing on end were turned into cemetery crosses. Robert Powell's Captain Walker was crucified on the shape of a bomber plane. (And Ann-Margret writhed around in baked beans and soap suds and rode a giant, sausage-shaped cushion between her legs. Nothing to do with Catholicism as such, but not the kind of thing a caring, nurturing mom usually did in movies).

---

91 'All my films have been Catholic films, films about love, faith, sin, forgiveness, redemption', except for *The Boy Friend*, Ken Russell remarked.

NAZISM.

World War Two is the spectre that haunts so much of Ken Russell's cinema, and also the rise of fascism, in particular National Socialism (Russell was 12 in 1939). Russell has attacked Nazism and anti-semitism many times in his movies (anti-fascism is a very potent ingredient in the cinema of Orson Welles, too). And the classical composers who became associated with the Nazis – Richard Wagner and Richard Strauss – were the object of some of Russell's angriest attacks.

Ken Russell was not alone in sending up Nazism in movies, and deploying the imagery of fascism to comic and satirical effect. Two major, American Jewish filmmakers have often done the same thing: Woody Allen and Mel Brooks. The number of times that Brooks sends up Germany, German culture, Germans and in particular the Nazis is striking – not only most famously in *The Producers*, but also in films such as *Blazing Saddles*, *Spaceballs* and *Robin Hood*.

And critics have attacked Mel Brooks' films the same way they have attacked Ken Russell's pictures: for being too crude, too silly, and for taking on serious topics, such as Nazism, in a glib, superficial and vulgar fashion. And there are definite stylistic affinities between the way that Russell and Brooks send up Nazism – they can't resist to portray exaggerated Nazi salutes, or satirize the swastika or the German soldier's helmet, or produce grotesque satires on the fate of Jews in Nazi Germany.

THE KEN RUSSELL SCHOOL OF FILMMAKING:
RUSSELL'S COLLABORATORS

Ken Russell's films, like those of Francis Coppola or Orson Welles, were somewhat family affairs: for many years his costume designer was his wife Shirley Kingdon. His children (by Kingdon) appeared in and worked on many films (Victoria (b. 1963), Alex (b. 1959), James (b. 1958), Toby (b. 1964), Xavier (b. 1957), and Victoria and Xavier were part of the crew on later productions (as well as her dad's movies, Victoria

Russell has also designed the costumes for *Color Me Kubrick*).[92] Molly has acted in US TV shows. Alex is a painter. The family were involved with the production of *The Devils*.

Ken Russell's son Xavier has cut (or helped to cut) many of his later TV and film projects, including *A British Picture, Ralph Vaughan Williams, The Secret Life of Arnold Bax, The Insatiable Mrs Kirsch, The Mystery of Dr Martinu, Lady Chatterley, Ken Russell's Treasure Island, Alice In Russialand, Classic Widows*,etc.

Among the most important collaborators on Ken Russell's films were his producers – Roy Baird and Harry Benn and Ronaldo Vasconcellos and Dan Ireland (and also Sandy Lieberson and David Puttnam). Baird acted as producer, with Benn often doing production manager duties. (Baird co-produced *The Devils*).

SHIRLEY KINGDON.

The influence of Ken Russell's wife Shirley Ann Kingdon (1935-2002)[93] should not be under-estimated: presumably they would have discussed Russell's projects in great detail, with Shirley contributing all sorts of suggestions.[94] Kingdon was costume designer for *The Devils* –a huge undertaking (but a challenge which most costumiers would relish. It's not everyday you get to dress a huge cast of principals and extras in a stylized vision of 17th century France!).

And the importance of costume in Ken Russell's movies cannot be over-stressed: *all* of his movies are costume movies – not only in the usual sense of being historical films – but because they emphasize costume in every single shot (Russell described *Lisztomania*, for instance, as a costume film, a movie in which costume assumed prime significance). Taken as a whole, Russell's movies constitute some of the most impressive expressions of costume design in film history.

In their incredible book *Film Art*, one of *the* standard texts on cinema, David Bordwell and Kristin Thompson use

92 Most memorably, Victoria appeared as Sally Simpson in *Tommy*. Ken Russell's other children – Alex, Molly, Rupert, etc – have also appeared in his movies.
93 I have referred to Shirley Russell as Shirley Kingdon in this study to differentiate her from Russell when using just the surname.
94 John Baxter remarked that Kingdon was in on every stage in a production, and a vital member of Russell's coterie (Bax, 56).

the costumes and design in *Women In Love* to illustrate a good example of storytelling with colour:

> Ken Russell's *Women In Love* affords a clear example of how costume and setting can coordinate and contribute to a film's overall narrative progression. The opening scenes portray the character's shallow middle-class life by means of highly saturated primary and complementary colors in costume and setting. In the middle portions of the film, as the characters discover love on a country estate, pale pastels predominate. The last section of *Women In Love* takes place around the Matterhorn, and the character's ardor has cooled. Now the colors have become even paler, dominated by pure black and white. By integrating itself with setting, costume may function to reinforce the film's narrative and thematic patterns. (163)

And while we are mentioning *costume*, it's vital to include *hair* and *make-up* too: for instance, Charles Parker (makeup) and Ramon Gow (hair) on *The Devils*. That is, as well as being *costume* films, Ken Russell's films are also *hair* films, and *make-up* films. The importance of make-up (and special effects make-up) on a movie such as *The Devils* or *Altered States*, for instance, hardly needs to be stressed, while hairdressing is central to any costume movie. (Hair dressing took a special significance in *The Devils*, of course, requiring actresses to have their hair shaved. That's a big deal for some people, and no doubt some actors would never consider it).

Although he questioned the practicality and tensions of a husband and wife working together professionally (it's still very rare in cinema), there's no doubt that Ken Russell appreciated the enormous contribution that his wife Shirley Kingdon made to his movies. She was known as 'Second Hand Rose', someone who could find treasures in second hand (used) stores. In *A British Picture*, Russell writes:

> Undoubtedly, one of her greatest talents was the ability to sort through mountains of old clothes and unearth a Fortuni dress – the equivalent of coming across a Stradivarius in a junk shop. In fact, some of our happiest moments together were spent in junk shops with me as her willing assistant. And one has only to look at *Savage Messiah*, *The Music Lovers* and *The Boy Friend* to see that it all paid off. (BP, 95)

VIVIAN JOLLY.

Ken Russell's second wife, Vivian Jolly (they were married between 1983 and 1991), was an American working in England; she had been an assistant on *Savage Messiah*, and later studied film at Boston University. Russell met Jolly again when she filmed a documentary on the making of *Valentino*. Jolly became a key associate in the Ken Russell School of Filmmaking – collaborating on scripts, discussing projects in detail, and helping with productions (Jolly has a co-writing credit on *The Rainbow*).

STUART BAIRD.

One of the regulars on Ken Russell's production team was editor Stuart Baird (*The Devils, Savage Messiah, Tommy, Valentino, Lisztomania* and *Altered States*), one of the superstar editors in the British film industry. Baird is certainly one of the great editors of action movies: Baird went on to cut *Lady-hawke, Demolition Man, Maverick, Casino Royale, Outland, Superman 1* and *2, Gorillas In the Mist, New Jack City, Robin Hood: Prince of Thieves, The Omen, Revolution, Die Hard 2* and the first two *Lethal Weapon* flicks. Baird eventually turned to directing (*Executive Decision, US Marshalls* and my favourite of the *Star Trek* pictures, *Star Trek: Nemesis* [2002]).

The influence of editor Stuart Baird on Ken Russell's cinema should not be under-estimated. Baird and his editing team really punched up the rapidity of the imagery of movies such as *Tommy, Valentino* and *Lisztomania*, and made sure that the famous, Russell 'shock' cuts were really rammed home.

MICHAEL BRADSELL.

One of Ken Russell's regular editors was Michael Bradsell: he cut *The Devils, Women In Love, The Music Lovers, The Boy Friend, Mahler, Tommy* and *Savage Messiah*, and later movies such as *Gothic, Aria* and *Hot Pants*. Which makes Bradsell one of the absolutely vital contributors to Russell's cinema, because editing is a particularly important ingredient in Russell's filmic style. It's Bradsell and his team who would have worked out in detail the counter-pointing that Russell likes to employ, where one section or scene is played against another, and the editing techniques such as the famous, Russellian shock cuts.

Other regular editors included Peter Davies (*The Lair of the White Worm, The Rainbow, Lady Chatterley*), and Brian Tagg (*Crimes of Passion, Whore, Prisoner of Honor* and *The Strange Affliction of Anton Bruckner*). Terry Rawlings, Maurice Askew and Brian Simmons worked on the sound of Russell's films (Rawlings was sound editor on *The Devils*). Allan Tryer edited many of the early TV documentaries. (It's worth noting that Russell's movies have been pioneers in the realm of sound: *Tommy* was the first production to use the quintaphonic system; and *Lisztomania* was the first Dolby Stereo show; and *The Devils* has a truly idioisyncratic score).

DEREK JARMAN.

Derek Jarman (1942-1994) worked with Ken Russell in the early 1970s (on *The Devils* and *Savage Messiah*), and Russell's love of flamboyance and rich imagery is easily spotted in Jarman's cinema (think of the very Russellian *Caravaggio* , or films such as *Jubilee, The Garden* or *The Last of England*). While Jarman might have hated working out at Pinewood on Russell's films, his time with the older filmmaker was clearly crucial. Both artists employed 'shock' tactics; shared similar themes (the artist in society, religion, British traditions); both had highly idiosyncratic cinematic styles; both were rebels; both often worked on the margins of the industry; both were ostracized by film critics; both exalted British art (such as the Romantics, and early modernism); both loved the British landscape (Jarman's Dorset, London and Dungenness, Russell's beloved Lake District and the South Coast); both loved classical music (Jarman made a film of Benjamin Britten's *War Requiem*, while Russell was well-known for his classical composer biopics); and both enshrined the artistic calling.

'There was no better director to learn from', Derek Jarman said in *Dancing Ledge* of Ken Russell, 'as he would always take the adventurous path even at the expense of coherence' (105).

Although Derek Jarman became a cult icon in some circles, and his movies were lauded critically (but not by everybody – some loathed them as much as they loathed Russell's work), his movies now seem very minor compared to the output of giants like Ken Russell (or any of filmmakers that Jarman revered, such as Pier Paolo Pasolini). Jarman is not, in the end, a 'British Pasolini', or a worthy or significant successor to Russell. There's a fatal desperation to be trendy in Jarman's work, to be 'cool', to be self-consciously ironic and arch, which hampers his movies in particular, whereas Russell couldn't give a shit about all that. You always felt that Jarman yearned to be taken as seriously as Pasolini or Michelangelo Antonioni, but he didn't have the chops in cinema to achieve that. Jarman's sub-Kenneth Anger/ sub-Andy Warhol, trashy effects are over-worked and ill-conceived, his pop culture references are laboured, and he has little to no feeling for staging decent drama.

Christopher Hobbs, Derek Jarman's regular production designer (he worked on *Jubilee*, *Caravaggio*, *The Last of England*, *The Garden* and *Edward II*), also designed a number of Ken Russell films (like Jarman himself), including *The Devils*, *Savage Messiah*, *Salomé's Last Dance*[95] and *Gothic*.

THE OPENING SCENE

One of Ken Russell's specialities is the strong opening sequence. Many filmmakers, such as Orson Welles and George Lucas, have also cultivated the technique. It's the opposite of employing a s-l-o-w opening sequence which takes five minutes to get into the narrative. Not for Russell a montage of fifteen 2nd unit shots of the principal setting of the story, for example, accompanied by slow, depressing music. Or lengthy quotes or captions. Or a lot of exposition upfront. Russell gets right into it.

Orson Welles said that a movie should open powerfully, because the screen was dead, the thing was just film projected onto a screen. Theatre could get away with slower openings, as the audience settled into their seats. But a movie had to grab

---

95 And Michael Buchanan was production designer on both *Caravaggio* and *Salomé's Last Dance*.

the audience right from the beginning – the 'riderless horse' must enter the scene, as Welles put it. Hence the beginning of *Othello* (1952), with that extraordinary funeral on the battlements, or the unbeatable start of *Citizen Kane*.

The Big Beginning was a lesson that Ken Russell learnt from his television days,[96] when his documentaries for *Monitor* were broadcast in a Sunday evening slot after a movie. As Russell explained:

> I gradually learned that as we followed the main feature film on Sunday night when anyone saw *Monitor*, the average viewer would take x number of seconds to get up and turn it off, so if I had a film on we would drop the logo thing at the beginning and put it at the end and I would devise an opening sequence for my films which would stop them turning off.

So *The Devils* launches with a high camp musical number, a brilliant way of wrong-footing the audience, expecting a serious historical movie exploring Big Themes; *Lisztomania* starts with composer Franz Liszt and one of his lovers fucking (swiftly followed by a comic duel with swords); *The Debussy Film* (1965) has a beautiful woman being shot with arrows, in a St Sebastian skit; *Mahler* opens with a building by a lake exploding; *Tommy* starts with a man silhouetted against a mighty, orange sun. Russell also acknowledged that viewers tended to be desensitized by so much television viewing. They'd be talking while the news was on, or eating supper while watching a movie. Hence the shock effects, to wake up the audience.

---

96 The device comes from television, where it's called the 'short hook', typically a murder, car crash, or explosion, designed to stop people changing channels (A. Block, 433).

SOME OF KEN RUSSELL'S INFLUENCES

SYMBOLIST ART.

An important influence on the cinema of Ken Russell is late 19th century literary and artistic culture in Europe, including, in Britain, Oscar Wilde,[97] Aubrey Beardsley, and the Pre-Raphaelites. Wilde and his play *Salomé* and the figure of Salomé herself (particularly as enshrined by Beardsley), crop up in many places in Russell's output (even in unlikely places, such as a Michael Caine *Harry Palmer* movie).

SALOMÉ.

Direct references to Salomé can be found in *Delius: Song of Summer*, *Salomé's Last Dance*, *Billion Dollar Brain* and *Isadora Duncan*. Salomé is of course one of the key female figures of Symbolist and Decadent art. She is the *femme fatale* type who symbolically melds sex and death, desire and fear, contact and loss, for the (male) artist. *Femme fatales* are aplenty in Ken Russell's cinema (to cite just a few obvious examples: China Blue in *Crimes of Passion*, Lady Sylvia in *The Lair of the White Worm*, Nina Milyukova in *The Music Lovers*, Life in *Delius: Song of Summer*, etc). In Symbolism, the *femme fatale* is Medusa, Salomé, Delilah, Jezebel, the Queen of Sheba, Judith, Lilith, Ninuë (the lover of Merlin), Venus, Helen of Troy, the Mona Lisa, and Cleopatra. She's there in literary and poetic women such as Salammbô (in Gustave Flaubert), La Belle Dame Sans Merci (in John Keats' poem), Carmen (in P. Mérimée), Cécily (in the *Mystère de Paris* by Eugène Sue), Conchita (in Pierre Louÿs), Matilda (in M.G. Lewis) and Eustacia Vye (in Thomas Hardy's *The Return of the Native*). But the artist who completely made Salomé his own was the French Symbolist painter Gustave Moreau: Salomé dominates Moreau's art (and it was Moreau and his *Salomé* that Des Esseintes enthused over in the *Bible* of the Symbolist and Decadent period, J.-K. Huysmans' *À Rebours*).

---

97 Oscar Wilde became enamoured of French Symbolism, and employed its influences (Moreau, Huysmans, Louÿs), in his *Salomé*.

SURREALISM.

Ken Russell was a fan of Surrealism, and wanted to make a film about Salvador Dali. Jean Cocteau was another big influence on Russell's cinema, and it's easy to spot Cocteau's heightened, theatrical and fantastical elements in his films.[98]

Jean Cocteau's influence can be discerned all over the place – in the work of Jean-Luc Godard, Donald Cammell, Derek Jarman, Orson Welles, Francis Coppola, Kenneth Anger, and of course the Walt Disney Studios, who updated *Beauty and the Beast* in 1991 (as a Broadway musical). It's probably impossible to watch *La Belle et la Bête* or *Blood of a Poet* or one of Cocteau's *Orpheus* films and *not* be influenced. They are so beautiful and enchanting, they can't help but throw a spell over you.[99]

THE LAKE DISTRICT.

The Lake District was used many times by Ken Russell: his beloved Skiddaw, Castle Crag, Derwent Water and Borrowdale Valley (Russell first visited the Lakes in 1965, looking for locations for his Dante Gabriel Rossetti documentary, and later lived there for over 20 years). Cumbria was used for the scene where Oliver Reed solemnly consecrates Mass in the mountains and lakes in *The Devils*; for the crag that Roger Daltrey climbed at the end of *Tommy* (and the opening picnic scene); Robert Powell's lakeside retreat in *Mahler*; and the waterfall where Sammi Davis and Paul McGann made out in *The Rainbow* (and where Reed as Dante Gabriel Rossetti contemplated suicide in Russell's *Monitor* show about the Pre-Raphaelites).

The Lakes also featured in *Dance of the Seven Veils*, *Dante's Inferno*, *Song of Summer*, *A British Picture* and films on Wordsworth and Coleridge. The area stood in for Norway, Iceland, Bavaria and France. In *A British Picture*, Ken Russell described his first sight of the mountain Skiddaw:

---

98 'His films (*La Belle et La Bete, Orpheus*) made a big impact on me. The third amateur movie I made, *Amelia and the Angel* was heavily influenced by Cocteau. It was the one that got me into the BBC', Russell later said.
99 *The Red Balloon* (Albert Lamorisse, 1956) was also an inspiration for the young Ken Russell.

I jumped out of bed, pulled the curtains and froze. My heart pounded, my blood raced, I caught my breath, my eyes widened, my hair stood on end, an unseen orchestra played a tremendous chord. Only clichés can describe what no one has ever been able to portray – a vision of God. (BP, 130-1)

*

It's striking how much of Ken Russell's cinema deals with France and French culture: *The Devils, Always On Sunday, The Debussy Film, Don't Shoot the Composer, Delius: Song of Summer* and *Prisoner of Honor*, are either set in France or are about French art and culture. Meanwhile, French scenes appear in *Savage Messiah, Isadora Duncan,* and *Lisztomania*.[100]

Russia and Russian culture is found in many places in Ken Russell's cinema (as well as pro-Soviet politics): in *The Music Lovers* obviously, which takes on a Russian musical icon. Also: *Isadora Duncan, Billion Dollar Brain,* the unmade *Nijinsky,* and *Valentino* starred a famous, Russian ballet dancer. Germany and German society and art is another element in Russell's movies, from *Mahler* and *Lisztomania* to *Lotte Lenya Sings Kurt Weill* and *Dance of the Seven Veils*. And of course there are numerous references to German music (Beethoven, Wagner, Strauss) in Russell's cinema.

FILM INFLUENCES.

Ken Russell said in *A British Picture* that he consumed movies by the ton when he was young. Like Ingmar Bergman, Russell had his own film projectors, and played Fritz Lang, Leni Riefenstahl, Harold Lloyd, Charlie Chaplin, Felix the Cat, Mickey Mouse, Snub Pollard, Betty Boop, and, later, Jean Cocteau, René Clair, Jean Vigo and Orson Welles. The visionary epics *Die Niebelungen* (1924) and *Metropolis* (1926) were some of Russell's most beloved early influences. 'I'd seen thousands of films by then but never any that excited me as much as these', Russell recalled in 1973 (Bax, 62). *The Secret of the Loch* was another favourite. At the local flea pit he saw *Flash Gordon*, Felix the Cat, Betty Boop and Old Mother Reilley; later, he devoured F.W. Murnau, Jean Vigo, G.W. Pabst, Sergei Eisenstein, Jean Renoir and Jean Cocteau (BP, 16-17). Orson Welles was another inspiration for Russell:

---

100 But very few of Russell's Francophone flicks were filmed in France.

Orson Welles had that magic as well. I still think *Citizen Kane* is a masterpiece. There's nothing like that ever made in English cinema, not with that style and flair.[101]

There's so much one can say about *Citizen Kane*, of course, but here I'll emphasize one aspect in relation to the cinema of Ken Russell, and that's the feeling of *play*, of experimentation, of trying all sorts of stuff out in a movie. In short, the utter *joy* of making movies. Orson Welles had that, and Russell has it in spades. And it never leaves him (just as it never left Welles: Welles simply *adored* making movies).

The *sheer joy* of making cinema bounces out of *Citizen Kane*, and it does in Ken Russell's finest work. Even in *The Devils*, with its solemn subject matter and upsetting images. It's the pleasure of putting sounds and music and images together, which's an important aspect of the some of the best movies – you can see it in *An American In Paris* or *Contempt* or *Porco Rosso* or *Once Upon a Time In China*. The filmmakers' enjoyment undoubtedly helps to keep these movies alive in the very crowded world of cinema.

And in Ken Russell's movies and TV shows, you can see that he and the production teams were having a ball. True, there were productions that were fraught with problems, but you don't make as many movies and TV shows as Russell has unless you're crazy about the whole process (there are much less stressful ways of earning rent and food).

The Marx Brothers were favourites of Ken Russell's – who doesn't like the Marx Brothers? In 2007, Russell wrote in the London *Times* of his favourite male character in movies:

> that man for all seasons, Rufus T. Firefly, from *Duck Soup* –
> alias Captain Spaulding, the African explorer ("Did someone
> call me schnorrer?"), from *Animal Crackers* – played by
> Groucho Marx. That painted-on moustache, that crouching walk
> (like an inept private eye), that unlit cheap cigar (from which he
> continually flicks nonexistent ash), that knowing glance at the
> audience that lets us in on the gag, have kept me chuckling for
> more than 50 years.

In his films, Ken Russell, like many another filmmaker,

---

101 Ken Russell has cribbed the beginning of *Citizen Kane* a number of times –
consciously, of course. At the beginning of *Isadora Duncan*, for instance, or in
The Debussy Film, or the multiple viewpoint form of *Valentino*.

would create conscious nods to some of his favourite film-makers: silent comedy *à la* Harold Lloyd or Charlie Chaplin (in *Tommy*);[102] a slice of epic action from Sergei Eisenstein[103] (in *Billion Dollar Brain*); the Surrealism and dreamy fantasy of Jeans Cocteau and Vigo; or the deep focus, black-and-white cinematography of Orson Welles and Ingmar Bergman (in *Delius: Song of Summer* and *Dante's Inferno*), plus plenty of Bergman's penchant for angst and intensity.

In *The Devils* you can detect Cecil B. DeMille, Ingmar Bergman, D.W. Griffith, Jean Cocteau and the Surrealists, David Lean, Sergei Eisenstein and Federico Fellini.

It's clear that Ken Russell would've flourished in the early days of Hollywood, for instance – working alongside giants like D.W. Griffith or Cecil B. DeMille, or turning out knockabout comedy for Mack Sennett or Charlie Chaplin. Indeed, the melodrama and spectacle of Griffith's cinema has so many affinities with Russell's – such as *Intolerance*, with its grand-iose sets, its extravagant costumes, its parallel stories, its incredible climaxes, its eye-popping action, and the screen teeming with details and life.

In fact, silent comedy is an *enormous* influence on Ken Russell's cinema, and scenes filmed in a silent comedy manner can be found everywhere in his work. Silent comedy is one of Russell's default modes of filmmaking; it's something he can do as naturally as anything else. A *major* fan, a *passionate* fan of all of silent cinema – there are references to it in every single one of Russell's movies and TV shows.

Ken Russell would've been quite at home in the Germany of the 1920s, too, in amongst great productions such as *Nosferatu, Metropolis* or *Die Niebelungen.* The silent cinema era features prominently in *Mahler, Tommy, Lisztomania, Isadora Duncan, Dante's Inferno, The Dance of the Seven Veils, The Boy Friend*, and the whole of *Valentino*.

When considering Ken Russell's influences from the history of cinema, it's striking just how many were French and German: Fritz Lang, F.W. Murnau, Jean Vigo, René Clair, G.W. Pabst, Jean Renoir, Leni Reifenstahl, Jean-Luc Godard and

102 Ken Russell adores the silent comedy classics, and has references to Charlie Chaplin, Laurel and Hardy, Harold Lloyd, and Buster Keaton in numerous places in his movies.
103 There's quite a bit of Eisenstein in Russell's œuvre.

two Jeans (Vigo and Cocteau). So as well as consuming the usual North American and British movies (Disney, Chaplin, Lloyd, *Betty Boop*, *Fritz the Cat*, etc), Russell was very into European cinema.

SYMBOLS AND MOTIFS

> You can't shake your own sensibility. No matter what the concept is, the artist's eye decides when it's right... which is a notion of sensibility.
>
> Kenneth Noland

Among the numerous recurring symbols or motifs that Ken Russell employs are circles, the sun, mountains, mirrors, fire, water (lakes, rivers, waterfalls), the colour red, symmetry, trains, and crosses (and anything Catholic or Christian). Russell loves circular motifs, and they appear throughout his work; there are circular windows, circular staircases, circular mirrors, close-ups of mouths and eyes; and course buildings and rooms (Urbain Grandier's rooms in *The Devils* are circular; other physical circles include the giant wooden machines, and the wheels with corpses tied to them).

Linked to circles is Ken Russell's use of the spinning camera – when a scene gets really intense, the camera rotates wildly (and there are many upside-down shots too). There are circular dances (like around the Maypole penis in *Lisztomania*); carousels; and spinning pianos (also in *Lisztomania*, and in *The Music Lover*).

Mountains and spectacular landscapes such as lakes and rivers and the ocean are in Ken Russell's cinema embodiments of romantic, pantheistic, lyrical, life-affirming feelings. Russell becomes a late addition to the roster of Romantic poets: Urbain Grandier communing by the lake in *The Devils* (as if the movie is placing nature and pantheism above and beyond Christianity – pantheism – and animism – are, after all, *far* older spiritual beliefs than Catholicism); Tommy standing in the sun; Ursula and Skrebensky running around naked on the hills in *The Rainbow*; Edward Elgar on the Malvern Hills; Henri Gaudier at the Isle of Portland in *Savage Messiah*.

Often there's a character standing with their arms outstretched, embracing the natural world and fusing with it, in *The Devils, Tommy, Savage Messiah, Delius: Song of Summer, Women In Love, Dante's Inferno*, etc. As Ken Russell describes Tommy's act at the end of *Tommy* in the shooting script: it is 'an affirmation of Man's eternal divinity. Tommy raises his arms as if to embrace the life giving sun' (the image was put on Russell's coffin at his funeral).

Fire would typically connote chaos and destruction (as in *The Devils, Mahler*, and *The Music Lovers*): no one can forget the startling image of the burning fields in *The Music Lovers*, when Peter Tchaikovsky returns to his country estate to find himself locked out by Madame von Meck (after Count Chiluvsky has told von Meck that Tchaikovsky is gay). And *The Devils* becomes very fiery at the end, with fire evoking the self-immolation of a whole nation's beliefs, as well as the law, morality and organized religion.

Symmetry is a favourite visual motif: so often, Ken Russell and his cinematographers will place a character or subject of a scene dead centre. And Russell likes a frontal, *tableau* approach too, as part of his stylization of cinema (like Sergei Paradjanov or Pier Paolo Pasolini). That is, very often scenes will be staged with the characters, props and scenery arranged along lines at right angles to the direction of the camera. However, although the *tableau* approach can produce rather static cinema, Russell's films contain so much dynamism in other areas they are seldom static.

Although he began by making black-and-white movies (as so many have done), and some of his finest pieces, such as *Delius: Song of Summer* and *The Debussy Film*, are in black-and-white, Ken Russell is certainly a remarkable director of *colour* movies. From his first major colour movie – *Billion Dollar Brain* – onwards, Russell has devoted plenty of energy to colour. His techniques include highlighting a particular colour (with red as a favourite, as with Jean-Luc Godard in the Sixties), and also by selective colour, draining all of the colours out of a scene except for one (such as the '1812 Overture' fantasy in *The Music Lovers*, where the scene's reduced to the grey of Peter Tchaikovsky's statue).[104] *The Devils* was conceived in the extremes of black and white, which's reflected in the costumes, production design, props, etc.[105]

DEATH.

Examining the narratives of many of Ken Russell's movies, and the paths they pursue, reveals unusual results. Take the topic of death, for example. In the action-adventure movies and formula dramas, such as *Billion Dollar Brain* and *Dogboys*, one expects the bad guys to die. But many characters die in Russell's other movies, underlining the themes of tragedy, toxic personalities and self-destruction.

Urbain Grandier in *The Devils* has the lengthiest and most gruesome demise in Ken Russell's *œuvre*, in a movie literally littered with corpses; *The Devils* doesn't include the figure of the Grim Reaper, but it well have. At the end of *Women in Love*, Gerald Crich stalks off into the snowy mountains to die. Peter Tchaikovsky dies at the end of *The Music Lovers* (and his mother at the beginning). So does Gustav Mahler, and Henri Gaudier, and Rudolph Valentino, and Frederick Delius, and Franz Liszt. Tommy's parents are killed in front of him. 'The emphasis on death and violence in my films could be a reaction against death being hushed up', Russell mused in 1973 (Bax, 200).

Clearly, for his artist characters, Ken Russell uses death as the means of closing the piece dramatically *and* thematically. And these deaths are not tacked on to the piece, to give it some serious import, as lesser filmmakers do, they are signalled throughout the piece (with their death drives, their suicidal tendencies, their corrosive personalities which affect everyone around them).

We're not talking in terms of some viewers in the audi-

---

104 Jack Fisher wrote of the colours in *Women in Love* 'Ranging from the dark, suffocating browns, through red-golds, through the lush warm exteriors, to the green-white of the snow, the colors constantly reaffirm Russell's visual attitude to the events' (1976, 43).
105 Yet the five masterpieces Ken Russell made for television in the late 1960s – *Delius: Song of Summer, The Dance of the Seven Veils, Dante's Inferno, Isadora Duncan* and *The Debussy Film* – are all in black-and-white. And that's partly a cost issue, because the BBC wanted to keep costs low. Thankfully, they were filmed on 35mm film stock, because 16mm from that era looks horrible.

ence knowing that Gustav Mahler or Henri Gaudier-Brzeska died before their time. We're talking about *movie* logic. And by that same dramatic logic, other characters should really die – for instance, after that feverish night in 1987's *Gothic*, one of those crazy writers and poets should die (Lord Byron definitely, and perhaps Percy Bysshe Shelley, too). That would ram home the cost of creativity in the Russellian manner (of course, *Gothic does* end with a corpse – the dead baby, with its Frank-ensteinian features).

KEN RUSSELL'S INFLUENCE

You don't think of Ken Russell as an influential filmmaker, like, say, Orson Welles or D.W. Griffith, Stanley Kubrick or Jean-Luc Godard, filmmakers who have certainly influenced many, many film folk. But Russell has definitely had an impact on cinema, and not only in Blighty. Anyhoo, a filmmaker with such a strong style is bound to influence somebody.

For instance, when he was shooting what is perhaps the greatest war movie, *Apocalypse Now* (1979), Francis Coppola said he was directing it like a Ken Russell movie, operatic, with coloured flares. And Coppola again took up the Ken Russell approach when he adapted *Dracula* for the screen in 1992 (as critics such as Ken Gelder have pointed out in *New Vampire Cinema*).[106]

As well as Francis Coppola, you can detect Ken Russell's impact in the films of Oliver Stone (*The Doors*), Baz Luhrmann (*Romeo + Juliet, Moulin Rouge*), Rob Marshall (*Chicago*), Peter Jackson (*The Lord of the Rings*), Derek Jarman (*The Tempest, Caravaggio*), Peter Greenaway, Franc Roddam (*Quadrophenia*), Milos Forman (*Amadeus*), Alan Parker (*Pink Floyd: The Wall, Evita*), Bob Fosse (*All That Jazz*)[107] and

---

106 'The vision of scarlet blood splashing over Lucy's bed – as well as Lucy's writhing body, etc – probably owes something to the 'symphonic', camp/ apocalyptic set pieces found in the lurid horror films of Ken Russell, particularly *Gothic* and *The Lair of the White Worm* (2012, 6).

107 The fantastic biopic/ autobiopic *All That Jazz* (1980), for instance, is gleefully Russellesque (as well as, as critics noted, Felliniesque, being yet another version of *8 1/2* from a contemporary filmmaker).

Michelangelo Antonioni (*Blow Up*).108

Rainer Werner Fassbinder was also influenced by Ken Russell, according to Joseph Lanza (who discerns Russell's impact on *Berlin Alexanderplatz* it's easy to spot the affinities between Fassbinder and Russell!). 2001's *Moulin Rouge* is a Ken Russell movie in all but name (but not as good), as are *Amadeus* and *Shine*.

Sometimes filmmakers – and film critics – have used Ken Russell as an example of the kind of filmmaking they *don't* want to produce or to see more of. The socialist-realist school, those filmmakers who derive from the British 'kitchen sink', the 'Angry Young Men' and the documentary tradition, sometimes use Russell as the sort of filmmaking they want to avoid (even though Russell has of course produced many documentaries, and he also emerged from the documentary tradition in Britain of the early 1960s which also helped to form prominent filmmakers such as Ken Loach, Mike Leigh, Lindsay Anderson and Karel Reisz).

References to Ken Russell crop up all over the place. For example, in *The Complete Anime Guide* the Japanese cult *film noir* series *Wicked City* (1987) is described as possessing 'the noir feel of Raymond Chandler, combined with the rollercoaster horror thrill of John Carpenter and the sordid thrill of Ken Russell'.109

There's no doubt that in the realm of acting and performance, Ken Russell has had an influence. Russell has coaxed out some marvellous and memorable performances from his casts. For someone who says he doesn't really know how to direct actors, the performances mentioned below (there are many more) are proof that Russell must've been doing something right: Oliver Reed and Vanessa Redgrave in *The Devils*, Reed and Judith Paris in *Dante's Inferno*, Alan Bates, Glenda Jackson and Reed in *Women in Love*, Max Adrian in *Delius*, Richard Chamberlain and Jackson in *The Music Lovers*, Ann-Margret in *Tommy*, Robert Powell in *Mahler*, Roger Daltrey

---

108 The 1963 documentary *Watch the Birdie*, about the photographer David Hurn, apparently influenced Italian director Michelangelo Antonioni when he came to direct *Blow Up* in Londinium (according to Ken Russell [G, 44]). Antonioni used it for research into Swinging London.
109 T. Ledoux & D. Ranney. *The Complete Animé Guide* Tiger Mountain Press, Washington, DC, 1997, 57.

in *Lisztomania* and *Tommy*, Christopher Gable in *Dance of the Seven Veils* and Amanda Donohue in *The Lair of the White Worm*.

CLASSICAL MUSIC

> The combination of pictures and music has always been my favourite form of expression – surmounting all language barriers.

Ken Russell (BP, 209)

Music, for Ken Russell, is perhaps

the most incredible event in human history.[110]

I love that remark!

Ken Russell has never lost that sense of awe of music, and the ecstatic pleasure it gives. I totally agree with him:

I could not live without music.

Many times Ken Russell has employed music on set to get his actors (and crew) into a mood: for the 'rape of Christ' scene in *The Devils*, Russell

> found the most barbaric bit of *The Rite of Spring*, the music to which I had danced naked myself in my parents' house, and played it flat out. Without it the nuns were simply unable to cope: they were totally inhibited. There's a liberating force in music which, even if they don't appreciate the music as such, people can't help responding to, being primitive creatures at heart. If you let it take you over, as Glenda did, you can do anything you like. (Bax, 188-9)

The number of classical composers that Ken Russell made films about is very impressive:

Peter Tchaikovsky
Gustav Mahler
Richard Wagner
Franz Liszt

---

110 L. Langley, 1971.

Sergei Prokofiev
Claude Debussy
Frederick Delius
Richard Strauss
Edward Elgar (twice)
Ralph Vaughan Williams
Sir Arnold Bax
Anton Bruckner
Béla Bartók
Boshuslav Martinu
Gustav Holst

Extraordinarily, although most of those studies of classic composers were made for television, the first four were feature films (Wagner and Liszt appeared in *Lisztomania*).

And he staged operas by Igor Stravinsky (*The Rake's Progress*, 1982), Giacomo Puccini (*Madame Butterfly*, 1983 and *La Bohéme*, 1984), Gioacchino Rossini (*The Italian Woman In Algiers*, 1984), Bernd-Alois Zimmermann (*Die Soldaten*, 1984), Charles Gounod (*Faust*, 1985), Arrigo Boito (*Méphistophélès* 1989),[111] Gilbert & Sullivan (*Princess Ida*, 1992) and Richard Strauss (*Salomé*, 1993).[112] This's one reason why there were fewer movies in Russell's later years – he was working in live opera.

Ken Russell directed operas, but he could've had a career directing stage musicals for Broadway and the West End. His flair for combining images, sets, costumes, colours, lighting, movement, dance and dialogue with music is simply extraordinary (and *timing*, too: Russell has a showman's sense of timing, rhythm and pace, of knowing just when to slow a movie down, and when to ramp up the energy. He is also a master of the sudden reveal and the surprising jolt, the equal of Alfred Hitchcock or D.W. Griffith).

Then there was a documentary called *Classic Widows* (1995) about the wives of William Walton, Benjamin Frankel, Humphrey Searle and Bernard Stevens, a revisit to Edward Elgar on TV in 2002, a documentary about folk songs (*In*

111 This was filmed by Valiant SRL.
112 Ken Russell's approach to opera was to deliver a new interpretation – rather than a traditional take (BP, 227), and that sometimes led to controversy. In his autobiography, he waxes lyrical about particular singers.

Search of the English Folk Song, 1998), [113] and a guide to British music (1988).

And more recently, in the 2000s, Ken Russell embarked upon some fictionalized accounts of classical composers: essentially, they are novelizations of his movies (such as Frederick Delius, Ludwig van Beethoven, Johannes Brahms and Edward Elgar), focussing (inevitably) on their erotic relationships, in book form (and also as e-books).

In books such as *Elgar: The Erotic Variations*, *Delius: A Moment With Venus*, *Brahms Gets Laid* and *Beethoven Confidential*, Ken Russell was able to rework the research carried out for movies and TV documentaries into fiction. Viewers of Russell's films and TV shows will recognize many of the events in the books (some of these projects were unmade – publishing them in book form was a way for Russell to recycle material, which he, like everyone else, did all the time).

Ken Russell's books about famous composers were marketed in part by emphasizing their erotic elements. [114] But these were not 'sex lives of famous artists' stories. Rather, they were irreverent, witty, and entertaining. For Russell, they allowed him to include numerous details from the composers' lives that he hadn't been able to squeeze into the films and TV shows.

A novel followed, called *Violation* (2001), a self-conscious attempt at offence, involving Adolf Hitler, Eva Braun and a Jewish boy. [115] And a futuristic rewriting of the *Bible*, in *Mike and Gaby's Space Gospel* (1999).

Ken Russell has also produced radio plays – for example, *The Death of Alexander Scriabin*, which was broadcast on BBC Radio 3 in 1995, and featured James Wilby and Oliver Reed (this was the last Russell + Reed teaming).

Over the years, Ken Russell worked with many composers and conductors who were important figures in the British (and international) classical music scene: Peter Maxwell Davies,

---

113 Ken Russell's exploration of the British folk song included performances by a roll call of many big names of the time, including: Waterson Carthy, Eliza Carthy, June Tabor, Osibisa, the Albion Band, the Percy Grainger Chamber Orchestra, Donovan, and Fairport Convention.

114 The book covers of the British editions were by Paul Dufficey, the art director on movies such as *Lisztomania* and *Tommy*.

115 'It's a satire on Spielberg,' Ken Russell explained in 2000, 'a satire on concentration camps, a satire on schmaltz, a satire on Christmas, a satire on war movies, a satire on everything'.

Richard Rodney Bennett, André Previn and Carl Davis. Russell also collaborated with some of the big names in British pop music: the Who, Elton John, Eric Clapton (*Tommy*), Rick Wakeman (*Lisztomania* and *Crimes of Passion*), and Thomas Dolby (*Gothic*).

Presumably Ken Russell could have continued with films and TV shows about composers – moving onto Ludwig von Beethoven,[116] Alexander Scriabin,[117] Giuseppe Verdi, Robert Schumann, etc.

No other filmmaker I can think of has made such a passionate and lengthy exploration of classical music and composers (except Tony Palmer).[118] As to feature-length biographies, you can count the number on one hand. No, that's not true, there *have* been some biopics of composers, including some from the Classical Hollywood era and from more recent times: on Richard Strauss (*The Great Waltz*, 1938 and 1972, and *The Waltz King* 1963), on Giuseppe Verdi (*The Life of Verdi*, 1984), a TV series, on Richard Wagner (*Wagner*, 1984), on Ludwig van Beethoven (*Immortal Beloved*, 1994), on Frédéric Chopin (*A Song To Remember*, 1945, and a 2002 film), on Giacomo Puccini (1953 and 2001), on Robert Schumann (and Clara, of course): *Spring Symphony* (1983, and *Song of Love*, 1947), and on Alma Mahler (*Bride of the Wind*, 2001).

Probably the most famous (and certainly one of the most celebrated) of recent movies about a classical composer was *Amadeus* (1983), a film which clearly drew upon Ken Russell's landmark classical music and artists' biopics (that was Russell's Oscar really, not Saul Zaentz's or Peter Schaffer's). And more recent movies about performers, such as *Shine* (1996), about David Helfgott, and *Hilary and Jackie* (1998), about Jacqueline du Pré and her sister Hilary.

There was also a Russian biopic on Peter Tchaikovsky,

---

116 Ken Russell got very close to shooting *The Beethoven Secret* when the finances dematerialized.
117 Ken Russell had written a script about Alexander Scriabin, but couldn't find any backers.
118 Among British directors, Tony Palmer (b. 1941) has produced many documentaries about composers, including for the BBC. Palmer has covered Mozart, Rachmaninov, Dvorak, Handel, and Stravinsky, as well as pop acts like Tangerine Dream, Cream and a history of pop. Palmer was keen to work with Ken Russell in the 1960s, when he was starting out, and eventually helped Russell on the TV *Isadora Duncan*.

released a year after Ken Russell's own movie *The Music Lovers*, 1971. And Liszt had been the subject of a 1960 movie starring Dirk Bogarde (*Song Without End*).

However, *very* few biographies of classical music composers have taken an irreverent approach, like Ken Russell's. The opposite is the norm: total awe at the creative process (though the messy private lives are explored in some biopics). Russell's *ir*reverence is still unusual: that sort of attack on a Great Artist is still seen as disrespectful.

When he takes on a classical composer, it is the *music* that is primary for Ken Russell, not only the biography of the composer. *The music.*[119] This cannot be over-stated enough, but it's one of the main reasons for the misunderstandings that Russell's films lead to. He is *not* producing a 'realistic' film or even a standard documentary piece about an artist. He is looking at their *art*, and is regarding music (perhaps incorrectly) as expressing something of the inner life of the subject. As he explains about his approach to the 1974 movie *Mahler*: he 'searched for the soul of the man in his music' (BP, 141). That sums it up neatly: films such as *Mahler, The Music Lovers, Lisztomania, Delius: Song of Summer* and *The Debussy Film* are searches for the soul of the man in his music.

If it was possible, Ken Russell said he liked to start with the soundtrack first:

> I try to start with the soundtrack first – you see, that's the most difficult part. Because once you have the soundtrack, you have the movie. Music is architecture to me so I always try to get a musical or architectural sense for the film. (RC, 252)

Ingmar Bergman has said the same thing:

> When we experience a film, we consciously prime ourselves for illusion. Putting aside will and intellect, we make way for it in our imagination. The sequence of pictures plays directly on our feelings. Music works in the same fashion; I would say that there is no art form that has so much in common with film as music. Both affect our emotions directly, not via the intellect. And film is mainly rhythm; it is inhalation and exhalation in continuous sequence. Ever since childhood, music has been my great source of recreation and stimulation, and I often experience

---

119 The title itself – *The Music Lovers*– is clearly deeply personal for Ken Russell.

a film or play musically.[120]

Ken Russell also clearly *understands* music in depth –
very few film directors possess that level of understanding and
knowledge (many, many famous film directors knew absolutely
nothing about music, and weren't able to communicate with
their composers beyond simple suggestions. Many of the celebrated directors today can't get beyond statements such as: 'I
like the music'). Even when he is being outrageous and con-
juring out-size imagery and scenes, you can still tell that
Russell understands the music in his movies in an incredibly
detailed manner.[121]

Ken Russell's classical music movies and TV shows also
depict plenty of musicians at work: composers are seen composing, writing on manuscripts, playing at the piano, conducting,
performing live, singing, etc. The trappings of classical music
are everywhere, too: musical manuscript paper, the conductor's
baton, the metronome, the brass band, the violin, the piano
(the props guys must've humped 100s of pianos on and off sets
for Russell's movies).

Ken Russell remarked that raising finance for films about
classical music composers was difficult. I should say nearly
impossible (outside of television). Many of Russell's films were
about artists, and very few biopics about artists cross over into
the mainstream and become big hits. You need big stars and a
fantastic script and a really sexy subject for your biopic. Films
about movie stars or rock stars, well, that's different (*The
Doors, Ray, Rock Star, Almost Famous, Dreamgirls*).

But even then, biographical flicks rarely hit the big time,
in terms of box office rentals (like musicals nowadays. They
can revered by critics and the Academy of Motion Picture Arts
and Sciences – such as *Bird* (about Charlie Parker), *Walk the
Line, Sid & Nancy* (about Sid Vicious and Nancy Spungen),
What's Love Got To Do With It?(about Ike and Tina Turner),
*Shine, Amadeus, Almost Famous, Nashville, A Hard Day's
Night, The Doors* and *Ray* (about Ray Charles). But few do
really big business. The incredible thing is that Ken Russell

120 "Introduction", *Four Screenplays*, 1960.
121 However, Russell wasn't a musician. But being so knowledgeable about
music no doubt made it so much easier for his composers to talk with him about
film scoring.

and his producers managed to persuade United Artists to put money into a film about a classical music composer. We know the famous story about how Russell pitched it to UA: 'a story about a homosexual who fell in love with a nymphomaniac'. But there was clearly more to the pitch than that.

Even so, movies about classical music composers – that has to be a minority interest from the get-go (imagine it today: in a multiplex in New Jersey, what're audiences gonna see: a movie about a tortured, depressed artist set in Berlin in the 1840s or the latest popcorn, Summer blockbuster about super-heroes protecting the White House from aliens?). Which's why most of Ken Russell's films about classical music composers have been television-based productions, *not* movies. It's part of public service broadcasting (at least in Britain) that television should explore all of the arts, not just, if left to its own devices and the rampant commercialism of a capitalist social system, pop music and movies and fashion and celebrity gossip (with the occasional prestige drama rehashing Jane Austen or Charles Dickens yet again).

Or to put it another way: in Britain, public service television and radio (i.e., the BBC) is funded by the British tax payer. Everyone owning a television set must have by law a TV licence. And that pays for the British Brainwashing Corporation (there are other streams of revenue for the Beeb, of course, including rampant capitalism). And part of that deal between the BBC and the British government is that the BBC is beholden to broadcast all sorts of things a commercial broadcaster would not bother with. A classical music radio station (BBC Radio 3), for instance, or hundreds of hours of television programming on all sorts of minority interest topics, including most of the arts.

So Ken Russell's TV documentaries about classical music composers or architects or poets or painters came about very much because of the public service broadcasting tradition in Britain. Without that support from the British tax payer, those sorts of TV programmes would dwindle to a very small audience or a minor TV channel (in the age of cable and satellite TV).

And what's incredible about Ken Russell is that he

attempted to continue the public service broadcasting tradition of little, old Britain into the cut-throat world of internationally-distributed movies. And without television finance (which was the way to go in many cases from the 1980s onwards). That is, *The Music Lovers* and *Mahler* and *Savage Messiah* were conceived and produced in the era *before* video cassettes and DVDs (which would have brought in essential revenue), and also without backing from TV companies.

Or to put it another way: *The Music Lovers*, a biopic about a Russian, classical music composer, was paid for by a North American movie studio not a British broadcaster. However, United Artists had some provisos (if not guarantees) that at least some elements that would be included to encourage them to green-light the project: first, two stars, Richard Chamberlain and Glenda Jackson (and Jackson had recently won as Oscar). And a hot director. And a script that would promise to be talked-about if nothing else.

In recognition that the interest among the movie-going public will be small, many of Ken Russell's projects, in the dog-eat-dog world of global movie distribution, have been made with small budgets: *Savage Messiah, Mahler, The Rainbow, The Lair of the White Worm*, etc.

MORE ABOUT MUSIC AND MOVIES

> No other art can so sublimely arouse human sentiments in the innner-most heart of man. No other art can paint to the eyes of the soul the splendours of nature, the delights of contemplation, the character of nations, the tumult of their passions, and the languor of their sufferings as music can. Regret, hope, terror, meditation, consternation, enthusiasm, faith, glory, tranquillity, all these and more are given to us and taken from us thanks to her genius and according to the bent of our own.
>
> George Sand, *Consuelo* (1843)

One of Ken Russell's great passions is classical music. His memoirs abound with references to Tchaikovsky, Mahler, Strauss, Elgar, Liszt, Prokofiev, Beethoven and Bach. 'My imagery comes from listening to music,' Russell asserted (BP,

156). He is a 'slave of music', as Percy Bysshe Shelley put it.
In 1997, US chiildren's author Maurice Sendak remarked:

> To me, the best of all art forms is music and perhaps opera is
> my favourite, and the best best best of all that is Mozart.

'I was mad on music, and would rush out like a starving
man and get all the records I could afford,' Ken Russell
recalled of his youth. 'I couldn't get enough of it' (Bax, 82-83).
Well, we know that!: music saturates Russell's entire work, in
movies, television, books, newspaper articles, and photography. For Russell, music was like oxygen (Bax, 102).

The affinities between cinema and music are countless,
and filmmakers have been exploiting them since the birth of
cinema. The notion of all the arts moving towards the condition of one art (or as Walter Pater famously put it, towards
music), developed in the age of Romanticism. German poet
Novalis spoke of 'painting, plastic art are therefore nothing but
figurative music. Painting, plastic art – objective music. Music
– subjective music or painting'.

Huw Wheldon and *Monitor* was instrumental in getting
Ken Russell's ideas for biopics on great composers made –
building on the *Monitor* TV programmes, Russell continued
with feature films on musicians. Russell noted that there have
very few films on composers, apart from his own *The Music
Lovers* and Tony Palmer's *Testimony* (presumably he means *his*
sort of films about composers). 'What I've always been after is
the spirit of the composer as manifest in his music' (1993, 75).

Ken Russell's work for BBC's *Monitor* was vital in launch-
ing his career, and enabling him to explore classical music via
celluloid. The *Monitor* shows included *Pop Goes the Easel*
(about four young Pop artists), a biopic of Douanier Rousseau,
Two Scottish Painters, *The Biggest Dancer in the World* (on
Isadora Duncan), and *Dante's Inferno* (about Dante Gabriel
Rossetti and the Pre-Raphaelites). The *Monitor* programme on
Edward Elgar was a Russell success: it used the Malvern Hills
in Worcestershire as the backbone to a portrait of Elgar
(famous shots included Elgar staring out towards Wales, kite-
flying and horse-riding on the Hills).

Ken Russell said that he sent his three amateur films

(*Peepshow, Lourdes* and *Amelia and the Angel*) to the Beeb, which resulted in his being employed by *Monitor*. In *A British Picture*, Russell asserted that Edward Elgar had 'captured the spirit of England, past, present and future, more convincingly than any other artist, living or dead' (BP, 27).

Ken Russell's preference for making films about real people was seen as problematic for the BBC, who weren't sure about the ethics of this kind of dramatized documentary (it became widely adopted from the 1980s onwards). Russell said he learnt much from Huw Wheldon and *Monitor*, including how to stretch a budget, how to improvize within financial limits. Russell claimed that his talks with Wheldon were 'the only time I've been able to talk with someone about my work and really get something of fantastic value out of it' (Bax, 112-3).

Ken Russell spoke nostalgically of the discussions in the *Red Lion* pub near the BBC – '[t]hat was the most rewarding drinking I ever did… It was thrilling, believe it or not, and bloody instructive at the same time' (ib., 113). Russell called Huw Wheldon the 'guiding genius' of 'the one and only English experimental film school ever' (ibid.). For his part, Wheldon remarked that Russell had enormous powers of invention and imagination that required a strong producer or scriptwriter to rein them in (ib., 123). 'He had a leaping imagination and, as frequently happens with people of this kind, great tenacity and determination'.

BIOPICS.

Many of Ken Russell's films are drawn from biographies of real people – most obviously, classical composers. Some of those biopics are based on books, and some on extensive research. For the rest of his output, Russell has used, like almost all filmmakers, books and plays: literary works such as *The Rainbow, Women In Love, Lady Chatterley's Lover, Billion Dollar Brain, Altered States, The Fall of the Louse of Usher, The Lair of the White Worm, The Devils of Loudun* or plays such as *The Boy Friend, The Devils, Salome's Last Dance* and *Whore*.

So most of Ken Russell's films are not original screenplays

in the sense of original stories featuring characters that haven't been seen before. There is plenty of research in a Ken Russell movie. Like Francis Coppola and Stanley Kubrick, Russell enjoys that part of the preparation for a project. But that doesn't mean that the research will end up on screen undiluted by Russell's vision and style.

Before he begins a biopic, Ken Russell said he immersed himself in the

> iconography of the period, the photography, the painting, the literature. I absorb it like a piece of blotting paper and then I just go and do the film. (In F. Robbins, 1973)

For *Savage Messiah*, Ken Russell said he did an extensive amount of research, which included visiting Paris, seeing the library where he met Sophie Brzeska, explored Henri Gaudier's London, talked to people who knew him, read Brzeska's letters and art histories, etc (Bax, 222). And there's a point where all of that research snowballs into madness, and you say, no more! Enough! OK, I know *everything* about this guy. Then you move beyond it all, and start making the movie.

But that doesn't mean that the film is a straight translation of research to the screen (how could it be?). Indeed, like all filmmakers, Ken Russell constantly changes contexts, times, places, characters, etc: dialogue from one context or time is put into another time or context,[122] characters are combined, and if the budget won't allow it, some events have to be reduced to a much cheaper equivalent event.

Ken Russell's first biopic was of a classical music comp- oser, naturally – Sergei Prokofiev (*Portrait of a Soviet Com- poser*, 1961). Many of Russell's programmes for television were about music: *The Miner's Picnic* (brass bands), *Portrait of a Soviet Composer* (Sergei Prokofiev), *Variations On a Mechan- ical Theme* (mechanical instruments), *Guitar Craze*, *Lotte Lenya Sings Kurt Weill*, *Elgar*, *Bartók*, *The Debussy Film*, *Don't Shoot the Composer* (Georges Delerue), *The Dance of the Seven Veils* (Richard Strauss) and *Delius: Song of Summer*.

Two of Russell's early TV films were about dance: *Marie*

---

122 Ken Russell likes to use the actual things that real people said, or real quotes from novels, in his movies. Although the meanings and contexts may be different, sometimes whole scenes would be made up of real quotes (G, 112).

Rambert (1959) was about the Ballet Rambert company, and
The Light Fantastic (1960) was about dancing in England. And
Isadora Duncan was of course about one of Russell's favourite
artists (Duncan also influenced Gudrun's dancing style in
Women In Love and 'Gosh' Smith-Boyle in *Savage Messiah*).

Then there were shows on painters (*Pop Goes the Easel,
McBryde and Colquhoun,* the Pre-Raphaelite Museum in
Battersea, Dante Gabriel Rossetti, Henri Rousseau), poets
(John Betjeman, and, later, William Wordsworth and Samuel
Taylor Coleridge), and architecture (*Antonio Gaudi*).

Ken Russell said he was trying to do what music composers do – to express something inexpressible, to reach an area
of divine mystery.[123] You could put it another way: Russell's
movies tend towards the condition of music. Or that he is
trying to explore the same realms as music.

Life is a mystery for Ken Russell – and one reason why
artists were important was because 'artists somehow make
mysteries concrete, make them more tangible. They interpret
the ineffable for the rest of us' (RC, 246).

For Richard Eder (1976), Ken Russell's biopics are really
about Russell himself: they reveal more about the director than
they do about Mahler or Tchaikovsky or Liszt.

> As far as the audience is concerned, it is almost as if Tchai-
> kovsky, Liszt and Mahler had taken turns making films about
> Mr Russell.

You may not notice a significant omission from many of
Ken Russell's films and biographies about classical music
composers, and this is the standard *contextualization* of documentaries and biographies. In Russell's TV shows and films
about composers (and artists), there is no introductory segment
outlining the politics and key events of the period, no images
of kings and queens and politicians and big events such as wars
or coups or revolutions or assassinations or whatever. There
are few dates, too, saying what year it was that, say, Frederick
Delius contracted syphilis (it was 1922), or what year Franz
Liszt first met Richard Wagner (it was in 1849), or when
Gustav Mahler composed his *Ninth Symphony* (it was in 1908-

123 J. Walker, "Ken Russell's New Enigma", *The Observer,* Sept 8, 1974.

09).

All of that is simply left aside in Ken Russell's TV shows and movies – all of that pedagogical stuff which public service broadcasters such as the BBC and PBS put into their documentaries. Russell's films and television programmes don't lecture their audience, don't assume the role of a teacher or a nanny. (If you want that info, you can look it up in your own time – the movie or TV show won't do it for you).

Instead, the shows go straight for explorations of the artist themselves and their work. And they also assume that their viewers are fairly intelligent, and already know quite a bit about European history from 1800 to the present.

The BBC mandate to 'inform, educate and entertain', the Reithian mantra of the early days of the Beeb, are simply put to one side in Ken Russell's documentaries and biopics. Oh, you can learn plenty, and the films and TV shows are teaching you plenty, if you want to see it like that. And, yes, there is a huge amount of historical research in the films and shows. But these shows and movies are *not* historical lectures, they are not homework, their aims are quite different.

So many of the films and TV programmes of Ken Russell hope that the audience is going to do quite a bit of work themselves. As Joseph Gomez pointed out, re. *The Music Lovers* if the viewer isn't willing to unravel the complexities of the movie, it can lead to misunderstandings (G, 98).

DANCE.

Another Ken Russell passion was dance (at one time he had trained in ballet). He performed with the British Dance Theatre and the London Theatre Ballet, including going on tours, and also with the Norwegian Ballet (including a visit to Oslo). Russell has written of his times with touring dance companies in his autobiographies.

There was an enormous amount of dancing in *The Boy Friend*; *The Devils* contains some dancing during the execution of Grandier (by the circus players), and of course the nuns in their hysteria were choreographed; Glenda Jackson cavorted in front of the cattle in *Women in Love* (plus Hermione's dance, and the dance in Switzerland); Rudolf Nureyev, probably the world's foremost ballet dancer of the period, starred in *Valentino*; characters in *The Music Lovers* and *Mahler*, and *Savage Messiah*, and *The Debussy Film*, and many others move choreographically; dance runs throughout *Isadora Duncan* and *The Dance of the Seven Veils* movies which're wholly dance-oriented.

If there's a chance to squeeze in a dance number into a film, Ken Russell will do it. In fact, it'd be quicker to cite movies and TV shows directed by Russell which *don't* contain any dancing. (And there's plenty of ballet dancing, as well as more popular dancing in Russell's movies; films featuring ballet are a sub-genre of the dance genre. Some are records of performances, like *Swan Lake*, *A Midsummer Night's Dream* and *The Nutcracker Suite*, or ballet companies such as the Bolshoi Ballet. Russell contributed with ballet documentaries; and one of his key performers, Christopher Gable, was with the Royal Ballet).

'When you're dancing, you're really alive'.

So says Isadora Duncan in Ken Russell's and Sewell Stokes' 1966 BBC movie *Isadora Duncan*. It's certainly one of Russell's credos. No other British filmmaker, and probably no other filmmaker in the history of cinema, even including great dance directors such as Bob Fosse, Gene Kelly, Stanley Donen or Vincente Minnelli, has included so much dancing in their works. (Fosse, for instance, directed far fewer movies than Russell, and although Minnelli made more musicals than Russell, including some of the classics, Russell includes choreography even in straight melodramas. If Russell had directed a biopic of Vincent van Gogh, he would've been dancing thru the wheatfields).

In other movies, Ken Russell often favours physical acting, rather than verbal dexterity (*The Devils* displays some marvellous examples of physical acting from most of the main actors). Russell advocated a cinema of visual spectacle, not people sitting around talking. Like Michael Powell, Russell had admired Vaslav Nijinsky (he had planned a film on the Russian dancer, while Pressburger and Powell's *The Red Shoes* had a Sergei Diaghilev figure). Dancers such as Nijinsky and Duncan were touchstones for Russell, even tho' they died before his time. One can imagine that if a time machine were available, Russell would certainly have gone to see them dance, as well as met heroes such as Ludwig van Beethoven and Peter Tchaikovsky (and wherever Russell is now, maybe he's met some of his heroes!).

MADNESS.

There are more disturbing images of madness in Ken Russell's films than in the work of many a filmmaker. Nina Milyukova at the end of *The Music Lovers,*for instance, or the nuns in *The Devils* and the composer in *Delius: Song of Summer.* And not only insanity, but also hysteria. Richard Wagner at the end of *Lisztomania*, for instance, or the poets in *Gothic.* So many images, one wonders if there is some biographical reason for it. While the costs of being an artist for some dramatists might be death, in Russell's cinema it can lead to madness (a living death).

And in drama and cinema (as in life itself), the living death of madness can be much more disturbing than death itself. While death might give a character's story a tragic or noble or melancholy ending, insanity, like a severely disabling illness, is much more of a punishment (it sure ain't spiritual transcendence or an upward move into martyrdom). At the end of a Hollywood movie a character might end up heroically sacrificing themselves and dying, and saving the world in the process. But to have that same heroic figure becoming insane is very different.

And suicide is a recurring theme, too: characters take their life, or try to, in *The Music Lovers,Women In Love, The Debussy Film, Isadora Duncan, Dante's Inferno* and *The Devils.* And often those suicides are linked to the central characters, to the artists: they can't take anymore, so they find a way out.

MAKE YOUR OWN KEN RUSSELL MOVIE.

A do-it-yourself kit for a Ken Russell movie (and anyone aspiring to make a piece of Russellania), would require the following items:

✟ a piano
✟ candles
✟ smoke and fire
✟ 19th century costumes
✟ spangly modern costumes
✟ S/M gear
✟ Nazi uniforms
✟ nun costumes
✟ a horse (and maybe a carriage)
✟ crucifixes
✟ swastikas
✟ a whip
✟ a conductor's baton
✟ swords
✟ a banana,[124] bottle or other phallic totem
✟ a brass band
✟ masks & feathers
✟ a train
✟ a mirror
✟ a theatre
✟ a church
✟ an asylum
✟ a lake
✟ mountains
✟ a forest
✟ champagne
✟ a CD player or i-Pod plus giant speakers & amp (for music playback)

---

124 Bananas! In a Jean-Luc Godard movie, when actors are at a loss of what to do in a scene, they light a cigarette (again and again in French movies!). In a Ken Russell movie, when an actor asked, 'what shall I do here, Ken?', the maestro probably replied, 'well, I dunno, how about eating a banana?' And if the actor retorted, 'I did that in the last movie, Ken!', the exasperated director might have replied, 'phooey, love, no one will notice! Terry! Where's my champagne?!'

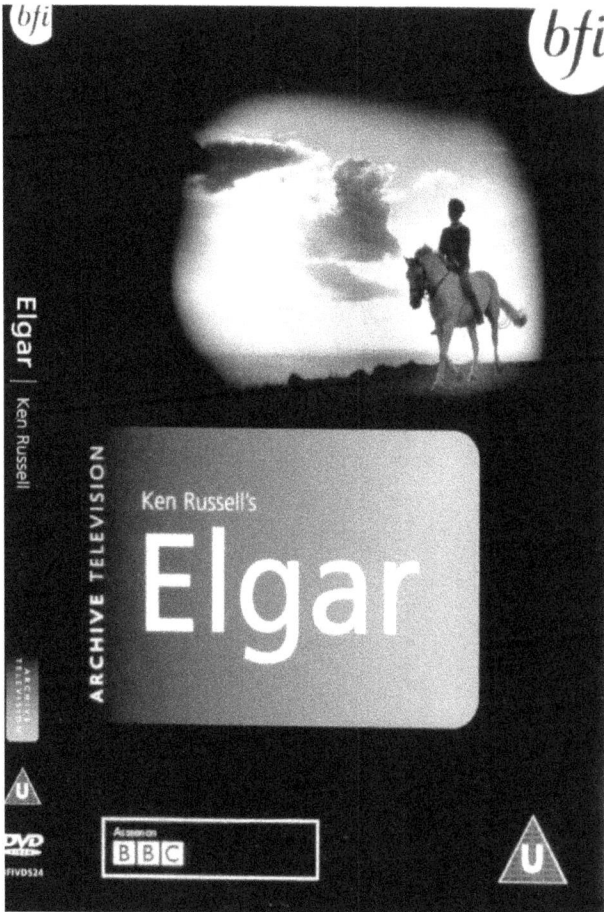

bfi

bfi

Elgar | Ken Russell

ARCHIVE TELEVISION

Ken Russell's

Elgar

U

DVD

FFIVD524

As seen on

B|B|C

U

One of the most celebrated of Ken Russell's BBC works,
the Elgar documentary from the early 1960s

Billion Dollar Brain, the 1967 entry in the Harry Palmer series

Dante's Inferno (1968)

WIDESCREEN EDITION

KEN RUSSELL'S Film

"THE MUSIC LOVERS"

RICHARD CHAMBERLAIN   GLENDA JACKSON   DVD

The Music Lovers (1970)

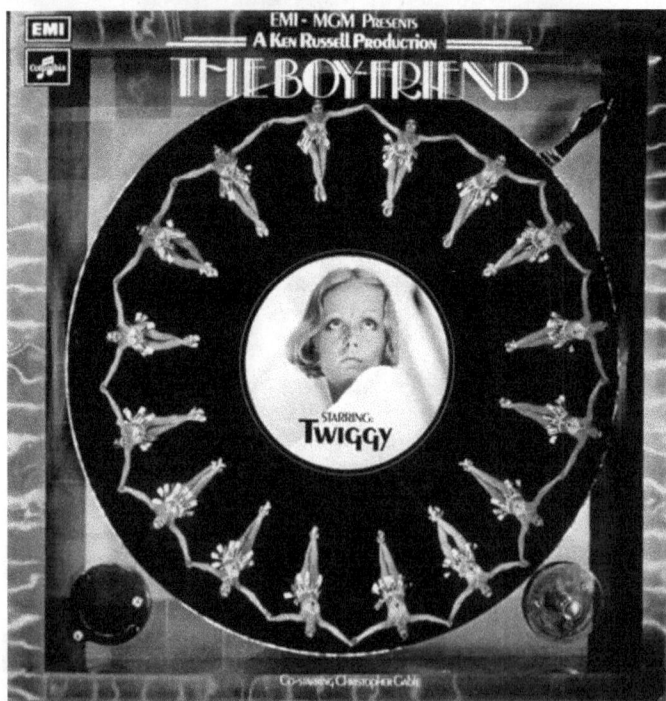

EMI - MGM Presents
A Ken Russell Production
THE BOY FRIEND

STARRING
TWIGGY

Co-starring Christopher Gable

Mahler (1974)

NUREYEV IS
VALENTINO

A ROBERT CHARTOFF-IRWIN WINKLER Production   A KEN RUSSELL Film

RUDOLF NUREYEV "VALENTINO"

LESLIE CARON · MICHELLE PHILLIPS and CAROL KANE

Associate Producer HARRY BENN · Written by KEN RUSSELL and MARDIK MARTIN
Directed by KEN RUSSELL · Produced by IRWIN WINKLER and ROBERT CHARTOFF

United Artists

1 SHEET "VALENTINO"

L'expérience la plus terrifiante
de l'histoire de la science
échappe à tout contrôle...
AU-DELA DU RÉEL
"ALTERED STATES"
"AU-DELA DU RÉEL" WILLIAM HURT · BLAIR BROWN · BOB BALABAN · CHARLES H
DANIEL MELNICK · JOHN CORIGLIANO · SIDNEY AARON · PADDY CHAYEFSKY
HOWARD GOTTFRIED · KEN RUSSELL

1984's Crimes of Passion

GABRIEL BYRNE   JULIAN SANDS   NATASHA RICHARDSON   MYRIAM CYR   TIMOTHY SPALL

A KEN RUSSELL FILM

GOTHIC

"A Visual Feast"
Sunday Telegraph

18

AMANDA DONOHOE ■ HUGH GRANT
CATHERINE OXENBERG

KEN RUSSELL'S

LAIR

OF THE

WHITE

WORM

ARTISAN

"A HOOT OF A HORROR FILM!"
— Peter Travers, PEOPLE

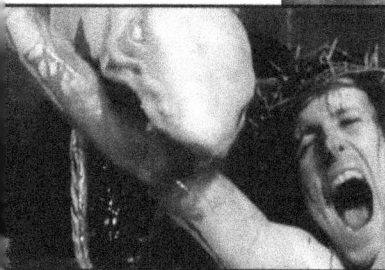

Lady Chatterley (1993)

The Crime Of One Nation.
The Courage Of One Man.

RICHARD DREYFUSS in

PRISONER of HONOR

Directed By
KEN RUSSELL

Powerfully
Convincing!
~New York Times

Dreyfuss Is Outstanding!
~Daily News

Two movies from the 1990s
directed by Ken Russell

FROM KEN RUSSELL THE ACCLAIMED DIRECTOR OF THE WHO'S "TOMMY" AND "ALTERED

Inspired by the amazing life story
of the controversial
URI GELLER

TERENCE STAMP

Mindbender

FEATURING THE MUSIC OF ELTON JOHN, THE MOODY BLUES, THE BEE GEES AND PETER GABRIEL

BRING YOUR BROKEN CLOCKS AND WATCHES TO THE TH

4
✝
THE CINEMA OF KEN RUSSELL:
SOME CONCLUSIONS

In this study about *The Devils* and Ken Russell's cinema – I
keep emphasizing the *difference* of Russell from all of his
contemporary filmmakers, and the uniqueness and brilliance of
Russell's talent and vision. None of Russell's contemporaries
among British film directors – Ridley Scott, Alan Parker, Mike
Newell, Richard Attenborough, John Glen, Lewis Gilbert,
Bryan Forbes, Adrian Lyne, Richard Eyre, Bill Forsyth, Clive
Donner, Jack Clayton, Alan Bridges, Roy Ward Baker, Terence
Fisher, Michael Apted, Ken Annakin, Neil Jordan, Roland
Joffé, Mike Leigh, Ken Loach, Michael Lindsay-Hogg, John
Madden, Gavin Millar, Anthony Mingella, Ronald Neame, Pat
O'Connor, Michael Radford, Karel Reisz, Franc Roddam, Tony
Scott, Charles Sturridge, J. Lee Thompson, Michael Winner,
Peter Yates, Terence Young, Charles Crichton, Lindsay Ander-
son and Nic Roeg – would open a savage exploration of
religious and political hypocrisy set in plague-ridden 17th
century France with a dance number featuring the King of
France dressed as the Goddess Venus! None of those contemporary film directors have made a movie about a tortured, gay,
classical composer!

I am also exalting Ken Russell's cinema for its unique
take on life, its enshrinement of art and artists, its love of the
British landscape, and its wild and ceaseless devotion to music,
because contemporary cinema coming out of Britain nowadays
is so fucking *dull*, and because contemporary culture in Britain
now is so fucking *dull*. Conservative, unoriginal, safe, *tame*.

Since the 1990s, I've found culture and society in Britain
more conservative than ever – to the point where it's stifling in

its banality and unadventurousness, combined with its aggress-
ive consumerism. Ken Russell feels the same: in 2001 he
lamented 'the *Daily Mail* mentality' of modern Britain, 'where
everything is safe and yet prurient'.

'Passion in British films worries some people', claimed
Ken Russell, and adds that British cinema is thin on religion
and music biopics (1993, 75). In England, it's embarrassing to
talk about art and artists. As Bernardo Bertolucci put it:

> I think the problem in England is embarrassment. People in
> England keep using the term embarrassment. It's part of Eng-
> lish reticence, and the famous English understatement. You find
> art embarrassing. This is quite unlike the French who have no
> sense of embarrassment, otherwise they wouldn't use words like
> *sublime* and *sublimissime*[1]

Ken Russell was cast in British cinema as a rebel, an outsider, a vulgarian,[2] a wayward talent who hadn't made much of
merit since his 'golden age' of the early Seventies (*Women In
Love* is routinely regarded as Russell's best film, but certainly
not by the director himself, or most of his acolytes). Russell
was all contradiction (which he actively encouraged): though
regarded as vulgar his films were about intellectuals and artists;
his artistic ambitions were continually undercut by camp, over-
the-top performances (both in front of and behind the camera);
his anti-naturalism did not fit in with the quasi-social realism
of much of British cinema (in this he resembled filmmakers
such as Peter Greenaway[3] and Derek Jarman, who also worked
on the margins and advocated anti-realism). Russell complained:

> I sometimes think I would fare better in the hands of British
> critics if I was called Russellini. They may forgive Fellini his
> excesses, but I am chastised for being theatrical. (1993, 82).

1 Quoted in I. Halberstadt, *Pix* , 2, BFI, 1997.
2 Viewers who feel assaulted by the imagery and shock tactics probably miss
some of the subtlety in Ken Russell's movies, but there is subtlety there: for
instance, the level of *detail* in the *mise-en-scène* or the amount of cultural
allusions and references in the films.
3 Ken Russell did not like Peter Greenaway at all – maybe because his filmic
territory was too similar (mixing art with sex, art with violence, art with philo-
sophizing, and so on). 'What is it about Greenaway's films that makes the flesh
crawl?' Russell asked in *Fire Over England*. Remarking on Greenaway's technique of cutting up Michael Nyman's music into 'arbitrary chunks according to
his needs', Russell said that 'Greenaway treats the human race in much the same
way. And he is more interested in shit than soul' (1993, 168).

There is some truth in this: somehow, it's OK if European *auteurs* go wildly over-the-top, with exaggerated, flamboyant or plain bizarre movies, such as: Luchino Visconti (in *Ludwig* and *Death in Venice*), Pier Paolo Pasolini (in *Salò* or *Pigsty*), Jean-Luc Godard (in *Weekend*, Volker Schlöndorff (in *The Tin Drum*) or Werner Herzog (in *Nosferatu* or *Fitzcarraldo*), but not a British director. Like the MGM musical, the Western, or the space opera, Ken Russell's kind of cinema was seen as 'un-British', too brash, noisy, lurid, camp, etc. It was over-the-top and sensual like some of the cinemas of Europe. Russell's work had most in common, perhaps, with Italian cinema: with the Italian combination of vulgarity and intellectualism, high camp and high art, sensuality and spirituality, found in the films of Visconti, Fellini and Pasolini. There is also a tradition in Japanese animation for including silly, over-the-top moments of humour right in the middle of 'serious' scenes (but that doesn't affect the impact of the serious intent of the movies or TV shows).

And as the comedies of Mel Brooks, Zucker-Abrahams-Zucker, Woody Allen, the Marx Brothers and many others have demonstrated, you can make all of the serious points you want to make in a movie by using comedy and humour. A movie sure doesn't havta be 'serious' or solemn to explore any issue you fancy. Unfortunately, critics continually under-value comedy movies, and revere 'serious' or drama movies.

Vulgarity and art were part of the same thing for Ken Russell. But the vulgar didn't mean the commercial – that was a vulgarity that Russell despised:

> It's a strange thing that people can't reconcile vulgarity and artistry. They're the same thing to me. But an exuberant over-the-top larger-than-life slightly bad taste red-blooded thing. (Bax, 131)

But the finest filmmakers have been dubbed too baroque and theatrical: Orson Welles is the classic example. He made the two greatest American films ever – *Citizen Kane* and *The Magnificent Ambersons*(and a clutch of other films which are simply staggeringly spectacular – *The Trial, Chimes At Midnight, The Lady of Shanghai* and *Othello*) – but he was attacked non-stop for being too baroque, too self-conscious and too flamboyant.

Flamboyant, over-the-top, baroque, coarse, vulgar – you can fling the same epithets at Steven Spielberg, Gore Verbinski, Alfred Hitchcock, Roger Corman, Werner Herzog, Akira Kurosawa, etc.

Like some other filmmakers, Ken Russell will switch genres and moods from one film to another: after *The Devils*, which left some of the cast and crew exhausted, Russell jumped at the chance of directing a film version of *The Boy Friend*. Unfortunately, the filming of *The Boy Friend* proved to be an unhappy experience, with major fall-outs among the cast and crew, and technical obstacles, such as the sound stages, which weren't tall enough for the sets the production wanted to use.[4]

Ken Russell thinks you can have comedy and satire at the same time in a serious and dramatic film: it's quite OK to have sudden shifts from seriousness to comedy, or from literary dialogue to vaudeville fooling about. Some audiences find this mix confusing, or irritating, or tiring. Russell's films continually play around with the viewer's perceptions. For instance, fantasies are merged with the present tense of a movie, so the audience isn't sure if what they're seeing is meant to be taken straight, or if it's a fantasy (not a *dream* – Russell doesn't use *dreams* nearly so much as *fantasies*).

As well as fantasies, Ken Russell's films also employ a fantastical or exaggerated form of filmmaking – this may be the mode or approach that confuses viewers most, and which critics find particularly annoying. That is, the mode is not the fantasy of a particular character, but is the filmmakers' fantasy. Conventional dramatic modes such as memories and flashbacks are also employed, which further complicate the narratives of Russell's movies. (You could argue that all cinema is dream-like and fantastical – and Russell's works simply draw attention to it, or exaggerate it).

Certainly some of the confusions and irritations that some

4 It also appeared that the British film crew weren't used to staging a musical on this large scale. (But some of 'em must have worked on big musicals – quite a few were made in Britain in the 1960s, the period when the Hollywood studios were investing heavily in the British film scene: *Oliver!*, *Half a Sixpence* and *Chitty Chitty Bang Bang*).

viewers and critics have with Ken Russell's movies is that they are not sure how to take a particular scene or mode of narration. Is this scene meant to be serious or comic? Is this a fantasy of the main character, or is it the filmmaker fantasizing about the character's state of mind? Is this scene an ironic commentary on the situation? The movies say: yes, all of the above.

And, crucially, Ken Russell and the production teams don't necessarily indicate where one mode of address ends and another begins: they take away the signposts (no dissolves to shaky, black-and-white footage, for instance, to indicate a newsreel-style memory, and no watery, optical effects to indicate a dream).

At their most intense moments, when the montage sustains an apparently chaotic mix of music, images, dances, designs, stunts, looks and visual effects, nothing in a Ken Russell movie seems to be 'real', or is intended to be 'real', or has any link to 'reality'. Of course not! It's a movie! It's a piece of entertainment! Nothing about movies is 'real', was ever 'real', could ever be 'real'. It is movie-making as a mystery play from the Middles Ages, as Russell explained:

> You see, I think of my films as sort of modern mediaeval mystery plays. In the days of mystery plays, they took religion, bashed it over the head, cocked a snook at it, blasphemed it, sent it up, treated it melodramatically, comically... all in one act. And people liked it. (In P. Mezan, 1973

I agree wholeheartedly with Ken Russell when he says that he's not that interested in 'reality', that there's plenty of 'reality' around as it is. No need to add to it.

In a Ken Russell movie, some audiences are not sure where the filmmaker is coming from, or aiming at, nor where the film is headed. And they don't like that: they want to know if what they're watching is a comedy, if it's *meant* to be a comedy, and if it's OK to laugh, or if they are *meant* to laugh (consequently, you can see that Russell's movies would be tough to preview, and why a college audience might be a better bet than a shopping mall audience).

But Ken Russell is clearly a filmmaker who can happily send up his subject even as he celebrates it or takes it seriously (and some viewers find that hard to accept). Thus, Russell and his team take Peter Tchaikovsky or Henri Gaudier very seriously, but they also spoof them, in the same movie.[5] As Joseph Gomez noted, sometimes in Russell's films 'the importance of the image out-weighs the action' (40). A useful remark, because it means that the *image itself* (maybe the beauty of it, or the compelling nature of it, or just the photographic quality of it) can have more value or more juice in the movie than the *action* or the *narrative*. 'I am eaten up with the image, with the way things look,' Russell has said.

Some critics and some spectators want a film to have *meanings* or *actions* or *characters* or *ideas*, and to have these organized into a logical flow, so that cause leads to effect. But all of that traditional dramaturgy, while valuable, isn't always what a Ken Russell movie is about, or is interested in pursuing.

In other words, in a Ken Russell picture, the question is not: 'what does this mean?', or: 'why did that character do that?', or: 'what is this character saying?', or even: 'what is happening?'. The question is, rather: 'what does it feel like?', or: 'what is the mood of this scene?', or: 'what is the movement within this shot?', or: 'don't ask questions, just look at the costumes! the lighting! the sets! the make-up! and listen to that music!' (Again and again and again: *listen to that music!*).

Ken Russell's cinema simply reminds movie-goers that films are not only about *stories* and *characters* and *themes*, that they are also about the look of things, the sound of things, the links between things, and the stupidity or humour of things.

In this sense, a movie directed by Ken Russell might be usefully thought of in terms of the classic Hollywood musical. When I'm watching a Gene Kelly musical movie or a Vincente Minnelli musical, I'm not always asking questions like: 'what does that line of dialogue mean?', or: 'how will the next scene relate to this one, will the dramatic conflicts be resolved?', or: 'what was that character's motivation in that scene?'

Instead, I am looking at Gene Kelly – what a beautiful, nimble, athletic man! And I'm thinking: 'wow, that is such a fabulous movement!' Or: 'look at the way Kelly dances across the floor and leaps up onto that wall. So graceful!' Or: 'oh man,

5 Being amongst artists like Tchaikovsky, Shelley and Byron, Ken Russell said, was like being among old friends, his contemporaries (RC, 246).

look at the way the camera glides with Kelly as he spins and ends up framed in that doorway!'

And when I'm enjoying a Ken Russell movie, I'm reacting along the lines of: 'isn't it cool the way that Roger Daltrey grinned at that moment?' Or: 'look at the way that Glenda Jackson dances under the trees!' Or: 'look at the colours in that set and those costumes!' Or: 'how does our Ken get away with such apparent simplicity and vulgarity?!' And: 'oh, why oh why isn't Ken Russell being fêted as a genius?'

APPENDICES
✝
SOME OF THE FINEST MOMENTS IN KEN RUSSELL'S MOVIES

- The chase on the frozen lake in *Billion Dollar Brain*.
- Strauss as Zarathustra dancing with the nuns in *The Dance of the Seven Veils*
- The Oxford mural sequence in *Dante's Inferno*.
- The ending of *Isadora Duncan*.
- The water party in *Women In Love*
- The *First Piano Concerto* sequence in *The Music Lovers*.
- Tchaikovsky visiting von Meck's home in *The Music Lovers*
- The fireworks party in *The Music Lovers*
- The *1812* fantasy in *The Music Lovers*
- The 'rape of Christ' sequence in *The Devils* (even in its truncated form).
- The procession in *The Devils*.
- The *Pierrot* dance in *The Boy Friend*.
- Gaudier-Brzeska working all night on the sculpture in *Savage Messiah*.
- 'The Convert' fantasy sequence in *Mahler*.
- The Acid Queen sequence in *Tommy*.
- The Pinball Wizard sequence in *Tommy*.
- 'Eyesight To the Blind' in *Tommy*.
- Richard Wagner's Superman rally in *Lisztomania*.
- The phallic dance in *Lisztomania*.
- The second hallucination (peyote/ Emily) in *Altered States*
- The nightmares in *Gothic*.

QUOTES BY KEN RUSSELL

✞

Reality is a dirty word for me, I know it isn't for most people, but I am not interested. There's too much of it about.

✞

It's a strange thing that people can't reconcile vulgarity and artistry. They're the same thing to me. But an exuberant over-the-top larger-than-life slightly bad taste red-blooded thing.

✞

With the first big feature film I made, *Billion Dollar Brain*, I could afford to have an army on an expanse of ice and have the army fall through the ice, well of course you couldn't do that on TV. Feature filmmaking was far freer and pictorially the sky was the limit, but the budgetary limitations of TV didn't bother me, it meant you were forced to use you imagination even more.

✞

I was always fairly lucky with the censors. John Trevelyan [head of the British Board of Film Classification in the late 60s and early 70s] was very good; he stuck his neck out to keep the nude wrestling scene in *Women In Love* He argued that it wasn't me who put the scene in it was the author D.H. Lawrence, so it wasn't for pure sensationalism; it was an integral part of the novel.

✞

Sacrifice is the central pivot of the Catholic faith and one of the best things about it. It comes into a lot of my films, especially *The Devils*.

✞

The television adman's trick of passing off his dream as an attainable and desirable reality is to my mind the great tragedy of our age.

VIDEO AND DVD: AVAILABILITY
✝

Here's a reminder about access to Ken Russell's movies and TV work, as listed in the filmography, because it's a fairly fundamental issue: some films are easy to buy or rent on home entertainment formats like video, Blu-ray and DVD, but some are either difficult to track down, or unavailable. Most of Russell's television work of the 1960s, for instance, is not available on DVD or video, and has only the occasional airing on television. And the LWT and *South Bank Show* pieces, which were terrific television, also aren't in print (altho' some *South Bank Shows* have more recently been released on DVD. I would highly recommend the stunning North American release *Ken Russell At the BBC*).

As to showings on television, very occasionally pieces are re-broadcast. But don't expect *Dance of the Seven Veils: A Comic Strip In Seven Episodes On the Life of Richard Strauss, 1864-1949* to be shown after another re-run of *Cheers* or *Friends* or *Letterman* on CBS or ABC or the BBC any time soon. (*The Devils* is very rarely screened on TV in Albion).

But some releases feature audio commentaries by Ken Russell, and these are by far and away the most valuable editions of Russell's work on the home entertainment market. I highly recommend the DVDs releases of *Lisztomania* and *Tommy*. *The Devils* came in 2012. *The Music Lovers*, Russell's own favourite movie, has recently been released.

FANS ON *THE DEVILS*
✟

A selection of reviews of *The Devils* on Amazon.com.
(I haven't included film critics on Russell's work – no need to dish out more bile here!).

Wonderful, visually confrontational film by Ken Russell. This movie takes on: religion, politics, sin, sex, lust, love and (yes, even) honor through compelling performances by an outstanding and outlandish cast, led by Oliver Reed and Vanessa Redgrave.

✟

Passionately made, *The Devils*, still resonates, morally and politically, 40 years later: it remains a relevant, enduring piece of film making. A searing experience.

✟

I first saw this Ken Russell masterpiece when I was 16, during its original release. Especially in retrospect, I can say that this is a film that changed the way I viewed films. I not only learned what acting and directing were about (from an astounding Oliver Reed and the unique Russell respectively), but also became aware of the impact of editing and, most of all from *The Devils*, what sets could do for a film. And what sets they were! Minimalist fortifications, virgin-white within and without, checkerboard tiling and nuns and their habits (never was black and white starker), claustrophobic yet open to the heavens. And the colour and the contrast, how they could render any scene surreal.

✟

Aside from the quality of the transfer, this version of *The Devils* is one of the most bizarre films I have seen. I love it for its impact and its grotesque and over-the-top visuals, and it is enjoyable to watch in a twisted sense. It's a nightmare, it's a dream. It's horrifying, it's alienating. Also, it is brilliant! Russell is no doubt the film industry's antichrist.

FILMOGRAPHIES
✝
THE DEVILS (1971)

Warner Bros. 111 minutes, 117 minutes (restored). Technicolor.
Panavision. 1:2.35 (widescreen). Released: July, 1971 (G.B.), July
16, 1971 (U.S.A.)

CREW

Directed by Ken Russell
Written by Ken Russell
John Whiting – (play) and Aldous Huxley – (novel *The Devils of
    Loudon*)
Ken Russell – producer
Robert H. Solo – producer
Roy Baird – associate producer
Cinematography – David Watkin
Film Editing – Michael Bradsell
Production Design – Derek Jarman
Art Direction – Robert Cartwright
Costume Design – Shirley Russell
Tiny Nicholls – wardrobe supervisor
Music by Peter Maxwell Davies (and conductor)
David Munrow – period music arranger and director
Ramon Gow – hair stylist
Charles E. Parker – makeup artist
Graham Ford – unit manager
Neville C. Thompson – production manager
Ted Morley – assistant director
Nicolas Hippisley-Coxe – second assistant director
Terry Apsey – construction manager
George Ball – property manager
Bryn Siddall – property buyer
Ian Whittaker – set dresser
Alan Tomkins – assistant art director
Stuart Baird – assistant editor
Gordon K. McCallum – sound mixer
Terry Rawlings – dubbing editor

Brian Simmons – sound recordist
Rowland Fowles – boom operator
John Hayward – sound re-recording mixer
John Richardson – special effects
Peter Brayham – stunts
Harry Fielder – stunts
Peter Ewens – assistant camera
John Swan – electrical supervisor
Ronnie Taylor – camera operator
Robin Browne – director of photography: second unit
Harry Benn – production controller
Terry Gilbert – choreographer
Ann Skinner – continuity
Geoff Freeman – unit publicist

CAST

Vanessa Redgrave – Sister Jeanne
Oliver Reed – Urbain Grandier
Dudley Sutton – Baron De Laubardemont
Gemma Jones – Madelyn le Brou
Murray Melvin – Mignon
Michael Gothard – Father Barré
Georgina Hale – Philippe Trincant
Max Adrian – Ibert
Brian Murphy – Adam
Christopher Logue – Cardinal Richelieu
Graham Armitage – King Louis XIII
John Woodvine – Magistrate Trincant
Andrew Faulds – Rangier
Kenneth Colley – Legrand
Judith Paris – Sister Judith
Catherine Willmer – Sister Catherine
Iza Teller – Sister Iza
Imogen Claire – Nun
Selina Gilbert – Nun
Doremy Vernon – Nun
Cheryl Grunwald – Cameo
Alex Russell

KEN RUSSELL
✝

Films as director

Peepshow (1956)
Knights on Bikes (1956)
Amelia and the Angel (1957)
Lourdes (1958)
French Dressing (1964)
Billion Dollar Brain (1967)
Women In Love (1969)
The Music Lovers (1970)
The Devils (1971)
The Boy Friend (1971)
Savage Messiah (1972)
Mahler (1974)
Tommy (1975)
Lisztomania (1975)
Valentino (1977)
Altered States (1980)
Crimes of Passion (1984)
Gothic (1986)
Aria (1987) (Segment: Nessun Dorma)
Salomé's Last Dance (1988)
The Lair of the White Worm (1988)
The Rainbow (1989)
Whore (1991)
Tales of Erotica (1996) (Segment: The Insatiable Mrs. Kirsch)
Mindbender (1996)
The Lion's Mouth (2000)
The Fall of the Louse of Usher (2002)
Trapped Ashes (2006) (Segment: The Girl With Golden Breasts)
Hot Pants (2006)

Television work as director

Scottish Painters (1959)
Variations on a Mechanical Theme (1959)
Guitar Craze (1959)
Gordon Jacob (1959)
Poet's London (1959)
Portrait of a Goon (1959)
Journey Into a Lost World (1960)
Marie Rambert Remembers (1960)
Cranko at Work (1960)
The Light Fantastic (1960)
Shelagh Delaney's Salford (1960)
A House in Bayswater (1960)
The Miner's Picnic (1960)
Architecture of Entertainment (1960)
London Moods (1961)
Old Battersea House (1961)
Lotte Lenya Sings Kurt Weill (1961)
Antonio Gaudi (1961)
Pop Goes the Easel (1962)
Preservation Man (1962)
Mr. Chesher's Traction Engines (1962)
Elgar (1962)
Prokofiev: Portrait of a Soviet Composer (1963)
Lonely Shore (1964)
The Dotty World of James Lloyd (1964)
Watch the Birdie (1964)
Bartók (1964)
Diary of a Nobody (1964)
The Debussy Film (1965)
Always On Sunday (1965)
Isadora Duncan, the Biggest Dancer in the World (1966)
Don't Shoot the Composer (1966)
Dante's Inferno (1967)
Song of Summer: Frederick Delius (1968)
A House in Bayswater: Prokofiev (1968)
Dance of the Seven Veils (1970)
Clouds of Glory: William and Dorothy (1978)
Clouds of Glory: The Rime of the Ancient Mariner (1978)
The Planets (1983)
The South Bank Show: Vaughan Williams: A Symphonic Portrait (1984)
Faust (1985)

Ken Russell's ABC of British Music (1988)

A British Picture (1989)

Méphistophélès (1989)

Women and Men: Stories of Seduction (1990) (Segment: Dusk Before Fireworks)

The Strange Affliction of Anton Bruckner (1990)

Road To Mandalay (1991)

Prisoner of Honor (1991)

The Secret Life of Arnold Bax (1992)

Lady Chatterley (1993)

The Mystery of Dr Martinu (1993)

Classic Widows (1995)

Alice in Russialand (1995)

Treasure Island (1995)

In Search of the English Folk Song (1997)

Dogboys (1998)

Brighton Belles (2001)

Elgar: Fantasy of a Composer on a Bicycle (2002)

Revenge of the Elephant Man (2004)

A Kitten For Hitler (2007)

Boudicca Bites Back (2009)

BIBLIOGRAPHY
✟

KEN RUSSELL

" *The Music Lovers*", *Filmfacts*, 14, 1971
"Conversation With Ken Russell", in T. Fox, *Oui*, June, 1973
"Mahler the Man", *Mahler Brochure*, Sackville Publishing, London,
   1974
A British Picture: An Autobiography Heinemann, London, 1989
Altered States, Bantam Books, New York, 1991
Fire Over England: The British Cinema Comes Under Friendly Fire
   (a.k.a. *The Lion Roars*), Hutchinson, London, 1993
Mike and Gaby's Space Gospel Little, Brown, 1999
Violation, Authour House, 2001
Directing Film, Brassey's, Washington DC, 2001
Elgar: The Erotic Variations and *Delius: A Moment With Venus* Peter
   Owen, London, 2007
Beethoven Confidential and *Brahms Gets Laid*, Peter Owen, London,
   2007
"Ken Russell, the master director", *The Observer*, Aug 30, 2009

OTHERS

Y. Allom *et al*, eds. *Contemporary British and Irish Film Directors*, *A
   Wallflower Critical Guide*, Wallflower, London, 20001
R. Armes. *A Critical History of British Cinema*, Secker & Warburg,
   London, 1978
J. Ashby & A. Higson, eds. *British Cinema, Past and Present*,
   Routledge, London, 2000
T. Atkins, ed. *Ken Russell*, Monarch/ Simon & Schuster, New York,
   1976
S. Au. *Ballet and Modern Dance*, Thames & Hudson, London, 2012
M. Auty & N. Roddick, eds. *British Cinema Now*, British Film
   Institute, London, 1985
M. Barker, ed. *The Video Nasties: Freedom and Censorship In the
   Media*, Pluto Press, London, 1984
—. & J. Petley, eds. *Ill Effects: The Media/ Violence Debate* Rout-
   ledge, London, 1997

J. Baxter. *An Appalling Talent: Ken Russell,* M. Joseph, London, 1973

—. "The Television Films", in T. Atkins, 1976

L. Bawden, ed. *The Oxford Companion To Film*, Oxford University Press, Oxford, 1976

M. Beja. *Film and Literature: An Introduction,* Longman, London, 1979

R. Bell-Metereau: *"Altered States"*, *Journal of Popular Film and Television,* 9, 4, 1982

E. Blom, ed. *The New Everyman Dictionary of Music,* J.M. Dent, London, 1988

C. Bloom, ed. *Gothic Horror,* Macmillan, London, 1998

G. Bluestone. *Novels Into Film,* University of California Press, Berkeley, CA, 1961

D. Bordwell & K. Thompson. *Film Art: An Introduction,* McGraw-Hill Publishing Company, New York, NY, 2001

—. *et al*. *The Classical Hollywood Cinema: Film Style and Mode of Production To 1960*, Routledge, London, 1985

—. *Narration In the Fiction Film*, Routledge, London, 1988

—. *The Way Hollywood Tells It,* University of California Press, Berkeley, CA, 2006

F. Botting. *Making Monstrous: Frankenstein, Criticism, Theory,* Manchester University Press, Manchester, 1991

—. *Gothic,* Routledge, London, 1996

C. Bowen & B. von Meck. *Beloved Friend,* Random House, New York, 1937

J. Brady. *The Craft of the Screenwriter,* Touchstone, New York, 1982

M. Bragg. *The Seventh Seal*, BFI Classics, British Film Institute, London, 1993

A. Britton *et al*. *American Nightmare: Essays On the Horror Film,* Toronto, 1979

H. Brodzky. *Henri Gaudier-Brzeska,* Faber, London, 1933

J. Brosnan. *Primal Screen: A History of Science Fiction Film,* Orbit, London, 1991

P. Buckley. "Savage Saviour", *Films and Filming*, Oct, 1972

S. Bukatman. *Terminal Identity: The Virtual Subject In Postmodern Science Fiction,* Duke University Press, Durham, NC, 1993

G. Burt. *The Art of Film Music,* Northeastern University Press, 1994

I. Butler. *Religion In the Cinema,* A.S. Barnes, New York, NY, 1969

Ross Care, *Film Quarterly*, Spring, 1978

K. Carroll. "The Dark Brilliance of Ken Russell", *Sunday News*, March 30, 1975

M. Carter, ed. *Dracula: The Vampire and the Critics,* UMI Research Press, Ann Arbor, MI, 1988

D. Cavallaro. *The Gothic Vision,* Continuum, New York, NY, 2002

N. Cawthorne. *The Who and the Making of Tommy,* Unanimous, London, 2005

I. Christie. *Arrows of Desire: The Films of Michael Powell and*

Emeric Pressburger, Faber, London, 1994

M. Cloonan. *Banned! Censorship In Popular Music In Britain, 1967-92*, Arena, Aldershot, 1996

D.A. Cook. *A History of Narrative Film*, W.W. Norton, New York, NY, 1981, 1990, 1996

P. Cook & M. Bernink, eds. *The Cinema Book*, 2nd ed., British Film Institute, London, 1999

J. Crist, ed. *Take 22: Moviemakers On Moviemaking* Continuum, New York, NY, 1991

R. Crouse. *Raising Hell*, ECW Press, 2012

J. Curran & V. Porter, eds. *British Cinema History*, Weidenfeld & Nicolson, London, 1983

W. Darby & J. Du Bois. *American Film Music*, McFarland, Jefferson, NC, 1990

E. De Grazia & R.K. Newman. *Banned Films: Movies, Censors and the First Amendment*, Bowker, New York, NY, 1982

M. Dempsey: "The World of Ken Russell", *Film Quarterly*, 25, 3, 1972

—. "Ken Russell Again", *Film Quarterly*, 31, 2, 1977-78

L. Denham. *The Films of Peter Greenaway*, Minerva Press, London, 1993

R. Serge Denisoff & W. Romanowski. *Risky Business: Rock In Film*, Transaction, 1991

W.W. Dixon, ed. *Re-viewing British Cinema*, State University of New York Press, Albany, NY, 1994

K.J. Donnelly, ed. *Film Music*, Edinburgh University Press, Edinburgh, 2001

O. Doughty. *Dante Gabriel Rossetti*, Yale University Press, New Haven, 1949

S.C. Dubin. *Arresting Images: Impolitic Art and Uncivil Actions* Routledge, London, 1992

R. Durgnat. *A Mirror For England: British Movies From Austerity To Affluence*, Faber, London, 1970

J. Eberts. *My Indecision Is Final: The Rise and Fall of Goldcrest Films*, Faber, London, 1990

H.S. Ede. *Savage Messiah*, 1931

R. Eder. "The Screen: Ken Russell's *Mahler*", *New York Times*, Apl 5, 1976

J. Eszterhas. *The Devil's Guide To Hollywood*, Duckworth, London, 2006

S. Farber, "Russellmania", *Film Comment*, 11, 6, Nov, 1975

E. Fenby. *Delius As I Knew Him*, Icon Books, London, 1966

J. Finler. *The Movie Director's Story* Octopus Books, London, 1985

A. Finney. *The Egos Have Landed: The Rise and Fall of Palace Pictures*, Heinemann, London, 1996

J. Fisher. "Three Masterpieces of Sexuality", in T. Atkins, 1976

Kevin M. Flanagan, ed. *Ken Russell: Re-Viewing England's Last*

Mannerist, Scarecrow Press, 2009

G. Flatley. "I'm Surprised My Films Shock People", *New York Times*, Oct, 1972

T. Fletcher. *Dear Boy: The Life of Keith Moon*, Omnibus, London, 1998

G.E. Forshey. *American Religious and Biblical Spectaculars* Praeger, Westport, CT, 1992

T. Fox. "Conversation With Ken Russell", *Oui*, June, 1973

K. French, ed. *Screen Violence* Bloomsbury, London, 1996

L. Friedman, ed. *Fires Were Started: British Cinema and Thatcherism*, UCL Press, London, 1993

H. Gal, ed. *The Musician's World* Thames & Hudson, London, 1965

K. Gelder. *Reading the Vampire*, Routledge, London, 1994

—. ed. *The Horror Reader*, Routledge, London, 2000

—. *New Vampire Cinema*, BFI/ Palgrave Macmillan, London, 2012

J. Gelmis. *The Film Director as Superstar*, Penguin, London, 1974

R. Gentry: "Ken Russell", *Post Script*, 2, 3, 1983

L. Gianetti. *Understanding Movies*, Prentice-Hall, NJ, 1982

R. Giddings *et al*. *Screening the Novel: The Theory and Practice of Literary Dramatisation*, Macmillan, London, 1990

—. & E. Sheen, eds. *The Classic Novel From Page To Screen*, Manchester University Press, Manchester, 2000

D. Gifford. *The British Film Catalogue, 1895-1985*, David & Charles, London, 1986

H. Mark Glancy. *When Hollywood Loved Britain*, Manchester University Press, Manchester, 1999

J. Gomez. *Ken Russell* Muller, 1976

—. "Russell's Methods of Adaption", in T. Atkins, 1976

—. "Russell's Images of Lawrence's Vision", in M. Klein, 1981

C. Goodwin, *Evil Spirits*, Virgin Books, 2001

B.K. Grant, ed. *Planks of Reason: Essays on the Horror Film*, Scarecrow Press, Metuchen, NJ, 1984

—. ed. *The Dread of Difference: Gender and the Horror Film*, University of Texas Press, Austin, TX, 1996

S. Grantley & A. Parker. *The Who By Numbers* Helter Skelter, London, 2010

J. Green. *The Encyclopedia of Censorship* Facts on File, New York, NY, 1990

L. Greiff. *D.H. Lawrence: 50 Years On Film* Southern Illinois University Press, Carbondale, IL, 2001

Elizabeth Grosz. *Sexual Subversions* Allen & Unwin, London, 1989

—. "Lesbian Fetishism?", *differences* 3, 2, 1991

—. *Volatile Bodies*, Indiana University Press, Bloomington, IN, 1994

—. *Space, Time and Perversion* Routledge, London, 1995

J. Hacker & D. Price, eds. *Take 10: Contemporary British Film Directors*, Oxford University Press, Oxford, 1991

L. Halliwell. *Halliwell's Filmgoer's Companion*, 7th edition, Granada,

London, 1980

—. *Halliwell's Film and Video Guide*, 15th ed, ed. J. Walker, Harper-Collins, 2000

K. Hanke. *Ken Russell's Films*, Scarecrow Press, New Jersey, 1984

P. Hardy, ed. *The Aurum Encyclopedia of Science Fiction*, Aurum, London, 1991

S. Harper. *Picturing the Past: The Rise and Fall of the British Costume Film*, British Film Institute, London, 1994

C. Heylin. *All the Madmen*, Constable, London, 2012

G. Hickenlooper. *Reel Conversations: Candid Interviews With Film's Foremost Directors and Critics*, Citadel, New York, NY, 1991

A. Higson. *Waving the Flag: Constructing a National Cinema In Britain*, Oxford University Press, Oxford, 1995

—. *English Heritage, English Cinema: Costume Drama Since 1980*, Oxford University Press, Oxford, 2003

J. Hill *et al*, eds. *Border Crossing*, British Film Institute, London, 1994

—. *British Cinema In the 1980s*, Oxford University Press, Oxford, 1999

J. Hillier. *The New Hollywood*, Studio Vista, London, 1992

L. Hunt. *British Low Culture: From Safari Suits To Sexploitation*, Routledge, London, 1998

I.Q. Hunter. *British Science Fiction Cinema*, Routledge, London, 1999

A. Huxley. *The Devils of Loudun*, Chatto & Windus, London, 1970

I. Inglis, ed. *Popular Music and Film*, Wallflower Press, London, 2003

G. Jackson. *Esquire*, May, 1972

D. Jarman. *Dancing Ledge*, Quartet, London, 1984

D. Jones, ed. *Meaty Beaty Big & Bouncy! Classic Rock & Pop Writing From Elvis To Oasis*, Hodder & Stoughton, London, 1996

P. Kael, *Kiss Kiss Bang Bang*, Bantam, New York, NY, 1969

—. "Hyperbole and Narcissus", *The New Yorker*, Nov 18, 1972

—. *Taking It All In*, Marion Boyars, 1986

—. *State of the Art*, Marion Boyars, London, 1987

—. *Movie Love*, Marion Boyars, London, 1992

K. Kalinak. *Settling the Score: Music and the Classical Hollywood Film*, University of Wisconsin Press, Madison, WI, 1992

F. Karlin. *Listening To Movies*, Schirmer, New York, NY, 1994

B.F. Kawin. *How Movies Work*, Macmillan, New York, NY, 1987

P. Keough, ed. *Flesh and Blood: The National Society of Film Critics on Sex, Violence, and Censorship*, Mercury House, San Francisco, CA, 1995

M. Kermode. "Raising Hell", *Sight & Sound*, 2002

—. *Hatchet Job*, Picador, 2013

C. Kipps. *Out of Focus: Power, Prejudice: David Puttnam In Hollywood*, Century Hutchinson, London, 1989

M. Klein & G. Parker, eds. *The English Novel and the Movies*, F.

Ungar, New York, NY, 1981

P. Kolker. *The Altering Eye: Contemporary International Cinema*, Oxford University Press, New York, NY, 1983

—. *A Cinema of Loneliness: Penn, Stone, Kubrick, Scorsese, Spielberg, Altman*, Oxford University Press, New York, NY, 2000

J. Kristeva. *Powers of Horror: An Essay on Abjection*, tr. Leon S. Roudiez, Columbia University Press, New York, 1982

—. *Tales of Love*, tr. Leon S. Roudiez, Columbia University Press, New York 1987

—. *Black Sun: Depression and Melancholy* tr. L.S. Roudiez, Columbia University Press, New York, 1989

—. "A Question of Subjectivity: an interview" [with Susan Sellers], *Women's Review* 12, 1986, in Philip Rice & Patricia Waugh, eds. *Modern Literary Theory: A Reader* Arnold, 1992

L. Langley, "Ken Russell", *Show*, Oct, 1971.

J. Lanza. *Fragile Geometry: The Films, Philosophy and Misadventures of Nicolas Roeg* PAJ, New York, NY, 1989

—. *Phallic Frenzy: Ken Russell and His Films* Aurum Pres, London, 2008

D.H. Lawrence. *The Letters of D.H. Lawrence* ed. A. Huxley, Heinemann, London, 1934

—. *Selected Essays* Penguin, 1950

—. *A Selection from Phoenix,* ed. A.A.H. Inglis, Penguin, 1971

P. Leprohan. *The Italian Cinema*, tr. R. Greaves & O. Stallybrass, Secker & Warburg, London, 1972

J. Lewis. *Hollywood v. Hard Core: How the Struggle Over Censorship Created the Modern Film Industry*, New York University Press, New York, NY, 2000

C. Lyons. *The New Censors* Temple University Press, Philadelphia, PA, 1997

T.D. Matthews. *Censored*, Chatto & Windus, London, 1994

R. Manvell. *New Cinema In Britain*, Dutton, New York, NY, 1968

G. Mast *et al*, eds. *Film Theory and Criticism: Introductory Readings*, Oxford University Press, New York, NY, 1992a

—. & B. Kawin, *A Short History of the Movies* Macmillan, New York, NY, 1992b

J.R. May & M. Bird, eds. *Religion In Film*, University of Tennessee Press, Knoxville, 1982

—. *New Image of Religious Film*, Sheed & Ward, London, 1996

S.Y. McDougal. *Made Into Movies: From Literature To Film*, Holt, Rinehart and Winston, New York, NY, 1985

B. McFarlane, ed. *An Autobiography of British Cinema* Methuen, London, 1997

P. Mezan, "Relax, It's Only a Ken Russell Movie", *Esquire*, May, 1973

M. Miles. *Seeing and Believing: Religion and Values In the Movies* Beacon, Boston, MA, 1996

F. Miller. *Censored Hollywood: Sex, Sin and Violence On Screen*, Turner Publishing, Atlanta, 1994

K. Millett. *Sexual Politics*, Doubleday, Garden City, 1970

G. Mulholland. *Popcorn: Fifty Years of Rock 'n' Roll Movies*, Orion Books, London, 2011

R. Murphy. *Realism and Tinsel: British Cinema and Society, 1939-48*, London, 1989

—. *Sixties British Cinema*, British Film Institute, London, 1992

—. ed. *British Cinema of the 90s*, British Film Institute, London, 2000

—. ed. *The British Cinema Book*, Palgrave/ Macmillan, London, 2nd edition, 2009

R. Murray. *Images In the Dark: An Encyclopedia of Gay and Lesbian Film and Video*, Titan Books, London, 1998

S. Neale & M. Smith, eds. *Contemporary Hollywood Cinema*, Routledge, London, 1998

K. Newman. *Nightmare Movies*, Harmony, New York, NY, 1988

—. *Millennium Movies*, Titan Books, London, 1999

—. ed. *Science Fiction/ Horror: A Sight & Sound Reader*, British Film Institute, London, 2002

G. Nowell-Smith, ed. *The Oxford History of World Cinema*, Oxford University Press, Oxford, 1996

W. Ober. *Boswell's Clap and Other Essays*, Southern Ilinois University Press, IL, 1979

M. O'Pray, ed. *The British Avant Garde Film, 1926-1995*, University of Luton Press/ John Libbey, London, 1996

J. Orr. *Contemporary Cinema*, Edinburgh University Press, Edinburgh, 1998

C. Paglia. *Sexual Personae: Art and Decadence From Nefertiti To Emily Dickinson*, Penguin, London, 1992

J. Park. *Learning To Dream: The New British Cinema*, Faber, London, 1984

—. *British Cinema*, B.T. Batsford, London, 1990

D. Parkinson. *The Rough Guide To Film Musicals*, Penguin, London, 2007

D. Peary, ed. *Omni's Screen Flights, Screen Fantasies*, Doubleday, New York, NY, 1984

C. Penley, ed. *Feminism and Film Theory*, Routledge, London, 1988

—. *et al*, eds. *Close Encounters: Film, Feminism and Science Fiction*, University of Minnesota Press, Minneapolis, 1991

G. Perry. *Life of Python*, Pavilion, London, 1983

—. *The Great British Picture Show*, Pavilion, London, 1985

D. Petrie. *Creativity and Constraint In the British Film Industry*, Macmillan, London, 1991

—. ed. *New Questions of British Cinema*, British Film Institute, London, 1992

—. *Screening Europe: Image and Identity In Contemporary European*

Cinema, British Film Institute, London, 1992

—. *The British Cinematographer*, British Film Institute, London, 1996

G. Phelps. *Film Censorship*, Gollancz, London, 1975

G. Philips. "Ken Russell as Adaptor", *Literature/ Film Quarterly*, 5, 1977

—. *Ken Russell* Twayne, Boston, MA, 1979

D. Pirie. *A Heritage of Horror: The English Gothic Cinema* Gordon & Fraser, 1973

M. Powell. *A Life In the Movies* Heinemann, London, 1986/ 1992

—. *Million-Dollar Movie*, Heinemann, London, 1992

R. Prendergast. *Film Music*, W.W. Norton, New York, NY, 1992

S. Prince, ed. *Screening Violence* Athlone Press, London, 2000

D. Puttnam. *The Undeclared War: The Struggle For Control of the World's Film Industry*, HarperCollins, London, 1997

M. Pye & Lynda Myles. *The Movie Brats: How the Film Generation Took Over Hollywood*, Faber, London, 1979

J. Pym. *Film On Four*, British Film Institute, London, 1992

D. Quinlan. *The Illustrated Guide To Film Directors* B.T. Batsford, London, 1983

T. Reeves. *The Worldwide Guide To Movie Locations* Titan Books, London, 2003

J. Richards, ed. *Films and British National Identity*, Manchester University Press, Manchester, 1997

M. Richardson. *Surrealism and Cinema*, Berg, New York, NY, 2006

F. Robbins, "The Savage Russell", *Gallery*, May, 1973

J. Robertson. *The British Board of Film Censors*, Croom Helm, 1985

—. *The Hidden Cinema*, Routledge, London, 1989

W.H. Rockett. *Devouring Whirlwind: Terror and Transcendence In the Cinema of Cruelty*, Greenwood Press, New York, NY, 1988

J. Romney & A. Wooton, eds. *Celluloid Juke Box*, British Film Institute, London, 1995

V. Sage. *The Gothick Novel: A Casebook* Macmillan, London, 1990

D. Schaefer & L. Salvato, eds. *Masters of Light*, University of California Press, Berkeley, CA, 1984

T. Schatz. *Old Hollywood/ New Hollywood*, UMI Research Press, Ann Arbor, MI, 1983

—. *The Genius of the System: Hollywood Filmmaking In the Studio Era*, Pantheon, New York, NY 1988

R. Sellers. *Oliver Reed* Constable & Robinson, London, 2013

T. Shaw. *British Cinema and the Cold War*, I.B. Tauris, London, 2001

D. Shipman. *The Story of Cinema*, Hodder & Stoughton, London, 1984

—. *Caught In the Act: Sex and Eroticism In the Movies* Hamish Hamilton, London, 1986

T. Shone. *Blockbuster: How the Jaws and Jedi Generation Turned Hollywood Into a Boom-Town*, Scribner, London, 2005

L. Sider *et al*, eds. *Soundscapes: The School of Sound Lectures 1998-2001*, Wallflower Press, London, 2003

N. Sinyard. *Filming Literature: The Art of Screen Adaption*, Croom Helm, Beckenham, Kent, 1986

A. Slide. *'Banned In the USA': British Films In the United States and Their Censorship, 1933-1960* I.B. Tauris, London, 1998

J. Smith. *Withnail and Us: Cult Films and Film Cults In British Cinema*, Tauris, London, 2010

J. Squire, ed. *The Movie Business Book*, Fireside, New York, NY, 1992

G. Stewart. *Between Film and Screen: Modernism's Photo Synthesis*, University of Chicago Press, Chicago, IL, 1999

S. Street. *British National Cinema*, Routledge, London, 1997/ 2009

D Strerritt, "Whole Film Is 'One Flash' In His Mind", *Christian Science Monitor*, June 2, 1975

J. Stringer, ed. *Movie Blockbusters*, Routledge, London, 2003

P. Swann. *The Hollywood Feature Film In Postwar Britain*, Croom Helm, 1987

K. Thompson & D. Bordwell. *Film History: An Introduction*, McGraw-Hill, New York, NY, 1994

—. *Storytelling In the New Hollywood*, Harvard University Press, Cambridge, MA, 1999

D. Thomson. *A Biographical Dictionary of Film,* Deutsch, London, 1995

C. Tohill & P. Tombs. *Immoral Tales: Sex and Horror Cinema In Europe 1956-1984*, Titan Books, London, 1995

P. Townshend & D. McAnuff. *The Who's Tommy*, Pantheon, London, 1993

—. *Tommy, the Musical*, Vintage, London, 1999

—. *Who I Am*, HarperCollins, London, 2012

G. Tremlett. *Rock Gold: The Music Millionaires*, Unwin Hyman, London, 1990

J. Trevelyan. *What the Censor Saw*, Michael Joseph, London, 1973

P. Tyler. *Screening the Sexes: Homosexuality In the Movies*, Doubleday, New York, NY, 1973

K. Van Gunden. *Fantasy Films* , McFarland, Jefferson, NC 1989

G. Vincendeau, ed. *Encyclopedia of European Cinema*, British Film Institute, London, 1995

—. ed. *Film/ Literature/ Heritage: A Sight & Sound Reader*, British Film Institute, London, 2001

H. Vogel. *Entertainment Industry Economics*, Cambridge University Press, Cambridge, 1995

R. Wakeman. *Grumpy Old Rock Star*, London, 2008

—. *Further Adventures of a Grumpy Old Rock Star*, Arrow, 2010

A. Walker. *National Heroes: British Cinema In the Seventies and Eighties*, Harrap, London, 1985

—. *Hollywood, England: The British Film Industry In the Sixties*,

Harrap, London, 1986

J. Walker. *The Observer*, Sept 8, 1974

J. Walker. *The Once and Future Film: British Cinema In the 1970s and 1980s* , Methuen, London, 1985

—. *Art and Artists on Screen*, Manchester University Press, Manchester, 1993

P. Webb. *The Erotic Arts*, Secker & Warburg, London, 1975

E. Weiss. & J. Belton, eds. *Film Sound: Theory and Practice*, Columbia University Press, New York, NY, 1989

O. Welles. *Orson Welles: Interviews* ed. M. Estrin, University of Mississippi Press, Jackson, 2002

C. Wilson. *Ken Russell*, Intergroup, London, 1974

M. Wolf. *The Entertainment Economy*, Penguin, London, 1999

L. Wood, ed. *British Films, 1971-1981*, British Film Institute, London, 1983

J. Wyatt. *High Concept: Movies and Marketing In Hollywood*, University of Texas Press, Austin, TX, 1994

A. Yule. *Fast Forward: David Puttnam, Columbia Pictures and the Battle For Hollywood*, Delacorte, New York, NY, 1989

A.L. Zambrano: *"Women In Love", Literature/ Film Quarterly* 1, Jan, 1973

J. Zipes, ed. *The Oxford Companion To Fairy Tales*, Oxford University Press, 2000

—. *The Enchanted Screen: The Unknown History of Fairy-tale Films*, Routledge, New York, NY, 2011

—. *The Irresistible Fairy Tale*, Prince University Press, Princeton, NJ, 2012

WEBSITES

Savage Messiah/ Ken Russell: iainfisher.com/Russell
Aldous Huxley: somaweb.org

Jeremy Robinson has written many critical studies, including *Hayao Miyazaki, Walerian Borowczyk, Arthur Rimbaud,* and *The Sacred Cinema of Andrei Tarkovsky,* plus literary monographs on: William Shakespeare; Samuel Beckett; Thomas Hardy; André Gide; Robert Graves; and John Cowper Powys.

It's amazing for me to see my work treated with such passion and respect. There is nothing resembling it in the U.S. in relation to my work.
Andrea Dworkin (on *Andrea Dworkin*)

This model monograph – it is an exemplary job, and I'm very proud that he has accorded me a couple of mentions… The subject matter of his book is beautifully organised and dead on beam.
Lawrence Durrell (on *The Light Eternal: A Study of J.M.W. Turner*)

Jeremy Robinson's poetry is certainly jammed with ideas, and I find it very interesting for that reason. It's certainly a strong imprint of his personality.
Colin Wilson

Sex-Magic-Poetry-Cornwall is a very rich essay… It is a very good piece… vastly stimulating and insightful.
Peter Redgrove

Thomas A. Christie

JOHN HUGHES
& EIGHTIES CINEMA
Teenage Hopes & American Dreams

hn Hughes (1950-2009) is one of the best-loved figures in 1980s American
nmaking, and considered by many to be among the finest and most celebrated
comedy writers of his generation. His memorable motion pictures are
sightful, humanistic, culturally aware, and paint a vibrant picture of the United
States in a decade of rapid social and political change.

Bibliography, notes, illustrations   372pp.
ISBN 9781861713896 Pbk   ISBN 9781861713988 Hbk
Also available: *Ferris Bueller's Day Off: Pocket Movie Guide*

Walerian Borowczyk

Cinema of Erotic Dreams

by Jeremy Mark Robinson

Walerian Borowczyk (1923-2006) was a Polish artist, animator and filmmaker who lived in France for much of his life. He is the author of European art cinema masterpieces *Goto: Island of Love, Blanche* and *Immoral Tales*, some surreal animated shorts, and controversial films such as *The Beast*. This new book concentrates on Borowczyk's feature films, from *Goto* to *Love Rites*, which contain some of the most extraordinary images and scenes in recent cinema. Erotica for some, porn for others, Borowczyk's films are highly idiosyncratic and unforgettable.

Bibliography, notes, 110 illustrations 252pp.
ISBN 9781861713674 Pbk ISBN 9781861713124 Hbk
Also available: *Walerian Borowczyk: The Beast: Pocket Movie Guide*

andy goldsworthy
touching nature

WILLIAM MALPAS

ontemporary British sculptor Andy Goldsworthy makes land and
vironmental art, a sensitive, intuitive response to nature, light, time,
owth, change, the seasons and the earth. Goldsworthy's sculpture is
coming ever more popular, appearing in TV documentaries, public works,
d Holocaust memorials. Goldsworthy has exhibited around the world, and
s become one of the foremost contemporary sculptors in Great Britain.

e book has been updated and revised for this new edition.

3N 9781861714122 Pbk   ISBN 9781861714138 Hbk
lly illustrated   www.crmoon.com

ANDREI TARKOVSKY

JEREMY MARK ROBINSON

POCKET GUIDE

Andrei Tarkovsky is one of the great filmmakers of recent times.

This book covers every aspect of Tarkovsky's artistic career, and all of his output, concentrating on his seven feature films: *Ivan's Childhood, Andrei Roublyov, Solaris, Mirror, Stalker, Nostalghia* and *The Sacrifice*, made between 1962 and 1986.

Part One of this study focusses on the key elements and themes of Andrei Tarkovsky's art: spirituality; childhood; the film image; poetics; painting and the history of art; the family; eroticism; symbolism; as well as technical areas, such as script, camera, sound, music, editing, budget and production.

Part Two explores Tarkovsky's films in detail, with scene-by-scene analyses (in some cases, shot-by-shot). Tarkovsky emerges as a brilliant, difficult, complex and poetic artist.

Fully illustrated. This new edition has been revised and updated.
ISBN 19781861713957 Pbk   9781861713834 Hbk

MAURICE SENDAK

& the art of children's book illustration

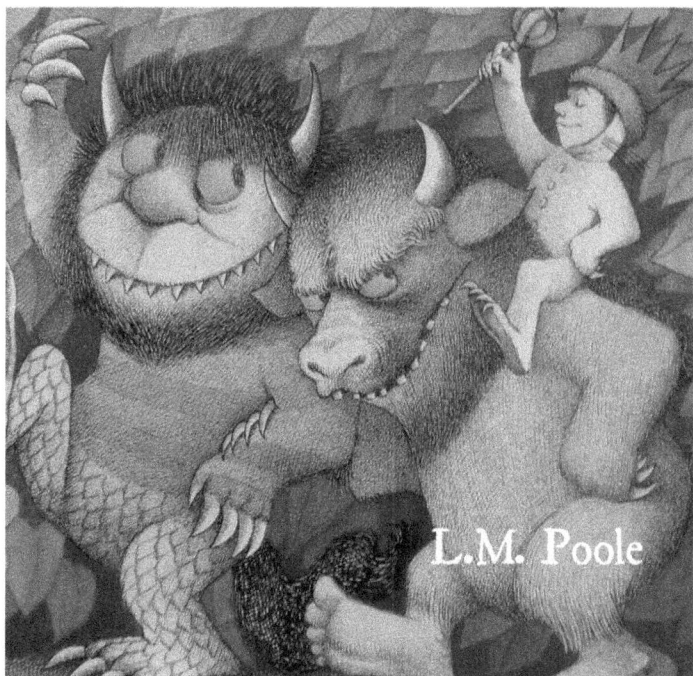

L.M. Poole

Maurice Sendak is the widely acclaimed American children's book author and illustrator. This critical study focuses on his famous trilogy, *Where the Wild Things Are*, *In the Night Kitchen* and *Outside Over There*, as well as the early works and Sendak's superb depictions of the Grimm Brothers' fairy tales in *The Juniper Tree*. L.M. Poole begins with a chapter on children's book illustration, in particular the treatment of fairy tales. Sendak's work is situated within the history of children's book illustration, and he is compared with many contemporary authors.

Fully illustrated. The book has been revised and updated for this edition.
ISBN 9781861714282 Pbk   ISBN 9781861713469 Hbk

Beauties, Beasts, and Enchantment

CLASSIC FRENCH FAIRY TALES

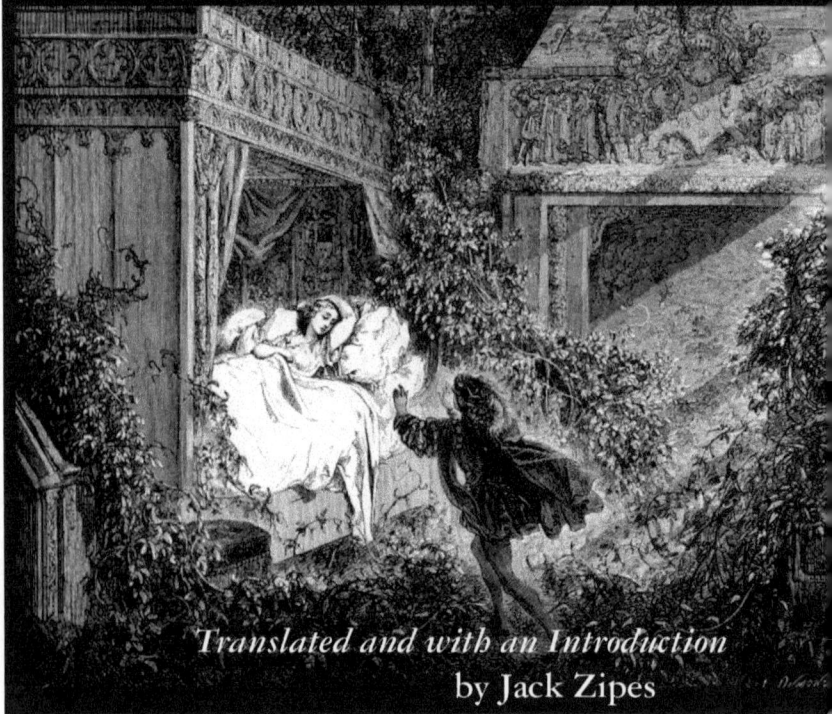

Translated and with an Introduction
by Jack Zipes

A collection of 36 classic French fairy tales translated by renowned writer Jack Zipes. *Cinderella, Beauty and the Beast, Sleeping Beauty* and *Little Red Riding Hood* are among the classic fairy tales in this amazing book.
Includes illustrations from fairy tale collections.
Jack Zipes has written and published widely on fairy tales.

'Terrific... a succulent array of 17th and 18th century 'salon' fairy tales'
- *The New York Times Book Review*
'Enjoyable to read... a unique collection of French regional folklore' - *Library Journal*
'Charming stories accompanied by attractive pen-and-ink drawings' - *Chattanooga Times*

Introduction and illustrations   612pp.   ISBN 9781861712510 Pbk   ISBN 9781861713193 Hbk

ARTS, PAINTING, SCULPTURE

web: www.crmoon.com • e-mail: cresmopub@yahoo.co.uk

The Art of Andy Goldsworthy
Andy Goldsworthy: Touching Nature
Andy Goldsworthy in Close-Up
Andy Goldsworthy: Pocket Guide
Andy Goldsworthy In America
Land Art: A Complete Guide
The Art of Richard Long
Richard Long: Pocket Guide
Land Art In Great Britain
Land Art in Close-Up
Land Art In the U.S.A.
Land Art: Pocket Guide
Installation Art in Close-Up
Minimal Art and Artists In the 1960s and After
Colourfield Painting
Land Art DVD, TV documentary
Andy Goldsworthy DVD, TV documentary
The Erotic Object: Sexuality in Sculpture From Prehistory to the Present Day
Sex in Art: Pornography and Pleasure in Painting and Sculpture
Postwar Art
Sacred Gardens: The Garden in Myth, Religion and Art
Glorification: Religious Abstraction in Renaissance and 20th Century Art
Early Netherlandish Painting
Jasper Johns
Brice MardenLeonardo da Vinci
Piero della Francesca
Giovanni Bellini
Fra Angelico: Art and Religion in the Renaissance
Mark Rothko: The Art of Transcendence
Frank Stella: American Abstract Artist
Alison Wilding: The Embrace of Sculpture
Vincent van Gogh: Visionary Landscapes
Eric Gill: Nuptials of God
Constantin Brancusi: Sculpting the Essence of Things
Max Beckmann
Gustave Moreau
Caravaggio
Egon Schiele: Sex and Death In Purple Stockings
Delizioso Fotografico Fervore: Works In Process 1
Sacro Cuore: Works In Process 2
The Light Eternal: J.M.W. Turner
The Madonna Glorified: Karen Arthurs

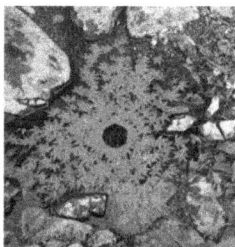

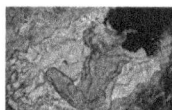

LITERATURE

J.R.R. Tolkien: The Books, The Films, The Whole Cultural Phenomenon
J.R.R. Tolkien: Pocket Guide
Beauties, Beasts and Enchantment: Classic French Fairy Tales
Tolkien's Heroic Quest
Brothers Grimm: German Popular Stories
Sexing Hardy: Thomas Hardy and Feminism
Thomas Hardy's *Tess of the d'Urbervilles*
Thomas Hardy's *Jude the Obscure*
Thomas Hardy: The Tragic Novels
Love and Tragedy: Thomas Hardy
The Poetry of Landscape in Hardy
Wessex Revisited: Thomas Hardy and John Cowper Powys
Wolfgang Iser: Essays and Interviews
Petrarch, Dante and the Troubadours
Maurice Sendak and the Art of Children's Book Illustration
Andrea Dworkin
Cixous, Irigaray, Kristeva: The *Jouissance* of French Feminism
Julia Kristeva: Art, Love, Melancholy, Philosophy, Semiotics and Psychoanalysis
Hélene Cixous I Love You: The *Jouissance* of Writing
Luce Irigaray: Lips, Kissing, and the Politics of Sexual Difference
Peter Redgrove: Here Comes the Flood
Peter Redgrove: Sex-Magic-Poetry-Cornwall
Lawrence Durrell: Between Love and Death, East and West
Love, Culture & Poetry: Lawrence Durrell
Cavafy: Anatomy of a Soul
German Romantic Poetry: Goethe, Novalis, Heine, Hölderlin
Novalis: *Hymns To the Night*
Feminism and Shakespeare
Shakespeare: *The Sonnets*
Shakespeare: Love, Poetry & Magic
The Passion of D.H. Lawrence
D.H. Lawrence: Symbolic Landscapes
D.H. Lawrence: Infinite Sensual Violence
The Ecstasies of John Cowper Powys
Sensualism and Mythology: The Wessex Novels of John Cowper Powys
Amorous Life: John Cowper Powys (H.W. Fawkner)
Postmodern Powys: New Essays on John Cowper Powys (Joe Boulter)
Rethinking Powys: Critical Essays on John Cowper Powys
Paul Bowles & Bernardo Bertolucci
Rainer Maria Rilke
Joseph Conrad: *Heart of Darkness*
In the Dim Void: Samuel Beckett
Samuel Beckett Goes into the Silence
André Gide: Fiction and Fervour
Jackie Collins and the Blockbuster Novel
Blinded By Her Light: The Love-Poetry of Robert Graves

POETRY

Ursula Le Guin: *Walking In Cornwall*
Peter Redgrove: Here Comes The Flood
Peter Redgrove: Sex-Magic-Poetry-Cornwall
Dante: Selections From the *Vita Nuova*
Petrarch, Dante and the Troubadours
William Shakespeare: *The Sonnets*
William Shakespeare: Complete Poems
Blinded By Her Light: The Love-Poetry of Robert Graves
Emily Dickinson: Selected Poems
Emily Brontë: Poems
Thomas Hardy: Selected Poems
Percy Bysshe Shelley: Poems
John Keats: Selected Poems
John Keats: Poems of 1820
D.H. Lawrence: Selected Poems
Edmund Spenser: Poems
Edmund Spenser: *Amoretti*
John Donne: Poems
Henry Vaughan: Poems
Sir Thomas Wyatt: Poems
Robert Herrick: Selected Poems
Rilke: Space, Essence and Angels in the Poetry of Rainer Maria Rilke
Rainer Maria Rilke: Selected Poems
Friedrich Hölderlin: Selected Poems
Arseny Tarkovsky: Selected Poems
Paul Verlaine: Selected Poems
Novalis: *Hymns To the Night*
Arthur Rimbaud: Selected Poems
Arthur Rimbaud: *A Season in Hell*
Arthur Rimbaud and the Magic of Poetry
D.J. Enright: By-Blows
Jeremy Reed: *Brigitte's Blue Heart*
Jeremy Reed: *Claudia Schiffer's Red Shoes*
Gorgeous Little Orpheus
Radiance: New Poems
Crescent Moon Book of Nature Poetry
Crescent Moon Book of Love Poetry
Crescent Moon Book of Mystical Poetry
Crescent Moon Book of Elizabethan Love Poetry
Crescent Moon Book of Metaphysical Poetry
Crescent Moon Book of Romantic Poetry
Pagan America: New American Poetry

MEDIA, CINEMA, FEMINISM and CULTURAL STUDIES

J.R.R. Tolkien: The Books, The Films, The Whole Cultural Phenomenon
J.R.R. Tolkien: Pocket Guide
The *Lord of the Rings* Movies: Pocket Guide
The Ghost Dance: The Origins of Religion
The Cinema of Hayao Miyazaki
Hayao Miyazaki: *Princess Mononoke*: Pocket Movie Guide
Hayao Miyazaki: *Spirited Away*: Pocket Movie Guide
The Peyote Cult
HomeGround: The Kate Bush Anthology
Tim Burton : Hallowe'en For Hollywood
Ken Russell
Cixous, Irigaray, Kristeva: The *Jouissance* of French Feminism
Julia Kristeva: Art, Love, Melancholy, Philosophy, Semiotics and Psychoanalysis
Luce Irigaray: Lips, Kissing, and the Politics of Sexual Difference
Hélene Cixous I Love You: The *Jouissance* of Writing
Andrea Dworkin
'Cosmo Woman': The World of Women's Magazines
Women in Pop Music
Discovering the Goddess (Geoffrey Ashe)
The Poetry of Cinema
The Sacred Cinema of Andrei Tarkovsky
Andrei Tarkovsky: Pocket Guide
Andrei Tarkovsky: *Mirror*: Pocket Movie Guide
Walerian Borowczyk: Cinema of Erotic Dreams
Jean-Luc Godard: The Passion of Cinema
Jean-Luc Godard: Pocket Guide
John Hughes and Eighties Cinema
Ferris Buller's Day Off: Pocket Movie Guide
The Cinema of Richard Linklater
Liv Tyler: Star In Ascendance
Blade Runner and the Films of Philip K. Dick
Paul Bowles and Bernardo Bertolucci
Media Hell: Radio, TV and the Press
Detonation Britain: Nuclear War in the UK
Feminism and Shakespeare
Wild Zones: Pornography, Art and Feminism
Sex in Art: Pornography and Pleasure in Painting and Sculpture
Sexing Hardy: Thomas Hardy and Feminism

The Light Eternal *is a model monograph, an exemplary job. The subject matter of the book is beautifully organised and dead on beam.* (Lawrence Durrell)
It is amazing for me to see my work treated with such passion and respect. (Andrea Dworkin)
Sex-Magic-Poetry-Cornwall *is a very rich essay... It is like a brightly-lighted box.* (Peter Redgrove)

CRESCENT MOON PUBLISHING P.O. Box 1312, Maidstone, Kent, ME14 5XU, Great Britain
0044-1622-729593 cresmopub@yahoo.co.uk www.crmoon.com

www.ingramcontent.com/pod-product-compliance
Lightning Source LLC
Chambersburg PA
CBHW062051080426
42734CB00012B/2609